WHY HAS JAPAN 'SUCCEEDED'?

Western technology and the Japanese ethos

Why has Japan 'succeeded'?

Western technology and the Japanese ethos

MICHIO MORISHIMA

CAMBRIDGE UNIVERSITY PRESS

CAMBRIDGE

LONDON   NEW YORK   NEW ROCHELLE

MELBOURNE   SYDNEY

Published by the Press Syndicate of the University of Cambridge
The Pitt Building, Trumpington Street, Cambridge CB2 1RP
32 East 57th Street, New York, NY 10022, USA
296 Beaconsfield Parade, Middle Park, Melbourne 3206, Australia

First published 1982

Printed in Great Britain at
the Pitman Press, Bath

Library of Congress catalogue card number: 81-15544

British Library Cataloguing in Publication Data

Morishima, Michio
    Why has Japan 'succeeded'?: Western technology
    and the Japanese ethos.
    1. Japan—Industries—History
    2. Japan—Civilization
    I. Title
    338.9′00952   HC462

ISBN 0 521 24494 3

Contents

Preface

This book contains the text of the Marshall Lectures which were given at the University of Cambridge in March 1981. Prior to this, in February 1981, I delivered an even more abridged version of these lectures as the Suntory–Toyota Public Lecture at the London School of Economics.

The question first of all was whether or not Japan had been successful, but no country is likely to be successful in all respects. Moreover success in one respect is closely connected to failure in another, and success and failure are often achieved in conjunction with each other. The theme of the present work is to attempt to clarify those respects in which Japan has been successful, and those in which she has met with failure, and to ask why this has been the case. In no chapter of the book, however, have I presumed to lay down in any categorical manner my own solutions to these problems.

This is in part due to my belief that, although I have purposely not written anything in the nature of a summary or conclusion, what I am trying to say is likely to be quite clear to the reader. It is also due to my believing that there cannot be a single correct solution to this sort of problem; there can at the most only be various different views. One should therefore not expound one's own personal conclusions in any ostentatious manner or impose them upon others. I am only too aware that the analysis I give only shows one side of the question, and that there is clearly a need for a comprehensive full-scale work on which a great deal of time has to be spent.

In this work we are not viewing Japan within the narrow vision of 'Japanese studies', but in much the same way as Max Weber viewed the capitalism of the West: Japan has had its own culture from ancient times, and the ethos of the Japanese people has been formed over many years within this cultural environment. Any temperament of this kind will of course gradually alter in accordance with any change in material conditions, and therefore any change in economic circumstances. The reverse is also true, however. Economic structures and economic relations are also strongly conditioned by the national ethos. It is often the case that even though material conditions may be the same what may be possible in Japan may not be possible in the West and vice versa. As we shall see later, a remarkably idiosyncratic ethos prevails in Japanese society, and as a result of these ethical feelings Japanese capitalism has to a considerable extent deviated from the typical free enterprise system. The question asked by this book is why the possessors of this kind of non-Western attitude came to gain such control over the industrial techniques produced by the West. Such examination of the economies of various countries under their respective ideologies is also possible in the case of China, in the case of the Soviet Union and in the case of India and the Near and Middle East, and the current significance of such work is considerable. Max Weber's work on the religions of the world was developed on the basis of such a grand conception as this, and though his individual conclusions might be mistaken large numbers of scholars should work together to promote studies of this kind.

Anything so grandiose as a comparative theory of economic systems based on comparative religious studies is, of course, far beyond my own capabilities; the present work has been written as the volume on Japan within this vast field of scholarship. The introduction and the first chapter are preliminary sections aimed at setting out the problem in a Weberian manner. These sections are for my purpose very important, but those who want information relating to modern Japan immediately are encouraged to read Chapters 2 to 5 first of all. If they are interested (and I hope that they will be) I hope they will subsequently read the introduction, Chapter 1 and conclusion.

Up until now I have written in English only in the field of mathematical economics, where so much is expressed with mathematical formulas, and the writing of this work would not have been possible without linguistic help from a large number of people. Mrs Prue Hutton and Mrs Luba Mumford (and my son, Haruo) corrected the English in the draft of the first chapter for me. The second chapter was written almost ten years ago with the aim of producing Japanese language teaching material for British students specialising in the study of Japan; it was subsequently translated into English by Dr Emi Watanabe. The third and subsequent chapters, the introduction and the conclusion were all translated from my Japanese language draft by Dr Janet Hunter. The 'assembly-line' with my wife making a clear copy of my own illegible draft and Janet then putting it into English has enabled me to save a great amount of time, to go far beyond the limitations of my own English and to write with much greater freedom. Her translation demonstrates the high level of Japanese language work in Britain. Moreover her specialisation in Japanese history meant that she could point out to me mistakes in my own memory and the existence of facts which I had forgotten.

I would finally like to thank those who read all or part of the manuscript and provided me both with encouragement and with instructive comments – Professor Ralf Dahrendorf of the L.S.E., Professor Roy Radner of the Bell Institute and Professor Masahiro Tatemoto of Osaka University. The comments made by those who acted as referees for the manuscript were also helpful. This work was written at the International Centre for Economics and Related Disciplines established at the L.S.E. in 1978, and I would like to take this opportunity of expressing my very deep gratitude to Mr Keizo Saji of Suntory Limited and Mr Eiji Toyoda of the Toyota Motor Co. Ltd, who donated the money for the establishment of the Centre. I would also like to thank Dr Yūjirō Hayashi of the Toyota Foundation, who was throughout a great source of help to me when the Centre was being established.

M.M.
May 1981

Acknowledgement

Ever since my days as a high school student I have been interested in history and sociology, but my knowledge in these disciplines is both narrow and shallow. This book is therefore indebted to the works of a great many authors although they have not been individually mentioned except where the reference is particularly significant. These works are all in Japanese and I do not intend to cite the names of the works, but I would like to record my thanks to these authors below as a whole.

Ando Yoshio, Aoyama Hideo, Arisawa Hiromi, Banpa Masatomo, Cho Yukio, Hayashiya Tatsusaburo, Hirschmeier Johannes, Hosoya Chihiro, Kaizuka Shigeki, Kanaya Osamu, Kawasaki Tsuneyuki, Kitayama Shigeo, Kobayashi Takashi, Matsumoto Seicho, Matsushita Kōnosuke, Murakami Shigeyoshi, Nagahara Keiji, Nagazumi Yoko, Nakayama Shigeru, Naramoto Tatsuya, Nozawa Yutaka, Oka Yoshitake, Ōkawa Kazushi, Ōtsuka Hisao, Sakamoto Taro, Sakudo Yōtaro, Shinohara Miyohei, Sugimoto Isao, Suzuki Ryōichi (the historian), Tamura Encho, Tanaka Sōgoro, Tōyama Shigeki, Tsuda Sōkichi, Wakamori Taro, Watanabe Shōkō, Watsuji Tetsuro, Yamaguchi Kazuo, Yasumoto Biten, Yui Tsunehiko.

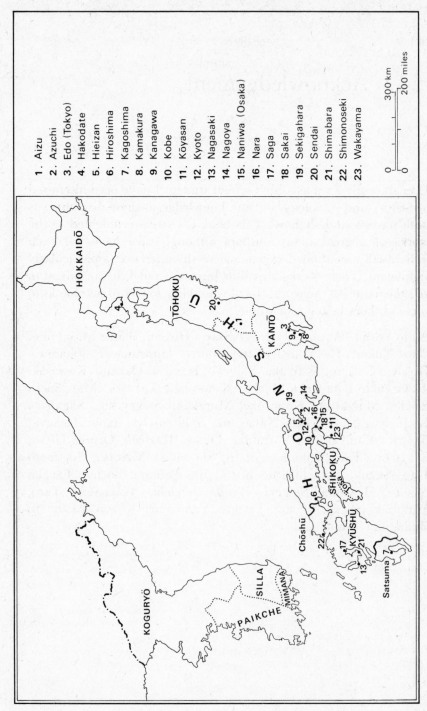

1. Aizu
2. Azuchi
3. Edo (Tokyo)
4. Hakodate
5. Hieizan
6. Hiroshima
7. Kagoshima
8. Kamakura
9. Kanagawa
10. Kobe
11. Kōyasan
12. Kyoto
13. Nagasaki
14. Nagoya
15. Naniwa (Osaka)
16. Nara
17. Saga
18. Sakai
19. Sekigahara
20. Sendai
21. Shimabara
22. Shimonoseki
23. Wakayama

Major places and areas of Japan and Korea mentioned in the text

Introduction

I

Whereas Karl Marx contended that ideology and ethics were no more than reflections of underlying material conditions – in particular economic conditions – Max Weber in his 'Protestant Ethic and the Spirit of Capitalism' made the case for the existence of quite the reverse relationship. He considered that it is the ethic that is given, and any type of economy which necessitates the people's possessing an ethos incompatible with that ethic will not develop; rather the emergence of an economy compatible with this ethic is inevitable. It was from this standpoint that Weber examined the world's major religions.[1]

Weber's conclusions concerning Confucianism can be summarised as follows. They are that Confucianism, like Puritanism, is

---

[1] Max Weber, *Gesammelte Aufsätze zur Religionssoziologie*, I (1920), II (1920), III (1921), J. C. B. Mohr (Paul Siebeck) Tübingen. The famous 'Protestant Ethic and the Spirit of Capitalism' (Die protestantische Ethik und der Geist des Kapitalismus) and 'Confucianism and Taoism' (Konfuzianismus und Taoismus) are both contained in the first volume.

There are, of course, criticisms of Max Weber's thesis; for example the idea that the capitalist spirit had already been in existence since before the birth of Protestantism put forward by L. Brentano. What Weber was interested in, however, was the relationship between the Protestant ethic and 'modern capitalism', and he believed that there existed a fundamental difference between Modern Capitalism and the capitalism which had previously existed. There is also the criticism made by R. H. Tawney that Weber not merely oversimplified both Calvinism and the spirit of capitalism, but that he also either underestimated or totally disregarded the part played by factors unconnected with religion (for example the political ideas of the Renaissance) in the intellectual movements conducive to the development of economic individualism. Even more criticisms can probably be brought forward by specialists in the case of Weber's work on China. What we are concerned with here, however, is not whether Weber was, or was not, right. The problem here is to consider the questions raised by Weber in relation to Japan. See L. Brentano, *Die Anfänge des Modernen Kapitalismus* (1961) and R. H. Tawney, *Religion and the Rise of Capitalism*.

rational, but that there exists a fundamental difference between the two in that whereas Puritan rationalism has sought to exercise rational control over the world Confucian rationalism is an attempt to accommodate oneself to the world in a rational manner. Furthermore, Weber concluded, it was exactly this sort of mental attitude among Confucianists that was a major factor in preventing the emergence of modern capitalism in China.

Despite this judgement Weber observed: 'The Chinese in all probability would be quite capable, probably as much as if not more capable than the Japanese, of assimilating capitalism which has technologically and economically been fully developed in the modern culture area.'[2] It must be said, however, that the ideology of Japan, or at least the most important of Japan's ideologies, is also Confucianism. Since Weber made very few positive observations on Japan, it is not at all clear, at least from his 'Confucianism and Taoism', whether or not he himself considers Japan to be a Confucian country.[3] Furthermore, whether or not Weber considers that the 'capitalism' which the Japanese have acquired is of the same kind as the 'modern capitalism' in conformity with the Protestant ethic is also very unclear. Here again no positive statement is made. However, despite these imperfections the above extract is in itself sufficiently suggestive of new lines of research.

In the following study I hope to throw light on the fact that in certain important respects Japanese Confucianism is very different from the Confucianism of China. In addition the Taoism which was introduced to Japan at the same time as Confucianism underwent considerable modifications and changed to emerge as Japanese Shinto. In Europe, Protestants split off from Catholics as a result of a different interpretation of the same bible; the rebels then built up a completely new work ethic – Weber's so-called

---

[2] M. Weber, *Gesammelte Aufsätze zur Religionssoziologie*, I, 1920, p. 535.

[3] In '*Die asiatische Sekten und Heilandsreligiosität*', however, Max Weber does discuss Japan. (See *Gesammelte Aufsätze zur Religionssoziologie*, II, pp. 295–309.) But his knowledge of Japan is not very extensive and his understanding would not appear to have been very deep. He regards the warrior class as having played the most important social role in Japan, and believes that the whole ethos and attitude to life of the Japanese was formed quite without regard to religion. However, as we will see later on, during the Tokugawa period the warrior class received a profoundly Confucian education (in the Kamakura period the samurai was deeply influenced by Zen Buddhism), and in the Meiji period compulsory education meant the people as a whole received a Confucian education. Weber makes no more than a passing reference to Japanese Confucianism, perhaps because he did not regard Confucianism as the principal ideology of Japan.

'spirit of modern capitalism'. In exactly the same way Japanese Confucianism started from the same canons as did Chinese Confucianism, and as a result of different study and interpretation produced in Japan a totally different national ethos from that prevailing in China. In Europe, with its contiguity of land between one country and another – and compared with the distance Japan lies from the Chinese mainland and the Korean peninsula even such countries as the British Isles, divided from mainland Europe by the English Channel, are as good as contiguous with their neighbours – because it was Catholicism which was first disseminated, any subsequent extrication from the arms of the Catholic faith necessitated a revolt or a revolution.

In an isolated Japan, however, it was impossible for Chinese Confucianism to spread in an unmodified form, and it was inevitable that from the very beginning the Japanese people should to a greater or lesser degree take over the doctrines in their own way and apply different interpretations to them. The religious revolution was carried out quickly, and probably unconsciously, on board the ships coming from China and Korea or on the beaches of the Japanese coastline. If one looks at things in this way the chain of events whereby differing interpretations of the same bible nurtured different ethoses among different peoples and helped to create totally different economic conditions can be said to have a certain validity not just when applied to the West but also when applied to the East.

Confucius regarded benevolence (*jen*), justice (*i*), ceremony (*li*), knowledge (*chih*) and faith (*hsin*) as among the most important virtues, but believed that of these it was benevolence (*jen*) which was the virtue which must be at the heart of humanity. Confucius believed that man's nature was fundamentally good, and considered in particular that the natural affection existing between relatives within one family was the cornerstone of social morality. According to Confucius the practice of morality did not lie in people's discharging the dispensations or commands of any transcendent being; it was when the natural human affection found within the family was extended without animosity beyond the confines of the family, both to non-family members and to complete strangers, that human nature had reached perfection and the social order was being appropriately maintained. Those who had acquired this kind of perfect love of humanity were spoken of as men of benevolence, or men of virtue (*jen-che*).

Confucius believed that to become such a person should be the ultimate objective of all moral cultivation. As might be expected, filial piety (*hsiao*) and the discharging of one's duty as a younger brother (*t'i*) became important virtues under Confucianism. Filial piety consisted of respecting one's parents, taking good care of them and acting according to their wishes; the obedience commensurate with a younger brother meant adherence to the wishes of elder brothers and seniors. In addition harmony (Ch. *ho*, Jap. *wa*) was essential for the achievement of benevolence. Harmony signified people's being in accord with one another and preserving accord within society, but this concept of *ho* also embraced a kind of harmony which was essentially harmful, being no more than one person's blindly following another. Similarly bravery (*yung*) was also frequently regarded as a precondition for this achievement of benevolence, but a brave person was not necessarily a benevolent person; bravery was something which must be directed towards the right ends. Confucius detested those people who, though they might be courageous, had no regard for courtesy.

Loyalty (*chung*) and faith (*hsin*) were the two virtues of sincerity. Loyalty implied sincerity vis-à-vis one's own conscience, i.e. an absence of pretensions or selfishness from the heart; faith meant always telling the truth. Faith was therefore the external expression of loyalty; whereas loyalty was a virtue which existed in relation to oneself, faith was a virtue which existed in regard to relationships with others. However, in just the same way as the keeping of a promise to commit an injustice was an act of wrongdoing, so loyalty by itself could not be considered perfect virtue. Loyalty could only be practised in conjunction with justice, or righteousness (*i*). Similarly the most important virtue, benevolence (*jen*), had to be tempered by justice and reinforced by knowledge; a simple, spontaneous humanity was not enough. Confucius described a true gentleman (a *chün-tzu*, or one replete with virtue) in the following manner:

> For the perfect gentleman there are nine considerations. These are a desire to see clearly when he looks at something; a desire to hear every detail when listening to something; a desire to present a tranquil countenance; a desire to preserve an attitude of respect; a desire to be sincere in his words; a desire to be careful in his work; a

willingness to enquire further into anything about which
he has doubts; a willingness to bear in mind the difficulties consequent on anger; a willingness to consider
moral values when presented with the possibility of
profit (*The Analects of Confucius*, chapter 16).

Confucius advocated what he called the principle of virtuous
government – meaning a method of government which would
strengthen the people by means of morality and serve naturally to
bring about order in society by raising the level of virtue among the
people. He strongly rejected any idea of constitutional government
on the grounds that under the principles of constitutionalism order
is imposed upon society by law and those who break the law are
penalised, so that people come to think how they can best avoid
punishment, and the resulting society has no sense of shame.
However, even in a society under the sway of the principle of
government by virtue something analogous to the laws found in a
constitutional society is essential. This was referred to by Confucius as *li*, or ceremony, by which he meant norms established by
custom but which were less rigid than laws. Confucius' maxim was
'guidance by morality, control by ceremony'. Given this he believed that 'people will come to have a sense of moral shame, and to
act correctly'. Confucius' belief was that it was especially incum-
bent on those in the upper levels of society to act in accordance
with the dictates of ceremony. A ruler must deal with his subordi-
nates in the fashion stipulated by custom; a rich man as well must
conduct himself with decorum and according to ceremony.

However the Confucianism which was understood and disseminated in Japan was not of this kind. It is also generally believed
that the differences between Japanese Confucianism and Chinese
Confucianism became greater and greater with the passage of time.
This can be shown by looking at the imperial injunction issued to
members of the Japanese armed forces in 1882. This injunction was
written from a Confucian standpoint, but was in no way a specific
ethical code allotted to a limited social group, i.e. members of the
armed forces. Following the establishment of the Meiji government
the traditional caste system had been abolished, the warrior class
had lost its prerogatives and a system of conscription had been
introduced. As a result the obligation of national defence fell to the
population as a whole, and all Japanese people were considered as

potential soldiers. The Imperial Injunction to Soldiers and Sailors was written on the basis of this sort of consideration, and was simultaneously an imperial injunction to the nation which had to be observed by the people as a whole. In this document five of the Confucian virtues were emphasised – loyalty, ceremony, bravery, faith and frugality; no special consideration was given to bene-volence, the central virtue in China. This neglect of the virtue of benevolence can be said to be quite natural in as far as the injunction was specifically aimed at members of the armed forces or the people as potential soldiers; but if we compare this with what was considered to be the essence of the soldierly or warrior spirit in China under Chiang Kai-shek or in ancient Korea certain charac-teristics of Japanese Confucianism become absolutely clear. In Chiang Kai-shek's army the major elements required for a soldierly spirit were wisdom, faith, benevolence, bravery and strictness; in the ancient Silla dynasty of Korea the qualities stipulated for soldiers according to the *hwa-rang do* (way of the perfect soldier – the Korean equivalent of Japanese *bushido*) were loyalty, filial piety, faith, benevolence and bravery.[4] Only faith and bravery are virtues common to all three countries. Benevolence is common to both China and Korea, but there is no mention of it in the case of Japan. Loyalty is common to both Japan and Korea but does not appear on China's list of virtues.

The neglect of benevolence in this fashion, and the emphasis placed on loyalty, must be regarded as characteristics peculiar to Japanese Confucianism. As mentioned earlier, benevolence was considered in China to be the central virtue of Confucianism. In Japan no especial importance was attached to it even in Shōtoku Taishi's Seventeen-Article Constitution of 604, which was written very much under the influence of Confucianism. It would not be true to say that the virtue of benevolence has continued to be completely disregarded throughout the history of Confucianism in Japan. However, this relative neglect of benevolence does not date only from the Meiji period; it is something which goes back a very long way. In Japan it was loyalty rather than benevolence which came to be considered the most important virtue, and this became more and more the case as Japan approached the modern period.

Furthermore the meaning of loyalty (Ch. *chung*, Jap. *chū*) was not

---

[4] See Ozaki Tomoe's essay (in Japanese) in *Dai-ikki Heika Yobi – gakusei no Ki*.

the same in both China and Japan. As previously mentioned, in China loyalty meant being true to one's own conscience. In Japan, although it was also used in this same sense, its normal meaning was essentially a sincerity that aimed at total devotion to one's lord, i.e. service to one's lord to the point of sacrificing oneself. Consequently Confucius' words 'act with loyalty in the service of one's lord' were interpreted by the Chinese to mean 'Retainers must serve their lord with a sincerity which does not conflict with their own consciences', whereas the Japanese interpreted the same words as 'Retainers must devote their whole lives to their lord.' As a result loyalty in Japan was a concept which, in conjunction with filial piety and duty to one's seniors, formed a trinity of values which regulated within society the hierarchic relationships based on authority, blood ties and age respectively. In Japan there was no question of the concept of loyalty and faith being considered two sides of the same coin, as was the case in China.

This concept of loyalty became more and more apparent from the Tokugawa period, and was especially obvious in its last years, becoming widely diffused among the Japanese people. This view of loyalty was not something of recent origin. As early as the time of the *Manyōshū* (an anthology of poems compiled in the latter half of the seventh century), poems spoke of loyalty towards the Emperor. In 749 Ōtomo no Yakamochi wrote:

> At sea be my body water-soaked,
> On land be it with grass overgrown,
> Let me die by the side of my Sovereign!
> Never will I feel regret.

It was in 753 that Imamatsuribe no Yosofu, a frontier guard, wrote:

> I will not from today
> Turn back toward home –
> I who have set out to serve
> As Her Majesty's humble shield.[5]

Loyalty in this sense of service to one's lord could frequently find itself in conflict with loyalty in the sense of being true to one's own

---

[5] Translations from Nippon Gakujutsu Shinkokai version of *The Manyōshū* (Tokyo, 1940).

conscience. However, in Japan this contradiction was not a serious one. In much the same way as conscientious pacifist activity was not permitted in Japan up to 1945 (and since then the Japanese constitution has nominally precluded the existence of a fighting force), so in Japan in earlier times the command of a lord counted for far more than the conscience of the individual. Throughout Japanese history up to the present individualism has never prospered, and, as a result, a strong, serious advocacy of liberalism has been virtually non-existent. The Japanese have been required to obey their rulers, to serve their parents, to honour their elders and to act in accordance with the majority factions in society. There has been little margin left over to grapple with problems of conscience.

Such an interpretation of loyalty could also conflict with the ideals of filial piety (Jap. *kō*)[6] and harmony (*wa*) (the Chinese virtues of *hsiao* and *ho*). This was because the orders of a ruler could conflict with parental wishes or with the majority opinion in society. As we shall see later,[7] Japan's first great political thinker, Shōtoku Taishi (573–621), prohibited dictatorship by the Emperor, so that his orders would not be in conflict with the majority opinion in society. Even so orders issued by the Emperor could still contradict parental wishes. Taira Shigemori (1138–79) encountered just such a paradoxical situation as this, and lamented it with the words: 'If I want to demonstrate my loyalty I must be deemed not to have filial piety; if I try to show filial piety I shall not be loyal.' But Japanese long after Shigemori would probably have chosen loyalty above filial piety. This was the case even when the Emperor's command might not reflect the feelings of the majority. When the Emperor issued a command which was unreasonable and tyrannical it was the man who overcame his own conscience and obeyed his master's injunction who was the loyal retainer, not the one who complied with the dictates of his own conscience and the will of the majority in society and refused to obey. The Japanese do not reproach such a person with an inadequate conscience; when he is in the wretched position of being unable to follow the dictates of his own conscience he attracts only their sympathy. While Chinese Confucianism is one in which bene-

---

[6] The structure of the Chinese family was very different from that of the family in Japan. The concept of filial piety, therefore, was quite naturally not precisely the same in both countries.

[7] See Chapter 1 below.

volence is of central importance, Japanese Confucianism is loyalty-centred Confucianism. Use of the word Confucianism in the first and subsequent chapters will normally refer to this kind of Japanese Confucianism.

II

Our earliest clear knowledge of Japanese history can be dated from about the fourth century. This gives us a historical era of some 1650 years from three centuries prior to the enactment of Shōtoku Taishi's Seventeen-Article Constitution in 604. The imperial family continued to be the ruling family of Japan throughout this period, but it was during no more than a third of this whole period that the Emperor was the ruler in fact as well as in name. For the remainder of the time essential control rested in the hands of regents (*sesshō* or *shikken*), chief advisers (*kanpaku*), retired Emperors (*hōō*), Shōguns (military chiefs) and others, and the Emperor was no more than a figurehead. At times there were prime ministers (*Dajō Daijin*) acting for retired Emperors, or regents acting for the Shōgun, so that even the retired Emperors or Shōgun were no more than figureheads themselves. However, even at such a time it fell to the Emperor to appoint the chief adviser, retired Emperor, Shōgun etc., so he remained nominally the ultimate ruler of Japan, and he continued to carry on his own administration, i.e. to maintain the imperial court. This means that some two thirds of the historical era in Japan were years of dual, and at times triple, government. Apart from antiquity and the years since the Meiji Revolution it has only been for a very few years, and intermittently, that there has existed a single government under direct imperial rule. Furthermore, for over 70% of this period of dual government, real political power was controlled by Shōguns, or prime ministers or chief advisers backed by military power. Under the influence of China a bureaucratic system was introduced into Japan's primal imperial government very early on and her dual military government also adopted a system of military bureaucracy; but there has been no tradition of civilian control of the armed forces.

China, in contrast, has had a purely civilian bureaucratic system. The Chinese continent, at least by the yardstick of premodern means of communication, was so vast that it rendered control by a single central government very difficult; but during a large proportion of the historical period the whole territory (the exact area varied according to the actual period) was, nevertheless, controlled by a single, unified Imperial regime. There were, of course, periods of disturbance in China as well, and also times when several dynasties divided the territory between them and existed side by side. The time when Confucius himself was living (551–479 B.C.) was one such period. It was a time when the Chou dynasty had lost its authority and several feudal city states were in conflict with each other. The Chou dynasty itself was no more than one of these. Following the Chou the first Emperor of the Ch'in dynasty united the whole region under his control, building a single large empire; the final imperial dynasty, the Ch'ing, fell some 2100 years later. While for about 500 years of this period the country was divided among different localised dynasties, for the remaining 1600 years it was unified under the control of various nationwide dynasties. Some of these dynasties, for example the Han, T'ang, Ming and Ch'ing, lasted over 200 years; others had short lives of no more than 30–40 years. Therefore the first consideration of any dynasty had to be how to prolong its own existence; whatever the situation the system of civilian bureaucracy was traditionally taken over by almost all the unified dynasties.

Confucius' greatest achievement probably lay in throwing open to a greater number of people the culture and education which had hitherto been the monopoly of the aristocracy. Confucius' disciples dispersed after his death, but one group of them took up service in the feudal states and became involved in politics as bureaucrats. Since Confucius himself had advocated the principle of government by virtue, and had been opposed to constitutionalism, his followers were not people who merely implemented laws and carried out administration; they were either politicians, or, if not, political advisers who suggested their own political ideas to their rulers. They also acted as teachers to the next generation. Thus in the period after Confucius' death when China was divided into several small states there appeared the small, feudal states which were civilian states run by officials fully trained in the principles of Confucianism, and on these states were modelled the vast majority of China's later unified dynasties.

However, the Ch'in dynasty (246–207 B.C.), the first unified post-Confucian dynasty, was opposed to Confucianism, and retreated from the principles of 'virtuous government'. The first Emperor of this dynasty prohibited the possession of books relating to Confucianism and other learning, ordered that all such books should be burnt and massacred large numbers of Confucians. He then drew up a series of regulations and orders, imposed a purely constitutional system of government, and ended up with a state which was an absolutist despotic monarchy resting on a centralised bureaucratic system. This first Emperor devoted his efforts to such things as constructing the thousands of miles of the Great Wall, and also created huge imperial palaces and detached palaces. He also engaged in frequent incursions outside China's borders. As a result large-scale disturbances among the harshly exploited peasantry broke out after his death and the great empire in which he hoped he had built the legal and military foundations for a strong country was eventually very short-lived, collapsing within a very short time.

The Han dynasty which followed the Ch'in (the early Han lasted 206 B.C.–A.D. 8, and the later Han dynasty A.D. 25–220) quite naturally learnt from the mistakes of its predecessor. The Han revived Confucianism and, moreover, actually recognised it as the orthodoxy of the state. Confucian intellectualism was respected; entry into the government was widened to include members of the intelligentsia and made more difficult for those related to the dynasty and the rich. At the same time the Han took over what they saw as the strong points of the Ch'in. The country was provided with a legal code and equipped with a system of bureaucracy. In addition regional governors were appointed by the central government. Under the ancient pre-Ch'in dynasties the provinces had been handed over to the relatives of the imperial family; the centre of the empire and the provinces were held together by the ties of imperial blood. The Ch'in had abolished this kind of Chinese feudal system and had instituted a 'prefectural' system whereby regional governors were appointed by the central government. At first the Han apportioned the provinces to members of the imperial family, but these regional branches of the imperial family were compelled to live in the capital. Their territorial rights became purely nominal and a prefectural system was implemented in full. The government was able to take in talented individuals from every class of society, because provided he had received sufficient Confucian training any man could become not only an ordinary official, but even Prime Minister or provincial governor. Moreover, it was civilian officials selected in this fashion who were in control of the army. Gradually a system of national examinations for entry into the bureaucracy was set up, a system which was more or less perfected by the early part of the T'ang dynasty (618–907).

This meant that the central government annually brought together school leavers from both the capital and the provinces, and individuals from all areas of the country who had obtained recommendations, and conducted examinations. Those who were successful were appointed to the bureaucracy.[8] The children of the nobility were at an advantage in these examinations because the things that were tested were, for example, how far an individual had mastered the Confucian classics, what were his literary powers of expression, whether he could write well and what were his powers of deduction. However, the sons of medium or small-scale landlords and other members of the lower classes did have the opportunity of being successful. Thus the prototype of the Chinese imperial state, with its laws and politics founded on the ideology of Confucianism, its prefectural system, its examination-appointed bureaucratic system and its civilian control of the army, was virtually complete by the end of the sixth century. China had already reached this stage when Japan first came into contact with her.

The forces which brought down this kind of dynasty were the peasantry, eunuchs and the peoples who lived on China's northern borders. It was sometimes just one of these factors which brought down a dynasty, but not infrequently two of these elements, or even all three, concurred to play a part in overthrowing the existing regime. The destruction of a dynasty might typically take the following pattern. The Emperor, for some reason or other, might die young. (Since Chinese Emperors showed a tendency to be addicted to a debauched lifestyle many of them did die young.) Since it was no longer the custom in China for succession to pass from one brother to another the Emperor would be succeeded by the Crown Prince, who was probably still a baby. Real political

[8] This kind of examination system was continued even when China was under the control of alien peoples. During the Yüan period (1280–1367) when China was under the control of a Mongol dynasty the examinations for entry into the bureaucracy was initially (to 1313) not conducted, but after that the examinations system was revived. The Ch'ing dynasty of the Manchus (1644–1911) was highly sinicised and consequently never took the step of abolishing the examinations.

power would pass into the hands of the Empress (Dowager Empress), or her parents or brothers. When the Empress herself was in control of the administration the voice of eunuchs in the running of affairs was often extremely great. (Apart from the official Empress, of whom there was only one, Chinese Emperors possessed over a hundred concubines, ranked in a carefully defined hierarchy, as well as thousands of court ladies. Affairs within the court were managed by eunuchs, who numbered several thousand. At times there were in excess of 10,000.) Furthermore, when it was the parents of the Dowager Empress who wielded power the influence of the eunuchs was frequently used to try and exclude such parental influence. Where it was the eunuchs who dominated nothing could be done without their agreement and for this bribery was invariably necessary. Officials would exact heavy taxes from the peasantry and bribe the eunuchs. As a result peasant uprisings and disturbances would break out, and in the ensuing confusion non-Chinese peoples would take advantage of the situation to cross over the Great Wall and make incursions into China proper. The army would be sent to repulse these enemies which in turn would necessitate the levying of further heavy taxes to meet the expenses of the campaign. The peasantry would thus become even more disaffected. In an agricultural country such as China, if the regime loses the support of the peasantry the power of the nation at once starts to decline, and the fall of the dynasty is inevitable.[9]

All dynasties met their downfall through a course of events very similar to these, though with certain variations. Whether or not a dynasty was able to endure was totally dependent on its agricultural policies, but appropriate measures were rarely taken. In ancient China there existed what was called the *ching-tien* (well-field) system. According to this each area of land of a given size was subdivided into nine smaller portions of equal size. These were in turn distributed to eight families, with the central section (the division was done on a 3 by 3 basis) being cultivated jointly by the eight families, with its produce being paid to the government as tax.[10] This system appears to have been implemented regardless of

---

[9] See, for example, Kaizuka Shigeki *Chūgoku no Rekishi* (History of China) vols. I, II, III (Iwanami Shoten, Tokyo, 1964, 1969 and 1970).

[10] The Chinese character for well (*ching*) consists of two vertical lines and two horizontal lines crossing each other (井). The division of a square field into 9 plots on a 3 by 3 basis meant that it was subdivided along the same lines as the shape of this character. Hence the system was called the well-field (*ching-tien*) system.

the locality. Both the Sui and T'ang dynasties had plans to try and implement this equal distribution of land on a nationwide scale, but all such ideas had finally been abandoned by the middle period of T'ang dynasty rule. Thus the poverty of agricultural policies provoked disturbances among the peasantry and eventually brought about the downfall of the dynasty. Typically, when the subsequent dynasty was established the Confucian literati would again occupy all the offices of the government and control would again be in the hands of the bureaucratic intellectuals. Measures to deal with the peasantry would be neglected very much as before, the Emperor would give himself over to debauched living, the exasperated peasantry would rise in revolt and this dynasty as well would finally collapse.

If we compare the political structure of Japan with the dynastic control of this kind that we find in China, certain points of broad similarity and dissimilarity can be indicated. Japan was throughout a dynastic country in the sense that the imperial family reigned unbroken, but, except for a few years, throughout the period from 1192 to 1867 the state was subject to dual government, with the Emperor's government (the court) and the Shōgun's government (the Bakufu) existing in parallel. The court was a civilian government controlled by civilian officials, the Bakufu a military administration controlled by soldiers. Since the court had been established long before the Bakufu (late sixth century–mid seventh century) and had taken China as its model it was a government with a code of laws (*ritsuryō*) and a system of civilian bureaucracy, whereas the Tokugawa Bakufu (1603–1867), which of all the Bakufu administrations was the most well-organised form of warrior government, was the government of a military bureaucracy founded on a hereditary status system. In Japan neither the imperial family nor the Shōgun's family ever possessed a harem on the scale of the Chinese Emperor's, and compared with the Chinese dynasties both the imperial and shogunal families led irreproachably frugal lives. Furthermore there were no eunuchs. The religion of the imperial family was Shintō, but the ideology of the bureaucracy of the Emperor's administration was Confucianism, as was that of the Tokugawa Bakufu. If one compares China and Japan during the Tokugawa period one is forced to conclude that China was a civilian Confucian country and Japan a military Confucian country. Chinese Confucianism, with its regard for 'benevolence' as the most important virtue, was well adapted to the sort of control structure that existed in China. Japanese Confucianism, according to which loyalty, in the sense of sacrificing one's whole life to one's lord, was regarded as the central virtue, was in accordance with Japan's warrior rule. Each country had therefore developed a ruling structure in conformity with its respective ideology.

The warriors of the Tokugawa period reconciled their moral obligation (loyalty to the Emperor) and the actual existence of dual government according to the following logic. They understood loyalty in genealogical terms. The ordinary warrior and the people owed allegiance to the *daimyō*, their immediate lord; each *daimyō* owed his allegiance to the Shōgun, who in turn owed loyalty to the Emperor. Given this hierarchy of loyalties the whole people owed loyalty to the Emperor either directly or indirectly. As long as the hierarchy in this loyalty system was maintained neither dual government nor the feudal system led to any ethical contradictions, and each person had only to think of his loyalty vis-à-vis the person immediately above him in the hierarchy. However there were occasions on which a *daimyō* failed to discharge his loyalty to the Shōgun or when a Shōgun disregarded the Emperor, and when this happened people began to wonder about this loyalty so important to Japanese Confucianism and to ask to whom this loyalty was due. When people concluded that this was a loyalty owed to the Emperor, calls for 'reverence of the Emperor' (*sonnō*) and 'destroy the Bakufu' (*tōbaku*) would emerge and the Bakufu would then find itself in a very difficult ideological situation. In fact in the later years of the Tokugawa period when Japan was under great pressure from the countries of the West to open her ports the Bakufu was at a loss to know how to deal with the crisis. On some occasions it disregarded the Emperor (the Court) and on others shifted the responsibility onto the Court for any mistakes. By its doing this the people began to realise that the Bakufu itself was not acting in accordance with Japan's ideology.

Chinese Confucianism is, at all events, humanistic, whereas Japanese Confucianism is remarkably nationalistic. This difference may well be a reflection of the inferiority complex which Japan developed in response to the 'Middle Kingdom' idea of China, the idea that China was the centre of the world, a country where civilisation blossomed like a flower in all its glory. Japan has perpetually been in the position where she has felt herself under pressure from a strong world empire and has, as a result, perhaps become excessively defensive. She has instinctively perceived that to continue to exist in her corner of East Asia she has to be both frugal and courageous. Since the cultural disparity which existed between China and Japan was probably at its greatest in the fifth and sixth centuries, when Japan first became aware of the existence of China and was still herself very much at a barbaric stage, defensive nationalism for the sake of survival was a salient feature of Japanese Confucianism from very early on. Japan was again made aware of the cultural disparity existing between herself and other countries in the sixteenth century, when contact with Western countries began.

These feelings of inferiority eventually led the Tokugawa Bakufu to adopt a policy of seclusion. There was a surge of nationalism at the end of the Tokugawa period when it became apparent that any further continuation of seclusion was impossible. The Japanese people changed course completely and devoted all their energies to the acquisition of Western technology. Whereas the Chinese bureaucracy consisted of men who had mastered the Chinese classics and who were skilled at poetry and literature, Japan's warrior bureaucrats were interested in weaponry, and hence in science and technology. Both countries may have been Confucian, but, whereas China's bureaucrats showed a stolid opposition to the sciences of the West, Japan's governments from the Tokugawa Bakufu through to the imperial government which followed the Meiji Revolution showed nothing but an enthusiastic desire to acquire this same science. While the motive power behind Western capitalism was the individual's demands for freedom, a forced march was begun in Japan to do away with the military and scientific–technological disparities which existed between Japan and the West. In this march the individual was expected to offer in sacrifice not merely his everyday life, but, if necessary, his death as well; this was his loyalty, his moral backbone.

When we look at Japan's development from this point of view then there are two particular periods in Japanese history which must catch our eye. These are, firstly, the period from the end of the sixth century to the middle of the seventh century when Japan was forced into an acute awareness of the pressure on her from the Chinese Empire, and, secondly, the last years of the Tokugawa Bakufu when she was subject to the advances of the Western

World War, Japan even developed an imperialist-fascist economy which disregarded the people's welfare by emphasising the build up of the military. In spite of her economic success in the postwar era, the prospects of individualism and liberalism blossoming and maturing in Japan are still extremely remote.

Finally, it seems remarkable that no significant religious revolution has occurred in Japan. The Japanese enriched their spiritual lives by changing the relative emphasis of their heterogeneous religions (or ethical doctrines). They emphasised the Shintō elements in times of national crisis and the Confucian elements after drastic changes in their political regime. In so doing, they acquired an ideological driving force for solving the problems with which their country has been confronted. Indeed, a flexible combination of the three ethical systems and not a single religion has contributed to Japan's cultural and economic development.

CHAPTER ONE

The Taika Reform and after

I

Throughout her history until the Meiji Revolution (1867–68) Japan was under the influence of Chinese culture; cultural stimuli and encouragement came from China either directly or through Korea. By adapting the imported culture to her own cultural heritage and to local conditions Japan was able to pursue her own unique development. Nevertheless, a huge cultural gap persisted between the two countries, and Japan had constantly to repeat the process of importing, digesting and amending Chinese culture in order to advance her own level of learning and civilisation. As is well known, after the Meiji Revolution a similar process occurred between Japan and the Western countries as she developed her culture and economy by importing their science and technology.

Buddhism, Confucianism and Taoism all came to Japan (from China via Korea) almost simultaneously in about the sixth century. In those times there were, apart from the imperial clan, two groups of clans, whose chieftains were called Muraji and Omi respectively. Muraji clans were in hereditary vassalage to the imperial clan and served the Emperor in religious affairs and the production of ecclesiastical and ceremonial ware, and in defence, according to the duties specific to each clan. Omi clans, however, were not originally the Emperor's lieges. In early history Omi clans held their own territories independent of the Emperor, but were later subjected to imperial rule. Leaders of powerful clans were called Ō-muraji (great Muraji), or Ō-omi (great Omi, which, if written in Chinese characters, means 'cabinet minister' in modern Japanese); the imperial clan already reigned over both these clans in the fourth century.

One must not regard Japan at that time as one would regard Japan today. At that time, both among the upper classes and among the people at large, husband and wife lived separately. The husband visited his wife but not the other way round. Naturally, the husband openly had several wives whom he visited in turn; the wife privately received several husbands in turn. Looked at from the present day point of view their sexual lives were in a state of confusion. The children were brought up by their respective mothers, so the children of different mothers were little more than strangers to each other. They could easily fall in love with one another, they could marry each other without any feeling that they were committing a crime, and at the same time they could easily kill each other. Therefore, an influential powerful chieftain could quickly establish a strong blood relationship with the imperial family by, for example, marrying his own daughter to an imperial prince, and then marrying their daughter to an imperial prince who was himself the offspring of a union between the first imperial prince and another of the chieftain's daughters. Moreover, at that time there was no primogeniture as there was later in Japan; the crown prince was often chosen from among the brothers of the emperor, so there was fierce fighting among them, and they frequently killed each other. However, when the so-called Great Tomb Age[1] ended the Japanese began to try and advance their culture.

During the sixth century the great nobles were increasing their political and economic power and of them the Soga and the Mononobe clans were the most powerful. The former (an Omi clan) respected the new culture (especially Buddhism which was then coming in from Korea) while the latter (a Muraji clan) was anti-Buddhist. Both clans enriched themselves by exploiting the colony which Japan held in Korea at that time. They often engaged in disputes about the succession to the throne and many possible candidates to the imperial throne were killed. In the end a civil war broke out between the two clans which brought about the decisive defeat of the Mononobe.

After this it was the Soga who chose which prince (or princess) of the imperial clan should be the Emperor (or Empress). The imperial clan was weakened and the throne became very unstable.

[1] Chieftains erected huge tombs for themselves; those built for the emperors were so big that it would not be an exaggeration to compare them with the Egyptian pyramids. So great were the numbers of people utilised in the construction of these tombs that agricultural production was affected.

Finally in 592 Umako of the Soga clan killed Emperor Sushun in order to let Empress Suiko accede to the throne. Sushun was Umako's sister's son and Suiko was the daughter of another of his sisters; both these sisters were the wives of the same Emperor Kinmei. As we have seen princes and princesses in the imperial family could not even trust their half brothers or half sisters. Many of the dynasties of Imperial China had been brought down by the power accruing to the Emperor's maternal relations, and the Japanese imperial family as well was at this time under pressure from the maternally related Soga clan. Eunuchs, who had frequently tyrannised over the court in China, were fortunately not introduced into Japan either at this time or at any time since. (The lack of existence of eunuchs was probably one of the important background factors which enabled Japan to preserve an unbroken imperial line.) However, in spite of all this, now that the Mononobe had been removed, the new culture flourished under the Soga.

In those days it was absolutely necessary for Japan to put the sovereignty of the imperial family on a firm basis and to reform her government machinery for both internal and external political reasons. Since about 370 the Japanese had occupied the southern tip of the Korean peninsula. This Japanese territory, which was called Mimana, adjoined Paikche and Silla which in turn adjoined Koguryö. Japan had also had extensive influence in Paikche and Silla from about the same time, and they paid tribute to her. The Mimanans gradually interbred with Koreans and made no effort to resist attacks from Paikche and Silla which plundered the colony, threatening its collapse. Though successive generations of Emperors tried to restore it they achieved little success. It must be remembered that at the same time as the setback in the peninsula, on the main island of Japan the imperial clan was losing control over the chieftains who were becoming more and more independent of the central government and who were claiming areas of land and the inhabitants therein as their own territory and vassals. Thus the strengthening of the government was necessary for both these internal and external reasons.

Prince Shōtoku Taishi (574–622), Heir Apparent and Regent to Empress Suiko, wanted to strengthen the imperial sovereignty but had to compromise with the then powerful Soga clan, especially since he himself was the son of Soga Umako's nephew (Emperor Yōmei) and niece (Princess Anahobe no Hashihito). He set about modernising the imperial government by introducing the Chinese administrative and judicial system which was far more advanced than the existing indigenous one. He instituted the Twelve-Cap-Rank System in 603 and promulgated a Seventeen-Article Constitution in 604. The former, which classified ministers and other officers into twelve ranks being marked by caps of prescribed pattern and colour, declared that officers should be appointed to appropriate positions not because of their genealogy but according to their ability. The latter may be considered as a kind of Public Service Regulations associated with the new Rank System. However, Shōtoku Taishi realised that the Chinese political philosophy underlying their system would conflict with his ultimate purpose which was to establish a strong state unified under a hereditary line of monarchs. In China it was believed that the mandate of Heaven could not be exercised by a sovereign without virtue; if an emperor was found to be lacking in charisma and was unable to govern the country satisfactorily, then God would not support him and would replace the ruling dynasty by another one. It was therefore considered that unless a rejection, or at least a revision, of this particular Chinese political practice was effected, it would be impossible to secure the Japanese imperial family from the possibility of revolution in the future since there had, in fact, been brutal and vicious emperors like Yūryaku and Buretsu in the past. Under the Chinese system such emperors would not have been tolerated.

'*Wa-kon Yō-sai*' (Japanese spirit with Western ability) was a Japanese slogan current after the Meiji Revolution when the nation was importing Western technology. Similarly, Shōtoku Taishi drew the distinction between the Chinese principle of thought and their practical ability, and carefully examined whether their spirit (or mental attitude) would suit the Japanese or not. If some elements of the Chinese philosophy were found to be unsuitable or undesirable, they were either entirely rejected or drastically revised. Although Shōtoku was keen to raise the level of education of the Japanese people up to the Chinese standard, he did not accept everything Chinese. He wanted to graft Chinese ability onto the stock of Japanese spirit.

However, in Japan a national spirit had not as yet been clearly and firmly formed. There were many blank spaces on the canvas for Shōtoku Taishi to fill in with his own colour; in fact, by doing so he became the first philosopher of thought in Japan. Although evidence is sparse, some historians claim that Shōtoku Taishi coined the name '*Tennō*' (Heavenly Emperor) for the Japanese emperor where before the title had been '*Ō-kimi*' (Great King). The change had far-reaching results; it implied that the Emperor was no longer a king, but was a Manifest God (*ara-hito gami*) and was thus identified with God. There could consequently be no possibility of conflict between God and Emperor and hence no revolution was admissible. The imperial throne was thus provided with divine right and established on a firm foundation. It was Shōtoku Taishi who provided the Japanese with the political axiom that in their country, as opposed to China, the claim to the throne could be made only with the authority of descent.

It is true that Shōtoku Taishi's view of the Emperor was not separable from his feeling of inferiority vis-à-vis the powerful Chinese empire; the identification of the Emperor with God was nothing else but an expression of the sense of crisis which was felt concerning the future of the imperial family. In the history of Japan Shōtoku Taishi played a role of great importance in promoting conservatism and loyalism; in fact, the idea of the 'Manifest God' has been repeatedly emphasised with the effect of encouraging fanatical rightists whenever the country has been confronted with a national emergency. But it is also true that Shōtoku Taishi made a great number of drastic changes which were progressive in character. For example, in the Seventeen-Article Constitution he proclaimed that in Japan there was no king or master other than the Emperor who ruled over all; every man was equal in front of the Emperor. He also wanted to establish a new Chinese-style bureaucratic system in which government officials were appointed not because of their pedigree but according to their character and ability. Offices were no longer inheritable, so the power of noble lineage was weakened.[2] Furthermore, Shōtoku proclaimed that no

---

[2] It is doubtful how far Shōtoku Taishi's ideals of the abolition of lineage and opening of offices to talent were realised under his rule. In fact one can consider it likely that all men of influence were given positions within the government commensurate with their respective political influence. However, this ranking of the existing heads of powerful families as government officers is highly significant. This was because if they were incorporated into the government then the Emperor's administration would also be extended within each clan. This is thought to be probably the only way in which the Emperor's government, which up to the time had not possessed overwhelming political power, could break down the defensive armour of the other clans and extend the imperial administration to within these families.

person would be allowed to exploit another; thus the prevailing situation of great nobles and chieftains having their own subjects and territories lost its legal basis. It was hoped that the caste and the old kinship system would therefore vanish.

Shōtoku's constitution stipulates in its first article that Japanese society should be constituted on the basis of the first principle of all communal societies which is *wa*: harmony among members. No one should be allowed to form a subgroup within the community in order to oppose others. Each person should calmly discuss matters to arrive at a decision which is reasonable and desirable from the viewpoint of the community as a whole. It is stated in Articles 10 and 17 that dictatorship should be rejected; that, to realise harmony within the society, governors at various levels should consult on important matters with the public and make decisions arrived at democratically. Article 2 states that Buddhism should be propagated in order to raise the moral level of individuals. Shōtoku Taishi considered that the *Tennō* regime could not be preserved unless this code of ethics was firmly observed throughout the country.

According to Shōtoku's model Japanese society consists of the Emperor, the civil servants and the people. Article 12 emphasises that local governors are no longer chieftains but rule their respective districts as government officials. They cannot therefore levy taxes or impose corvée on the people for private purposes. The remaining articles of the Constitution define the public service regulations. These are: civil servants must be obedient to the imperial edicts (Article 3); they should realise that propriety is the foundation of law and order (Article 4); they should administer political justice without which loyalty to the Emperor and benevolence to the people would not prevail (Article 6). Furthermore it is emphasised that civil servants should respect sincerity which is the mother of righteousness (Article 9); they should not act from selfish motives but should render service to the public (Article 15). Other articles giving detailed regulations for the conduct of civil servants say: Do not accept a bribe (Article 5); appoint the right man to the right position (Article 7); come to the office as early as possible and work overtime (Article 8); respect and carry out the principle of 'work-and-you-will-be-rewarded' (Article 11); perform public service smoothly by dispatching business quickly (Article 13); do not feel jealous over a colleague's good fortune (Article 14);

and, finally, avoid the busy farming season when setting farmers to non-farming work (Article 16).

Although the Constitution explicitly urges the people to respect Buddhism in its Article 2, as a whole it is very Confucian. The virtues of harmony, propriety, loyalty, benevolence, sincerity and righteousness which are highly advocated in the Constitution are all Confucian rather than Buddhist.[3] It also emphasises that a political decision should be made democratically whilst the people must obey the order of the Emperor unconditionally. This apparent paradox between democratic decision-making and the absolute rightness of the Emperor's orders can be resolved only by remembering that he is always right because he conveys to the people only those orders that are decided democratically. In Shōtoku Taishi's view, the Emperor was very much like a modern constitutional monarch and because of this character he was the God of the society as well as the Emperor (i.e. the Heavenly Emperor). In Article 10 Shōtoku Taishi stated:

> Man has his own will. One may disagree with what others agree to. Indeed, we may have different views. I may not be a saint; he may not be a fool. We are all ordinary people and no one can tell what is absolutely right. Each should accept the majority decisions even if he thinks that he alone is right.

Thus the Emperor can be the Heavenly Emperor only on condition that he gives up any notion of dictatorship. Shōtoku Taishi guarded the *Tennō* system from all danger of revolution by making the concession that the Emperor should be politically neutral. Bearing in mind the very critical situation in which the imperial clan was placed in those days, it could be that this concession was not Shōtoku Taishi's own spontaneous idea but a compromise forced on him in reaction to the then rapidly growing power of the non-royal members of the ruling class. But yet it may clearly be

---

[3] The words 'harmony is invaluable' used by Shōtoku in Article 1 come from Confucius' *Analects*. I agree with Watsuji Tetsurō's conclusion that Shōtoku Taishi was a Buddhist as far as the problems of the life of the individual were concerned, but a Confucian regarding the political problems of the state. (Watsuji, *Nihon Rinri Shisō Shi* (A History of Japanese Ethical Thought), vol. 1 (Iwanami Shoten, Tokyo, 1979), pp. 116–18). Shōtoku Taishi made considerable use of Buddhism for political purposes, but his political ideology was fundamentally Confucian.

seen how modern and progressive were some of his political ideas. As early as 604 he proposed (1) the *Tennō* system which resembles the modern constitutional monarchy, (2) democracy, and (3) bureaucracy.

Evidently measures which would logically lead to the abolition of the privileges enjoyed by the great nobles were unacceptable to men of high birth such as Soga Umako. To avoid a revolt Shōtoku Taishi had to conciliate them. Under the new Constitution the Emperor was not only restrained from having the state under his absolute rule, but he also had to consult with the ministers and high officials about every affair of the state he handled. Although, as some historians do (and as I have also done above), the constitutional-monarchic position of the Emperor could be highly regarded, it was actually a surrender, or at least a serious concession to the Soga clan on the part of Shōtoku Taishi. It was important to avoid any clash with the Soga. As a matter of fact, since many important positions in the government and at Court were already occupied by the Soga, the Emperors could do little without their consent. As has been said earlier, Empress Suiko was the daughter of the Emperor Kinmei by a wife from the Soga family. Moreover, she was set on the throne by Soga Umako after he had killed Emperor Sushun. Shōtoku Taishi himself was not only the son of Umako's nephew by Umako's niece but also his son-in-law. Clearly the Soga were already very powerful and it would be no exaggeration to say that they could have usurped the throne if they had really wanted to do so. The Constitution, insofar as it prevented the Emperor's personal dictatorship, was no more than a recognition and confirmation of this reality. Under the Constitution, the imperial clan established its special position as Divine Beings and acquired eternal sacredness and inviolability, while the Soga (as the maternal relatives of the imperial family) retained their real political superiority over all other chieftains. In spite of this Constitution there was no change in Soga Umako's position: he remained the chief minister of the Suiko government.

In order to deal with the internal and external problems with which Japan was faced, Shōtoku Taishi instituted a number of other positive programmes in addition to those of the 'cap ranks' and the promulgation of the Constitution. Being confronted with the more advanced culture of China, the Japanese in the late sixth century were divided into two groups. One insisted on opening up

Japan to China so as to promote cultural exchange between the two countries (though this would inevitably be a one-way exchange). The other insisted on closing the country to save it from being 'contaminated' by Buddhism. This was exactly the same as the reaction the Japanese had to the appearance of the powerful Western technology and science on the eve of the Meiji Revolution. It was not very hard for Shōtoku Taishi to promote his policies of cultural exchange as the dominant anti-Buddhist clan, the Mono-nobe, had already been defeated by the pro-Buddhist Soga. His purpose was the enlightenment of his country. He sent missions and students to China four times, not just because he was a believer in Buddhism, but also because he thought Chinese culture and Chinese institutions were indispensable for the development of Japan. He built a huge temple and guest palace in Naniwa (now Osaka) which was the main port to the then capital of Japan, Ikaruga near Nara. He started compiling official historical records of the imperial family, the great nobles (Omi, Muraji, etc.) and the people in general. He also planned an attack on Silla which was threatening the security of Mimana. However, all efforts to preserve the colony were in vain, and after his death in 621 Japan finally had to abandon it.

II

In spite of the new political ideas proposed by Shōtoku Taishi, who was a man of extraordinary talent and wisdom, there was no great change in actual politics. Shōtoku was more of a philosopher than a politician; he was too weak to carry out his epoch-making programmes and he therefore made a great many compromises with Soga Umako. Under Shōtoku Taishi's regency, it was Umako rather than Shōtoku himself who was really powerful; and after his death the Soga family became still more powerful and tyrannical. Revolutionaries were needed to implement Shōtoku Taishi's plans.

The Soga family was finally overthrown more than twenty years after Shōtoku's death. By this time those students who had been sent by him to China for study were coming home. Having seen that in China a new empire, the T'ang dynasty, was developing and flourishing, they were natural supporters of the policy of enlightenment. They insisted that the government should formulate codes of laws and ethics so as to establish as well-organised an administrative machinery as that possessed by the T'ang. Finally, in 645, the revolutionaries, Prince Naka no Ōe (later Emperor Tenchi) and Nakatomi no Kamatari (later Fujiwara Kamatari), carried out a coup d'état and killed Soga Iruka, the then head of the clan. They succeeded in establishing a system of centralised administrative power similar to that of the government of the T'ang empire. This was the Taika Reform (645–649); it was a revolution by the aristocracy based on the political doctrines of Shōtoku Taishi.

The main aim of the Taika Reform was to separate the chieftains from the land. It is clear that in the seventh century in an agricultural country like Japan no one could enjoy privilege to the detriment of others if the farmland was distributed evenly among the people by the state. Under the new regime the farmland of the nation was divided into equal lots each of which was further divided into nine equal plots in an exact copy of the Chinese system of land tenure. One lot was worked by eight men each being provided with one plot to work as his own. All eight men collectively farmed the remaining plot for the state. Chieftains were restricted to cultivating an allotment of land of the same size as that of the ordinary people, although if they worked as government officials they also received a certain stipend corresponding to their post in office. There could be no discrimination in their favour and against the populace. The chieftains lost their own private land and were appointed as administrators or governors of the central or local government of the state. Under a powerful central government a national prefectural system was established with an early socialist economy.

The people became equal before the law and, moreover, economically equal – at least in principle – by virtue of the nationalisation of land. Only the Emperor held a special position as the Manifest God and head of the nation, while the others were provided with equal opportunities. This was the case at least on the surface. The new government was progressive; its offices were open to talent. As an ideal, this system was not, of course, new; it was precisely the one which Shōtoku Taishi had elucidated, although he himself had not been able to realise it because of his need to compromise politically with Soga Umako. Prince Naka no Ōe accomplished the system conceived by Shōtoku in its more uncompromising and purified form, and when he at last liquidated Soga Iruka, grandson of Umako, the imperial family became the real power.[4]

After the promulgation of the Seventeen-Article Constitution, it took about forty years to establish this constitutional and bureaucratic government, which was in various respects similar to the government of the T'ang dynasty and adopted Confucianism as its official ideology.[5] It should be considered as the joint achievement of Shōtoku Taishi the philosopher, and Naka no Ōe the revolutionary; revolution cannot be accomplished simply by beautiful philosophy.

In spite of dissimilar characters, these two great men in some ways resembled one another. Firstly, they took a hawkish attitude towards Korea. Shōtoku Taishi, as we have seen, planned an attack on Silla in order to preserve Mimana. Naka no Ōe, while he was the Crown Prince under Empress Saimei, responded to Paikche's desperate plea for help to withstand an attack from the allied forces of T'ang and Silla by sending a large army to Korea. From Japan's viewpoint, this might be considered an unnecessary war because she had already lost her colony in Korea. The Japanese troops were convincingly beaten and had to retreat back to Japan. National prestige was heavily damaged and the Japanese government did not try to attack Korea again until Toyotomi Hideyoshi sent an expedition there in 1592–98. Naka no Ōe's mistake was comparable to Tōjō's which caused the devastating defeat of Japan in the Second World War, especially as far as both fought an unnecessary war. However, like Tōjō's, the mistake ironically brought about an unexpected bonus in the sense of postwar cultural prosperity. After the defeat many Koreans – politicians, scholars, priests and artists – extricated themselves from Paikche and came to Japan, where they contributed greatly to

[4] Following the Meiji Revolution the status system was abolished and all people became equal. However, as before, former feudal lords and former samurai were in a favourable position to obtain high rank in the new society. In the same way, in the case of the Taika Reform the chieftains for powerful families and their children found it far easier than the people at large to gain office in the new government. In Japan, reforms, revolutions and coups d'état have never been total, but rather moderate. Despite this one cannot deny that the Taika Reform was a reform of the utmost importance for Japan.

[5] As I have explained in the Introduction Japanese Confucianism is very different from Chinese Confucianism. In future where the word Confucianism is used by itself it should be taken as referring to this Japanese-style modified Confucianism.

the development of culture, as did the American occupation force after the Second World War.

Secondly, neither of these two able crown princes wanted to become Emperor. At first sight, this seems surprising, because both put their whole energy into providing the imperial system with a firm foundation and could easily have assumed the role. In fact, Shōtoku Taishi never held the throne and Naka no Ōe was Emperor for only four years, while he served as Crown Prince for twenty-three years. However, if one realises that the position of the Heavenly Emperor which they established was politically power-less (although sacred and inviolable), it is readily understandable why these two politicians, well aware of the new position of Emperor, were not interested in it.

After the Taika Reform, no chieftain, court noble or Shōgun (with the single exception of Archbishop Dōkyō) ever tried to become Emperor. From the long-run point of view, it was a very successful reform, and made secure the position of Emperor. Immediately afterwards, however, a serious mistake by Naka no Ōe himself led to an intense struggle for the throne developing within the imperial family itself. Naka, who had been Crown Prince under both Emperor Kōtoku and Empress Saimei, wished to retain the position following the death of the Empress; for the next six and a half years the position of Emperor remained vacant. Naka eventually succeeded to the throne in 668, but died only four years later. On his death bed he summoned the Crown Prince Ōama (his younger brother), and told him that he wished to be succeeded by his son, Prince Ōtomo. At the time, rather than the Emperor passing on the throne down to his son, it was more normal for the succession to be transferred sideways, i.e. to the Emperor's brothers. However, Ōama was in agreement and handed over the imperial throne to Prince Ōtomo, but after the death of Naka Ōama killed Ōtomo and came to the throne as Emperor Tenmu.

For 98 years after this only the Empresses Jitō and Genmei were exceptions to the fact that all Emperors were descendants of Tenmu. These empresses were daughters of Naka no Ōe (Emperor Tenchi), but were very closely tied to the Tenmu line. Jitō was the wife of the Tenmu himself and Genmei was the wife of his son. The last Emperor or Empress of Tenmu's line was Empress Shōtoku and no successor to her could be found among Tenmu's descend-

ants; as a last resort she recommended as her successor her lover
Dōkyō, but it is doubtful whether or not Dōkyō himself really
wished to become Emperor. After Shōtoku's death he did not resist
exile and Tenchi's grandson succeeded to the throne as Emperor
Kōnin. Tenmu's line came to a complete end and Tenchi's line was
eventually restored.

Thereafter, with the notable exception of Emperor Godaigo,
1288–1339, who wanted to restore the ancient regime in which the
Emperor directly ruled the country as the 'Great King' rather than
reigned over it as the 'Heavenly Emperor', most emperors were
constitutional monarchs and manipulated by a powerful regent,
prince, ex-Emperor (*hōō*), court noble or Shōgun. The times in
Japanese history when the imperial family was at the centre of the
power struggle were the period of a hundred years (671–770) when
the Tenchi and Tenmu lines fought each other, and the period of
the confrontation between the Northern and Southern dynasties
beginning with Godaigo (1331–92). Even at a time like this no
subject thought of himself trying to become Emperor. Those who
possessed political ambitions aimed at the positions of real power,
for example that of Shōgun, and not at a position which was
supreme purely in name. In this way as a result of the Taika
Reforms the position of Emperor became sacred, and the fact that
at the same time the Emperor had had to become politically
neutral meant that his position was not in effect one of political
importance. For politically ambitious nobles, warriors and priests
and others the imperial throne was not considered worth the
trouble of getting hold of, especially given that one ran the risk of
bringing on oneself dishonour as a traitor if one did capture it.
They desired rather to serve the Emperor, or, at least without
rebelling against him, to become a real wielder of power beneath
him. In this way, except at exceptional times, the Emperor was
installed outside the arena of political power struggles, and it is
beyond doubt that it was with this format that the Taika Reform
made a major contribution to stabilising the position of the
Emperor over the long term.

In spite of the political struggles between the Tenchi and Tenmu
lineages, culture developed very rapidly after the Taika Reform.
Comprehensive and detailed codes of laws and ethics were produced, and Japan became a country governed by law. The Taiho
Code, completed in 701, which covered criminal, administrative,

civil and commercial law remained in effect until approximately the eleventh century. It also continued to be formally valid until 1885 when the modern Cabinet Act went into effect. Following the example of China, national schools (*kokugaku*) and universities (*daigaku*) were established to educate future government officials, and a system of national qualifying examinations was also introduced. Confucianism greatly promoted the development of the legal, ethical and educational systems and remained the dominant moral principle of conduct and behaviour throughout subsequent history.

After the Taiho Code was enacted, the government initiated the publication of several important books including *Nihon-shoki* (702), a history of Japan modelled on the Chinese national Chronicles, *Kojiki* (published in 712) on the history of ancient Japan, and *Fudoki* (713) on the natural and cultural features of various regions of Japan. Also published was the *Manyōshū*, an anthology of poetry comprising some 4500 short and long poems from the earliest time to the year 760, many of which are today recognised as masterpieces in the Japanese language. All these efforts cannot be too highly praised, especially since the Japanese had had no writing system at all before the arrival of Confucianism and Taoism in Japan in the sixth century; they had to begin by Japanising Chinese characters and subsequently inventing a Japanese alphabetical system. This was an extremely difficult and adventurous project, because Chinese and Japanese were completely different and unrelated languages.

As we have said, the Japanese did not swallow Chinese culture whole but modified it to suit their purposes. The divine origin and absolute power of the Japanese imperial family are emphasised in *Kojiki* in a mythical form and in *Nihon-shoki* as history; many poems praising loyalty to the Emperor are also to be found in *Manyōshū*. While the belief in the Emperor's quasi-divine character as the Manifest God and the philosophy of the Heavenly Emperor were derived in part from the traditional indigenous cult, they were primarily inventions conceived by the Japanese after the arrival of the foreign political philosophy. It is important to note that these beliefs were recorded in writing only after these new ideas had been assimilated and Chinese culture and letters had been Japanised. Therefore, they were by this time in no way purely indigenous, having already been coloured by the Japanese reaction to China.

The institution of Heavenly Emperor may thus be interpreted as an ideological buttress against the Chinese theory of revolution, providing an eternally firm foundation for the Japanese imperial family so that it would forever be protected against all possible revolutions. Alternatively, it may be regarded as simply an indication of Japan's feelings of inferiority towards a powerful China; by promoting their Emperor to the rank of God, they felt they had acquired greater national prestige.

In fact, according to the *Nihon-shoki*, Shōtoku Taishi wrote an arrogant letter to the Chinese Emperor, saying in effect, 'The Heavenly Emperor in the East faithfully sends a message to the Emperor in the West.' However, there is no Chinese record that Shōtoku Taishi called the Japanese Emperor the Heavenly Emperor. On the other hand, a Chinese chronicle reports that the the then reigning Emperor was infuriated by a letter from Shōtoku Taishi to him saying, 'The Emperor of the country of the Rising Sun faithfully sends a message to the Emperor of the Declining Sun.'

In any case it is evident that a strong feeling of defensive nationalism developed in Japan in the face of the gigantic, powerful and culturally superior empire. There is no doubt that the concept of the Heavenly Empire planted its roots deeply in Japanese soil and had far reaching effects on the fate of the people. It is of course also true that it led to a number of conflicts within the imperial family, and many chieftains and feudal lords fought with one another for the Emperor's support. Over more than a thousand years, from the Taika Reform to the Meiji Revolution, Emperors were controlled by Kanpaku (the chief advisers to the Emperor), Shōgun (the commanders-in-chief of the expeditionary force against the barbarians) or Hōō (the retired emperors in holy orders) who were the real rulers of the country; the Emperor's political power was only nominal. Yet the idea of the Manifest God kept the line of sovereigns unbroken during that period. In times of national crisis such as the Mongolian Invasions (of 1274 and 1281), the visits of the powerful Western fleets to Japan during the closing days of the Tokugawa Shōgunate, and the Second World War, the people widely supported the concept and willingly sacrificed themselves for the nation because of it.

Japan's history is in great contrast to China's, where political changes frequently occurred and one dynasty replaced another. Even after the Second World War, the defeated Japanese people

remained loyal to their Emperor to such an extent that the Allied
Forces believed that they would sustain much loss of life because
the Japanese would put up a determined, fearful and persistent
resistance if the Tennō system were abolished. There is a surprising
continuity between the Seventeen-Article Constitution of Shōtoku
Taishi (604) and the present post-war Constitution (1946) as far as
the position and political role of the Emperor is concerned.
Although the Emperor's divinity has now been denied, he is still
the symbol of the State and of the unity of the Japanese people. He
is only a nominal ruler under both constitutions. Thus, in view of
China's history, where many dynasties, even those which had
established large empires covering the whole of the Chinese
mainland, did not last as long as 200 years, Japan could keep 'a line
of Emperors unbroken for ages eternal' by politically neutralising
the position of the Emperor and making it sacred and inviolable.

III

Confucianism and Taoism are said to have been originated by
Confucius and Lao-tzu respectively; both men belonged to the class
of literati.[6] During their early development, both ideologies provided the intelligentsia with more or less similar philosophies and
guiding principles in life. As a matter of fact, the word *tao* means
eternal order and course of movement of society (or the cosmos), so
that it is an orthodox Confucian concept. In China, however, after
Confucianism had established itself as the philosophy of the
government and won respect and support from the bureaucrats
and ruling class, Taoism became more and more anti-government
and remained a heterodoxy for most of the time. While Confucianism prevailed in the cities, many Taoists lived in seclusion in rural
areas. While Confucianism was intellectual in that it kept ghosts
and spirits at what it called a respectful distance (i.e. it never
positively embraced them although it did not actively attack them),
Taoism was mystical and shamanist, believing in and relying on
magic. Its main supporters were peasants in villages and illiterates
in towns.

In Japan as well the government adopted the ideology of

---

[6] Confucius was born in 551 B.C. and died in 479 B.C. He is said to have met with Lao-tzu
in 522 B.C., but some historians doubt whether Lao-tzu actually existed.

Confucianism. For example, as has already been pointed out, the Seventeen-Article Constitution and subsequent Imperial edicts were written from the Confucian point of view. Successive governments encouraged the people to cultivate such Confucian virtues as sincerity, righteousness, loyalty, propriety, wisdom and faithfulness. On the other hand, however, Taoism could not become established as an independent religion on the Japanese islands; instead there was Shinto. In fact, Taoism (which was sometimes called 'Suntaoism' in ancient China) was manifested as Shintoism in Japan; we may consider Shintoism as a disguised version of Taoism.[7] Indigenous religious beliefs and imported Taoist ones fused together in about the sixth century and cannot now be separated. (Incidentally, it is interesting that in Okinawa, which is outside the range of Shintoism, Taoism has existed as a religion since the fourteenth century and there are Taoist shrines in many places. This indicates that where Shintoism prevails Taoism does not appear and vice versa, suggesting that they belong to the same genus.)

Shintoism is usually considered to be truly indigenous to Japan. Although there may be many indigenous elements in it, it is extremely difficult to discover what Shintoism was in its pure and primitive form. There are no contemporary written records, since this was before the introduction of Chinese characters to Japan. All the written records which historians can use were already under some Chinese influence, so we can observe only Shintoism after the impact of Taoism. In fact, as Taoism emphasises its Chinese origins, the similar assertion of a Japanese origin for Shintoism may be considered very Taoistic. One may think of Shintoism either as a Japanised version of Taoism or as a combination of Taoism and primitive Shintoism; but if, as may well be, primitive Shintoism made a negligible contribution to the synthesis, the second view is virtually equivalent to the first.

It is interesting to see that some of the Taoist gods are found in a disguised form in Shintoism. Many services and rites of Taoism have been incorporated into the Shintoist rites of the imperial household

[7] This kind of view of Shintō has not yet been generally accepted among orthodox historians in Japan. However, after the draft of this chapter had been more or less completed I got hold of Fukunaga Kōji, Ueda Masaaki and Ueyama Shunpei, *Dōkyo to Kodai no Tennōsei* (Taoism and the Ancient Emperor System) (Tokuma Shoten, Tokyo 1978), where I found that a theory very close to my own way of thinking had been expounded. Fukunaga is a specialist in ancient Chinese history, Ueda in Japanese history and Ueyama in philosophy.

and into village festivals and rituals. Shintoism also contains such
Taoistic magical elements as fortune-telling, astrology, geomancy
and so on. 'To cleanse the mind from vice and reveal one's inmost
heart honestly' (seimeishin) is one of the virtues respected by both
religions. Moreover, we find many Taoist concepts in Japanese
fairy tales and folk stories. Indeed, most Japanese people have
been deeply affected by Taoism through its influence on primitive
Shintoism. For example, during the building of a house, they hold
ceremonies to mark each stage such as the ground breaking,
raising of the framework, etc., and these are all conducted by
Shinto priests. At Shinto shrines, visitors can draw sacred lots by
paying money and buying copies of the almanac to look up their
stars. All these actions are very Taoistic.

The Japanese myths compiled in *Kojiki* show that they were
written under considerable Taoist influence. It is stated that,
before the formation of the Japanese islands, the universe was in a
state of chaos. This view resembles the Taoist idea of the original
state of the universe, although a similar one may be found in
other religions such as Christianity, ancient Greek religion, etc.
During Japan's mythological age, political decisions are said to
have been made in Taoist–shamanist ways, and not according to
Confucianist–ritualist principles. Although most of the mythical
emperors (except Emperor Nintoku) were far from the Confucian
ideal, the editor of *Kojiki* writes in his preface that Emperor
Tenmu surpassed both Huang Ti (the ideal emperor of Taoism)
and Wen Wang of the Chou Dynasty (the ideal emperor of
Confucianism) in his ability to command respect and love,
whereas Empress Genmei was more famous than Yü, another
legendary emperor of China. This clearly suggests that the editor
was reflecting a feeling of inferiority to a more advanced Chinese
culture, particularly its Taoist and Confucian elements, and was
influenced by them.

In order to close the gap in cultural ability and political power
which existed between China and Japan, the Japanese Court and
government had to be drastically reformed. At the same time, an
ideology promoting the authority of the imperial family had to be
established. It is no exaggeration to say that the entire volume of
Kojiki is devoted to tracing the origins of the imperial family and
recording its history, and to establishing the sacredness of the
Emperor, which is based on his unbroken lineage. Only someone

who can prove descent from the Sun-goddess, Amaterasu, can claim the right of succession to the throne.

The throne is inviolable because the Emperor has Amaterasu's blood in his veins. This theory, however, does not rule out struggles for supremacy within the imperial family. In fact, the killing of a brother or a cousin, as we have pointed out, was not particularly exceptional among the members of the imperial clan in ancient Japan. Therefore, in spite of a rigid political regime and the unbroken line of sovereigns, useful reforms and innovations could be made. Someone who wanted to realise a new political ideal needed only to find – from within the imperial clan – a prince who would support the programme. The Taika Reform, a typical example of a Japanese coup or revolution, was completed when Prince Naka no Oe and Nakatomi Kamatari killed the Soga and Empress Kogyoku handed over the throne to her brother, Emperor Kotoku. By this Japanese rule of revolution, the Imperial line remained unbroken, although individual emperors were sometimes killed or forced to abdicate.

In the seventh century the Japanese reorganised the structure of government according to Confucian ideas and edited the myths, under the strong influence of Taoism, with the intention of implanting in people's minds an ideology supporting the imperial family. Since Confucianism is far more rational than Taoism, this can be regarded as an appropriate use of the two Chinese philosophies. Although court functions were Taoist, people understood them as Shintoist and thus believed that the imperial family respected the traditions of the country. Meanwhile, the government was Confucian and progressive. In response to pressure from the enormous Chinese empire, Japan established an efficient and powerful government and stimulated feelings of nationalism and patriotism among her people. It is ironic that the two Chinese philosophies in combination served both purposes. Shintoism, which was in effect Taoism, as we have seen above, promoted national spirit; in particular, during the late Tokugawa era, *kokugaku* (the study of Japanese classics), which originated from the study of *Kojiki*, and enthusiastically advocated the ancient Shinto beliefs, contributed greatly to the ultranationalistic and chauvinistic movement against the Western powers as well as against China.

It is tragic for the Japanese that the ideology which aroused the spirit of nationalism and urged the retention of the traditional polity has been irrational, magical and incantatory. In every national crisis, the Emperor prayed to his ancestor, the Sun-goddess Amaterasu, and turned to her for help. Luckily for Japan, during both of the Mongolian Invasions a typhoon hit the enemy's fleet and most of their ships were sunk. It was therefore called a kamikaze (a wind sent by God). Even during the Second World War, the Japanese prayed at Shinto shrines for another kamikaze. War tactics and strategies were not seriously reviewed with a cool critical eye, and the self-sacrifice of lives was fanatically supported.

In Japan, Shintoism is a religion primarily for the imperial family, although it has infiltrated the general population through various events such as village festivals, harvest festivals, and marriage, ground breaking and frame raising ceremonies. Thus, as in China, Japan adopted Confucianism as the ethical system for the official life of the elite, and Taoism (or its Japanese version, Shintoism) as the religion of the imperial family and the populace. (Note that, in China, Taoism was supported by the Imperial 'harem' as well as by the common people.) It must be emphasised, however, that there is a huge difference between Chinese Taoism and Japanese Shintoism. As I have pointed out, the latter supplied a religious rationale for the loyal and patriotic sentiments of the Japanese, while the former advocated in China that a person should retire from public life and live in seclusion, tranquillity and parsimony so as to attain the aim of ageless youth and immortality in the pursuit of earthly happiness.

The Japanese had thus transformed Taoism into its effective opposite. The genuinely Taoistic concepts of the Heavenly Emperor and the Divine Land (*shinkoku*, i.e. the land with supernatural powers) have been re-interpreted, in a way which is truly Japanese and very anti-Taoistic, so as to promote nationalism. Besides, Shintoists esteem self-sacrifice for the good of the Emperor rather than the pursuit of youth and longevity; they consider the eternity of the country but not the prolongation of an individual's life of the greatest importance, while Taoists emphasise the individual. It is therefore not surprising that these two countries, which have Shintoism and Taoism as their respective main heterodoxies, have followed completely different courses of historical development, in spite of Confucianism serving as their common orthodoxy.[8]

[8] As I have made clear in the Introduction, a detailed examination shows that Japanese Confucianism differs in many respects from Chinese Confucianism. The former was far more nationalistic than the latter.

Buddhism also came to Japan, although not directly from India but via China. It had already been adapted by the Chinese and therefore contained many elements in common with Confucianism and Taoism. The Japanese studied Buddhism in Chinese. However, in contrast with Confucianism, which provided a political philosophy for the monarch and his lieges, Buddhism was mainly concerned with helping people who were in distress – either mentally or materially. While Confucianism emphasised such virtues as loyalty and self-sacrifice, Buddhism regarded mercy towards all living creatures as the most important quality of human beings. During periods when Buddhists were active, they were concerned with various forms of social work such as relief for outcasts, the running of hospitals, various charities, construction and irrigation work. They influenced the government to undertake a number of welfare programmes; they went to towns and villages to propagate their religion among the populace.

Shōtoku Taishi's government, the first well-organised government in Japan, promoted Buddhism; Article 2 of his Constitution declared that, 'the people should respect Buddha, Buddhism and Buddhists'. Later, especially during the Nara period (710–794), Buddhism enjoyed the special protection of the government. It built huge temples and tall towers in many regions, on behalf of the religion and for the purpose of exalting national prestige. Leaders of the Buddhist hierarchy made inroads into the government and the Court and engaged in political manipulations. When Buddhism became influential in the government, Taoism, which had already established itself in the form of Shintoism as the religion of the Imperial family, was re-interpreted from the Buddhist point of view. The Gods of Shintoism were considered as manifestations of the Buddha and his distinguished disciples; Shintoism itself was regarded simply as a branch of Buddhism.

At the same time, however, Buddhism was being re-formulated from the Shintoist point of view. I have already mentioned that in Japan Taoism was transformed into Shintoism so that it accepted even that concept of the Emperor as the living god (Manifest God) of the nation which was very anti-Taoistic; Buddhism too, after it infiltrated the government, was Japanised by admitting the 'Divine Land' doctrine which states that Japan is the country of the 'Divine Land' in which the Manifest God reigns and should therefore be eternal as heaven and earth. In national crises such as the

Mongolian Invasions and the Second World War, Buddhist temples, like Shinto shrines, held devotional services to pray for the
enemy's surrender.

Unless it recognised this first principle of Japan, no Buddhist
sect could be publicly approved. A typically Japanised sect of
Buddhism is the Nichiren Sect, which arose in the latter half of the
thirteenth century. Although it claims to be Buddhist, it is in fact
shamanist (hence Taoistic) as well as ultranationalistic. (Christianity, which was warmly supported by Oda Nobunaga
(1534–82), then suppressed by Toyotomi Hideyoshi in 1587 and
finally prohibited by Tokugawa Iemitsu in 1635, might have had a
different history if the missionaries had been able to accept the
'Divine Land' doctrine; such a change, however, would have
entailed a serious transformation of Christianity.) Furthermore, it
must not be forgotten that when an advanced foreign culture is
introduced into a culturally less developed and poor country, the
following process of reception usually emerges. The ruling class of
the importing country takes an interest in the new ideas, while the
lower classes have few opportunities to come into direct contact
with the new thought. Because the masses are culturally unsophis-
ticated they can see it only through the eyes of the elites. As the
ideas gradually pass through the funnel of the ruling class, they
often degenerate. Japanese Buddhism was no exception; by the
latter half of the sixteenth century, when Oda Nobunaga became
dictator of the country, it seemed – at least to him – that the
religion was morally tainted and had lost its original spirit.

Although Nobunaga ruled for only a few years, he delivered a
devastating blow to Buddhism. He was a thorough rationalist, who
employed many experimental tactics in war; he did not fear defeat
in battle, but rather learnt from it how to develop a yet more
brilliant set of tactics for the next battle. He originated such
manoeuvres as battle formations using guns, starvation tactics,
inundation tactics, naval task force operations, the naval blockade
of ports, and bombardment by naval guns. He also developed a
number of new political ideas. He removed numerous check-points
and thus allowed a greater expansion of trade. He also abolished
the manors owned by nobles and Buddhist temples, and replaced
the hereditary manorial system (see Section IV below), which was
established about one hundred years after the Taika Reform, by an
advanced form of feudalism. Under this new system Nobunaga

could order lords and their warriors (samurai) to move from one fief to another in much the same way as modern bureaucrats are transferred. Such a 'modern feudalism' presupposes the existence of a class of specially trained professional samurai. They accompanied their lord to his new fief, while the peasants were tied to the land and concerned entirely with production. The samurai now became full members of the unproductive ruling class. Nobunaga's innovation of dissociating arms from farming was promoted and completed by his successors, Toyotomi Hideyoshi (1536–98) and Tokugawa Ieyasu (1542–1616); this lasted for about three hundred years until the Meiji Revolution.

The rationalist Nobunaga had no faith in God or Buddha; he also did not believe in the myth of the Divine Land. It is true that he respected the Emperor and helped the imperial family financially; however, at heart he considered that Shintoists and Confucianists were feeble and useless. Indeed, he was an entirely unconventional and exceptional Japanese, even liking the Western missionaries who in turn understood him. He praised them as brave men who had come from afar over the sea. Moreover, he could obtain from them useful information about the world situation and the development of science and technology in Europe. Nobunaga had a high regard for the rare and precious articles and new armaments which they brought. In short, he found the Christian missionaries useful.

On the other hand, Nobunaga considered the Buddhists, who had been parasites on successive governments, as the enemy. He found contemporary Buddhist thought riddled with reactionary conservatism and lacking even an iota of progressiveness. He burned to the ground the entire Enryakuji temple (which had exercised enormous political influence since its construction in 788) and massacred all the priests, their mistresses and anyone else connected with the temple, including children and its monk soldiers. Furthermore, he suppressed a civil war which the Buddhists of the Ikko Sect had started and punished traditionally respected temples such as Kōfukuji, Makioji and Kōyasan by destroying their buildings and killing their priests and followers.

Nobunaga was almost insane during the last years of his life. He had always been arrogant, big-headed, cruel, tenacious and capricious and these traits grew worse as he aged. Japanese Buddhists were horrified by the atrocities he had committed, especially the massacre at Enryakuji. After that event, they withdrew completely from any involvement in politics and charity and have never re-entered those areas.[9] Temples were reduced to serving as the executive organs of funeral ceremonies. The fact that most contemporary Japanese are atheistic and irreligious might partly be attributed to the appearance of this feared, radically atheistic rationalist tyrant early in Japanese history. Nevertheless, Buddhism remains a popularly-based religion although it is dubious whether the contemporary Japanese feel that Buddha is their salvation.

Looking at the whole history of Japanese Buddhism, the religion was at its most flourishing in the Nara perid (710–794) and the Kamakura period (1192–1333). Since, as has been mentioned before, it was the ruling class which had introduced Buddhism to Japan, Buddhism was utilised as a means of maintaining rule over the people; consequently it was not merely concerned with the happiness or misery of individuals, but rather to a far, far greater degree with the welfare of the state. This is especially true of the Buddhism of the Nara period. In contrast, during the Kamakura period, with the rise of the samurai, who were constantly confronted by death and who had to kill their adversaries if they themselves were to survive, it was only natural that these warriors should show a strong interest in Buddhism. One of the most extraordinary characters of the Kamakura period was Shinran. Shinran formed a religious order which dissociated itself completely from magic, permitted its members to marry and whose way of life was essentially secular. This led to the success of the sect founded by Shinran (*Jōdō Shinshū* – True Pure Land Sect) in becoming very widely disseminated among the people. At the same time the status of the hereditary priesthood changed and it became more and more of an aristocracy, and ultimately one of the great feudal powers. At first sight the True Pure Land Sect, as a secularised form of Buddhism, would appear to correspond to the Protestant sects within the sphere of Christianity, but it possessed little in the way either of a desire for social reform, or of a fierce indignation against evil or of popular salvation. The priesthood developed into a feudal power as a result of its struggle for worldly

[9] Sōka Gakkai obviously has its origins in the Nichiren sect of Buddhism, and now has a clear interest in politics. However, the behaviour of religions developed since the Meiji Revolution is in a rather different category from that of traditional Buddhist sects.

influence, and its leaders were able to indulge themselves in an extravagant, aristocratic lifestyle by means of contributions from the sect's adherents. Ikko sect was defeated by Nobunaga.

IV

The social disposition of ideologies established in the seventh century has existed in Japan to the present day. We may say in general that, even after the impact of Westernisation, Confucianism still prevails in the government, Shintoism in the imperial family, and Buddhism among the populace. However, the powerful constitutional state system which had been established by the Taika Reform was not long-lasting and its centralised organisation of the bureaucracy was gradually reduced to a shell.

We have mentioned above that the Japanese government suffered acutely from the decisive defeat of Prince Naka no Ōe's troops in Korea, although it ushered in important long-term cultural benefits. The weakened government had to struggle against the leading families which were gaining strength and was in fact forced to make serious concessions to them. Boys from distinguished families were given preferential treatment in appointment or promotion to an office in comparison with boys from ordinary families, and nobles occupied important positions in the government. The reformist government had to retreat substantially from its original progressive position.

Under this weak central government, local governors became increasingly independent of the Prime Minister. They behaved as if they were provincial kings rather than representatives of the central government in the respective provinces. They began to consider as their own territories the farmlands which they oversaw for the state. Moreover, even after the Taika Reform, wasteland, mountains and forests remained outside state ownership. In 723, the government agreed, in a compromise with the nobles, that any of this land which was reclaimed and cultivated might be privately owned by the developers while they lived. In 743 this lifetime ownership was converted into perpetual ownership. Thus, nobles were highly motivated to become local governors. They increased their landholdings by reclamation and disafforestation and became large landowners. Workers on these new private farmlands were

reckoned as retainers of the landlords. Thus the system of centralised bureaucratic government created by Shōtoku Taishi began to
collapse in the eighth century and was replaced by the pre-feudal
hereditary manorial system which was itself replaced by the
manorial feudalism which lasted until the time of Nobunaga in the
sixteenth century. Although the codes of laws and ethics enacted in
the Taika period were still formally valid, they were actually
ineffective and largely ornamental.

Historians regard manorial feudalism as having begun around
the end of the twelfth century and the beginning of the thirteenth
century. It was in 1185 that there occurred the downfall of the
Taira clan who had hitherto maintained overwhelming power at
court and had very much their own way. They were brought down
by the Minamoto. Both the Taira and the Minamoto were
offshoots of the imperial family, men who, with the Fujiwara
family's control of the government from the ninth century, had
gone out into the provinces as local governors. They had settled
there without returning to Kyoto when their terms of office were
completed, and become powerful provincial families. It was the
Taira clan that first rose to power and brought about the fall of the
Fujiwara family; they themselves were subsequently brought down
by the Minamoto. Apart from the Minamoto and the Taira there
were many other powerful provincial families. In order to protect
their own private land and the public land under their control from
the central government and other forces these families accumulated
military strength, and formed bands of warriors. The head of one of
these families became the lord of the domain (*ryōshu*), his relatives
the ruling council and the farmers under his control the soldiers. At
first the central nobility utilised these warrior bands to preserve
their own persons and property, but eventually quite the reverse
obtained, with the warriors in control.

The chief of the Minamoto clan at the time of the fall of the Taira
was Minamoto Yoritomo (1147–99). His real sphere of influence
was the Kantō area, but after the fall of the Taira he annexed the
territory which they had formerly controlled to become a national
influence. Yoritomo's government was initially a purely private
administration for the control of this territory, and his politics
nothing more than the domestic matters of the Minamoto clan.
The country as a whole continued just as before to be subject to the
system which had prevailed since the Taika Reform. When the

Taira had brought about the fall of the Fujiwara family they remained in Kyoto, monopolising all the important offices of the central government, but Minamoto Yoritomo did not leave Kamakura in his own personal territory of the Kantō. There existed the central government in Kyoto, and in Kamakura the machinery for the administration of the Minamoto's own family affairs, but in 1192 when Yoritomo was appointed to the office of *Sei-i Taishogun* (lit. Great Barbarian-subduing Generalissimo) his government (known as the *Bakufu* or military government) began to take on a public character and his personal troops came to be considered as a national army. Since with a private army and a private government he was likened to a monarch, the situation which had arisen was in violation of the 12th article of the Seventeen-Article Constitution, which stipulated: 'A country should not have two rulers, nor a people two lords.' However, since Yoritomo to the end retained the formality of being the supreme commander of an army under direct control of the Emperor and in Kyoto the bureaucracy (court nobility) from the Prime Minister downwards comprised the government under the Emperor this did not necessarily mean a breakdown of the existing state of affairs. In this way the Kamakura Bakufu (1192–1333) did not destroy the old system but secured its own legitimacy by recognising it and being recognised by it.[10] However, in practical terms neither the Emperor nor the government was able to control the Bakufu (military) and the Bakufu played more than just a purely military role; military government and court government were carried on in tandem. Thus with the era of Yoritomo Japan entered a period of dual government, but as time progressed the Bakufu gradually became the open government and the court a government very much in the shadow, a government in no more than name.

A concept of a warrior's devoted service to his leader is essential to the moral code of any warrior society. In China the Confucian virtue of *chung* (Jap. *chū*) referred to fidelity to one's own con-

[10] Those Bakufu which succeeded the Kamakura Bakufu (The Ashikaga and Tokugawa Bakufu) were likewise established by court appointment with court approval. A parallel can be seen in the case of Japan's modern army. From about 1920 the army began to assert its independence from the government as directly responsible only to the Emperor, and from about 1930 it started to play a role which was more than a purely military one. This time the formal existence of a Bakufu was not revived, but a correct understanding of trends in Japan at this time cannot be gained unless one considers this period as one of dual government.

science, or to oneself, but in Japan this virtue was interpreted as meaning loyalty to a ruler. I have already explained in the Introduction how such a belief in *chū* as a great virtue is to be found in the writings of Ōtomo Yakamochi and other poems of the *Manyōshū*.[11] However it was in the warrior society of the Kamakura period that this kind of 'Japanisation' of the concept of *chū* progressed apace. While the Taika regime was a constitutional regime founded on the three supports of public ownership of land, a system of bureaucracy and 'the principle of *wa* (harmony)' (Japanese style democracy), the Kamakura regime was a military regime based on the private ownership of land, patrimonialism and 'the principle of patronage and service' (in effect lord and vassal relationship). By this time the farmers on the estates had been freed from working on the land for the lord of the estate or a provincial family; provided they supplied a fixed amount of labour or paid to the lord tax in lieu there was no longer any objection to their working the land for themselves. It was due to the domain lords that it became possible for the farmers to live in this manner, and the fact that the domain lords themselves were able to carry on in this fashion, receiving labour service and taxes, was due to Yoritomo's confirmation of their land. Looked at from the point of view of each domain lord, in his role as Shōgun Yoritomo was no less than the protector of the system of private ownership of land within a public land ownership system. The peasants on the estates repaid the favours received from their lord by a willingness to sacrifice themselves whenever their lord might deem this necessary. The same was true of the relationship between the domain lord and the Shōgun.[12] The Shōgun had to extend his patronage widely within his own sphere of influence by permitting greater private ownership of land to those of his followers who had done him the greatest service. It was in this way that the Japanese feudal system

---

[11] The Ōtomo family was an ancient warrior clan.

[12] With the division of soldiers and farmers, professional soldiers naturally became bureaucratised. In the later period of warrior society (Tokugawa society) this lord and vassal relationship founded on 'the principle of patronage and service' continued to exist between the feudal lord (*daimyō*) and his retainers, but the favours of which a retainer was in receipt from his lord could no longer take the form of a lord's recognition of the retainer's private landholding; the favour bestowed was the receipt of a fixed hereditary stipend from the lord. In return for receiving from their lord such favours as these, which were not available to common people – either farmers, merchants or artisans – warriors gave loyal service to their lord as their form of repayment.

first emerged, and the Kamakura regime which followed this
pattern was in complete contrast to, and strongly conflicting with,
the Taika regime. A period of dual government in Japan does not
merely imply a period where two governments are in existence; it
means a period where the country is dualistically under the rule of
two completely diverse governments acting according to quite
diverse principles.

The country had now entered upon a period in which there were
clearly two rulers. Moreover it had embarked upon a period when
chū (loyalty) was the supreme virtue. Quite naturally it was a
problem as to what to do when loyalty to the Emperor proved
incompatible with loyalty to the Shōgun. In fact this problem is one
of the central themes of the *Tale of the Heike* (*Heike Monogatari*)
written at the beginning of the thirteenth century. In order for the
system of loyalties to be free of contradictions the Emperor's regime
and the Shōgunal one did not have to be totally separate; their
disparity had at the very bottom to be rooted in a common base. It
was as a result a necessary formality for the Shōgun to be awarded
by the Emperor the title of *Sei-i Taishōgun*, nor had the Shōgun to
show any hostility towards Confucianism, the basic ideology of the
imperial government. Above all the Shōgun had to be the protector
of justice. His task was not merely to bring about justice within his
own territories as a warrior leader, and to achieve impartiality
based on justice; as an imperial official entrusted by the Emperor
with military and policing powers over the whole country he was
under an obligation to bring about justice in Japan as a whole.
Bravery, fidelity, chivalry, honour and modesty were all esteemed
as warrior virtues, but during the Kamakura period the image of
the ideal warrior of this kind was very Confucian, and was the
original model of the image of the ideal soldier in the Imperial
Injunction to Soldiers and Sailors of the Meiji period.

In this kind of early warrior society where farming and arms
were not separable the distinction between soldiers and peasants
was not a clear one, consequently loyalty to the domain lord was
required of farmers as well. However, during the age of the civil
wars (1467–1567), such traditional forces were severely defeated by
Nobunaga's well-trained professional troops, so that a division of
labour between farming and fighting emerged within each feudal
clan. In this two-class society, consisting of warriors and farmers,
the production sector was later subdivided into the three classes of

Because of the influence of Shintoism and Confucianism, the Japanese people set much value on ancestor worship, self-sacrifice for the benefit of one's master and concord with other members of society. Therefore, in the Tokugawa era, both social and technological innovations were not welcomed with much enthusiasm; individuals rarely competed for promotion within a merchant house, and economic competition between businesses was not severe. As mentioned previously, it was not necessarily evil for merchants to pursue profits. Preachers of popular ethics advocated thrift, asceticism and integrity. However, they stressed that the pursuit of profits was distinct from the greed for profits, thus emphasising fair play in business. A few merchants made innovations in their businesses and became rich. Nevertheless, the society as a whole was conservative, paternalistic and anti-individualistic throughout the Tokugawa era. When the Japanese found that there existed a huge technological gap between their country and the West at the end of the era, they realised the need for change and thought seriously how to construct a national economy which could compete with the West. Thus it was in relation to foreign nations that the Japanese began to consider economic competition, efficient management and modern government. When faced by the overwhelmingly superior culture of China Shōtoku Taishi had recognised the necessity of building a strong state structure. In much the same way the patriots of the closing years of the Tokugawa period confronted by the powerful nations of the West eventually began to argue as to which of their two governments they should support.

CHAPTER TWO
The Meiji Revolution

I

This chapter will discuss the Meiji Revolution, or Restoration, (1867–68), which we may consider as a crucial event in the history of Japan. My interpretation of the Meiji Revolution diverges to a considerable extent from that held by most Japanese historians, but it has much in common with the interpretation of Western historiography, although there are differences in emphasis. The views widely accepted in Japan more or less adhere to Marxian historical theory, but I am of the opinion that modern Japanese history is too unique to be adequately explained by Marxist theory.

Most momentous events in history have particular central themes, and that of the Meiji Revolution is 'laying the foundation for the building of a modern state on the Western model'. The establishment of such a state has continued to be the earnest desire of the Japanese people, but it is such a difficult aim for them to achieve that even in the distant future they will continue to experience problems that arise from it.

The Japanese have interpreted this theme of building a Western-standard modern state in a material–physical, and not a spiritual, sense, and so, despite the rapid external and formal westernisation of science, technology, education, economics, the armed forces and political forms, spiritual changes have lagged far behind. Rather, as the phrase *wakon yōsai* (Japanese spirit with Western ability) indicates, the reaction has been an intense rejection of Western spiritual ideas. The Japanese have ardently desired to retain their culture, their way of life, the specific relationship between superior and inferior, and their family structure, yet simultaneously to build a modern nation endowed with power that is comparable to that of Western countries. This desire has persisted throughout the last century or more – on the eve of the Meiji Revolution; when fighting Russia in the latter part of the Meiji period; during the militaristic period when Nazi Germany was considered the ideal; when the country was in ruins after being defeated in the World War; and even today when Japan has become an economic giant.

Of course, it is not necessarily wrong to endeavour to build a state that is comparable to those in the West, and the fact that such a state is externally westernised and internally non-western does not call for criticism *per se*. But if the vacuum created by the rejection of the Western spirit is filled by one which is nothing more than a fanatical *Shinkoku-shugi* (literally, the 'land of gods' doctrine or the belief that Japan, being ruled by the Heavenly Emperor whose ancestors were the gods who created the universe, should be superior to all other countries), the resultant 'powerful nation comparable to the West' can pose a great threat to others.

As will be seen later, during the latter part of the Tokugawa period when there was a great debate in the country as to whether the *sakoku* (isolation and closure of the country) should be continued or Japan should open her doors (*kaikoku*), one may disregard the advocates of the anachronistic *joi* ('expel the foreign barbarians') brand of isolationism. However, even the majority of the progressive and realistic of the *kaikoku* policy supporters were not internationalists in the true sense. They urged the opening of the country only as an expedient. They too believed that the West was the land of 'foreign barbarians'; they felt it necessary to open the country for the present, but they thought that Japan would eventually become the mighty leader of all nations under whom the world could be unified.[1]

Such fanatical and chauvinistic ultra-nationalism declined in strength after the Meiji Revolution, but was resurrected *in toto* immediately preceding the Second World War as the 'theology' of the Greater East Asian Coprosperity Sphere, with its advocacy that all the peoples in East Asia should collaborate for their mutual prosperity under the leadership of the Japanese. With the World War defeat, the logical conclusion of such an ideology, Japan was obliged once more to adopt internationalism, and this resulted in Japan becoming a great power comparable to the West. However, it cannot be said that the problem of fanatical ultranationalism has

[1] Oka Yoshitake, *Kindai Nihon Seiji Shi* (Political History of Modern Japan), vol. 1 (Sōbunsha, Tokyo, 1967), pp. 29–57.

been entirely solved, for many Japanese still approve of the idea of 'Japanese spirit with Western ability' without being able to over-come the implication of the 'land of gods' doctrine which is central to the 'Japanese spirit'. This doctrine emerged as a reaction to the *chūka shisō* ('China as centre of the world' or 'Middle Kingdom' ideology) of China; an ideology with a similar function vis-à-vis the West was required.

Most Japanese today do not accept the conventional 'land of gods' doctrine in its entirety. But they have not discovered an alternative. This leaves an emotional vacuum in the 'Japanese spirit with Western ability' set-up; unless the means of filling this cavity is found, the possibility of future ominous developments remains.

When Japan came face to face with the West in the nineteenth century, she acknowledged the technology gap that existed, but at the same time she was unfortunately smitten with the idea of 'Japanese spirit with Western ability' because of her burning nationalistic sentiments. This, however, as will be seen later, was only natural from a historical point of view; that is, given the development of Japanese history, it is a way of thinking that arose quite spontaneously.

Concerning the technology gap first of all, the Japanese did not suddenly awaken to this gap between themselves and the West immediately prior to the Meiji Revolution. They knew about the powerful West long before; as early as 1543 the Japanese had obtain-ed a gun from a Portuguese merchant vessel. Japan at that time was in a state of warring confusion; the control of the Bakufu (the feudal military government) of the Ashikaga family was declining and war-lords of various provinces battled against one another. To be victorious during this warring period, it was vital to own effective arms. Many of these war-lords were acquainted to varying degrees with the extremely advanced science and technology of the West, but to obtain Western products through the purely economic means of importation was, if not impossible, exceedingly difficult. Christian missionaries were a prominent route through which they could be obtained. Thus, right from the beginning Western tech-nology was presented to the Japanese as inseparably linked to a Western spirit (Christianity). Many war-lords, therefore, became Christians, and the one who finally conquered the entire country was Oda Nobunaga (1533–82), who, although not a Christian

himself, had shown favour to Christianity and had skilfully capita-
lised on Western science, technology and arms. As has been
pointed out in Chapter 1 above, he gained the advantage in land
battles by his firearms strategy, and also established a high-speed,
mobile naval force. Furthermore, his modern strategies included
sailing a warship fitted with cannons into Osaka Bay to blockade
the city of Osaka from the sea.

We have also mentioned in Chapter 1 that Nobunaga successfully suppressed Buddhism, which had become totally corrupt by
clinging to traditional forms of power and which also did not bring
with it any valuable technology, while he took protective and
favourable measures toward Christianity. The Enryakuji temple on
Mount Hiei, which had ruled over the Buddhist world in Japan for
eight hundred years, exercised such religious and secular authority
that no war-lord had previously dared to attack it. But when
Nobunaga's opponents Asakura and Asai sought refuge on Mount
Hiei, Nobunaga surrounded the mountain. The two sides made
peace temporarily, but in the following year, when Asai moved his
forces, Nobunaga without hesitation ordered an attack on the
Enryakuji temple, destroying the whole mountain by fire and
massacring many monks, men and women. Similarly, when he put
down the Ikkō Sect Uprising, he crucified all the 20,000 believers.
Thus Nobunaga on the one hand favoured Christianity, regarded
Western technology with the greatest respect and was extremely
keen on its assimilation. On the other hand, his devastation and
mass killing of the Buddhists who opposed him led to a loss of
vitality in the Buddhist faith.

Despite these acts of savagery, Nobunaga should be evaluated
highly as Japan's first modern statesman. If Nobunaga, with his
insight into the future, had ruled for longer, Japanese history would
probably have unfolded along a totally different path. But primarily because of his personality and his 'premature' emergence in
history, he was assassinated in 1582 by one of his retainers, Akechi
Mitsuhide. The latter was in turn immediately murdered by
another retainer, Toyotomi Hideyoshi (1536–98) who in this way
unexpectedly gained supremacy over the country.

Toyotomi Hideyoshi arose from the position of Nobunaga's
low-ranking servant to that of his successor. Compared to Nobunaga he was a timid and conservative ruler, in spite of the fact that
he is considered to have had a bold personality, distinguishing

himself in Nobunaga's campaign of unification. After Hideyoshi re-unified the country himself upon coming to power after the death of Nobunaga, he launched an offensive on Korea, built the grandiose and lavish Osaka Castle, and enjoyed a life of luxury. At the same time Hideyoshi administered various policies which discouraged the creative and pioneering spirit of the Japanese.

Firstly, as he himself arose from the peasantry, he feared that a second Hideyoshi might emerge from among the farmers. Thus, when he became Chief Minister (*kanpaku*) he proclaimed the 'Sword Hunt Edict', confiscating all arms from farmers and townspeople. He also prohibited movement between the four classes of warrior, farmer, artisan and merchant, to prevent the recurrence of his own good fortune. In this way, the warriors became the ruling class with a monopoly over the possession of arms. At the same time Hideyoshi promoted meritorious retainers to the post of *daimyō* (feudal lord), and positioned them in various conquered provinces among the territories of the long-established feudal lords. The relationship between these new feudal lords and their subjects differed from that between the old ones and their subjects which was traditionally intertwined by kinship and territorial ties. This is the beginning of feudal rule based on a new type of lord–vassal relationship. When the feudal lord was moved to another province due to a transfer or a demotion, only he and his retainers moved, and not the peasants. Thus the relationship in these domains between the ruler and the ruled was similar to that within a modern bureaucratic state. Throughout the following Tokugawa period feudalism appropriated more characteristics of bureaucracy, and it was Hideyoshi who firmly established this trend initiated by Nobunaga.

Secondly, Hideyoshi consistently adopted an active posture towards China (Ming Dynasty), Korea and Taiwan, but did not welcome contacts with the West. This does not necessarily imply that Hideyoshi did not value Western science, technology and civilisation as highly as Nobunaga had done. On the contrary, it was precisely because he had such a high regard for them that he was greatly alarmed at the prospect that the Western invasion of the Orient (the Spanish had already conquered the Philippines) would be extended to Japan. He therefore prohibited the propagation of Christianity in 1587, and in 1594 crucified Christians in

Nagasaki. This suppression, though, was not on religious but on strictly political grounds. In other words, since the Christianity of the day was inseparably linked to Western technology, it is likely that he decided to ban the faith in order to prevent the political perils to which Western technology might lead.

Following the death of Hideyoshi, Tokugawa Ieyasu (1542–1616) began to rule in 1603. The Tokugawa family were the most cautious and defensive of Japanese rulers; they completed the conservative policies initiated by Hideyoshi. Firstly, the Tokugawa Bakufu purposefully stationed *fudai daimyō* (loyal hereditary lieges of the Tokugawa family) amongst the *tozama daimuō* (literally, 'outer lords', those who recognised Ieyasu's rule only after his victory in the crucial battle of Sekigahara), so that the former could watch the latter closely. At the same time, they administered a rigid caste system and thereby established a centralised feudal structure.

Secondly, for the Tokugawa, who had already unified the country, Western science and technology became nothing other than hazardous. They reasoned that if Japan continued her relations with the West, apart from the possibility of a direct attack, there was the likelihood that a provincial feudal lord could acquire powerful weapons from the West and strike against the Tokugawa family. It was therefore necessary that the Tokugawa maintain a permanent lead in the arms import race in order to retain their dominance. However, considering the state of transportation at that time, the capital of the Tokugawa, Edo (now Tokyo), could hardly be considered advantageous. In fact, it was such border districts as the western tip of the main island of Japan (Chōshū), the west and south coast of Kyūshū (Nagasaki and Satsuma), or the southern coast of Shikoku (Tosa) that had the upper-hand geographically. Therefore the Tokugawa deemed it advisable to ban all further relations with Western countries. Moreover, they were afraid of a *daimyō*'s allegiance to an alien doctrine coming before allegiance to the Bakufu. Thus they increasingly suppressed Christianity and limited trade, and finally in 1639 prohibited the entry of all Westerners, except for Dutch merchants, embarking on the so-called *sakoku* (closure or isolation) policy. International trade was subsequently completely controlled by the Bakufu at Nagasaki. The only exception to the seclusion rule was Holland which, on the grounds that it was Protestant rather than Catholic, was permitted to trade under the strict control of the Bakufu just at the small island of Deshima in Nagasaki.[2]

II

This isolation lasted for 220 years until in 1859 the Tokugawa Bakufu committed itself to opening the three ports of Kanagawa, Nagasaki and Hakodate to Russia, Britain, France, Holland and the United States. During this period of isolation, the Bakufu initially reinforced the class system and securely established the centralised feudal structure. In order to fortify their control over the provincial feudal lords, the Bakufu introduced in 1635 the *sankin kōtai* (alternate attendance) system, whereby the lords had to maintain residences in the capital which they occupied for several months every year or every alternate year, the length of time depending on such factors as the distance of the fief from Edo, and whether it was *fudai* or *tozama*. When they returned to their domains, they were obliged to leave their wives and children behind, as hostages to the Bakufu. On the one hand, this system put tremendous financial pressure on the feudal lords, making them incapable of accumulating sufficient military power to plot or scheme for independence from the centre. On the other hand, it led to the organisation of a countrywide road network and established the basis for the creation of a nation state. Japan was able to form a modern, unified nation state immediately after the Meiji Revolution because internal communication and exchange during the 200-odd years of isolation had resulted in the near completion of the foundation work necessary for Japan as a whole to become a single community, namely, the standardisation of language, the

[2] The isolation policy can also be regarded as something which was urged on the Bakufu by the Dutch. Holland did not just wish to exclude Portugal from the Japan trade, but also to monopolise trade with Southeast Asia by a cessation of trading activities on the part of Japanese who were active in the area at the time. Holland persistently disparaged the Portuguese to the Bakufu. When the news of the seclusion decision was announced the Dutch Governor-General in Batavia is said to have held a big party in celebration. See, for example, Iwao Seiichi, *Sakoku* (Seclusion), vol. 14 of *Nihon no Rekishi* (History of Japan) (Chuō Kōronsha, 1974). Also, see Hayashi Yujiro, *Watakushi no Seijuku Shakai Ron* (A Personal View of the Mature Society) (Sangyō Nōritsu Daigaku Shuppanbu, 1981).

There are those who believe that the Shimabara Rebellion by Christians in 1637–38 was the immediate cause of the complete closure of the country in 1639, but the trend towards national isolation was very marked even before the rising.

acceptance of similar ways of thinking and acting by the people of various provinces and the consequent similarity in social rules and customs and so forth.

Furthermore, Japanese capitalism – although, as will be seen later, it took a unique form – was able to function more or less as a market economy from the start. This was because, under the Tokugawa feudal system, castle towns developed in the provinces, and markets and relay-station communities along the highways were opened, due to the system of 'alternate attendance'. In the final two decades of the Tokugawa period (1850–68), Edo (Tokyo) was already as large as London with a population of more than one million. Osaka and Kyoto had 300,000 and 200,000 people respectively, and Nagoya and Kanazawa contained populations of about 100 thousand each. Towns and urban communities had also been established in many other places such as Hiroshima, Sendai, Wakayama, Kagoshima, Sakai and Nagasaki. When we compare this with the following description by Marx in the 1850s of the current state of urbanisation in Great Britain, we find that Japan was in a comparatively very advanced stage of development in the Tokugawa era: 'Except London, there was at the beginning of the 19th century no single town in England of 100,000 inhabitants. Only five had more than 50,000. Now there are 28 towns with more than 50,000 inhabitants.'[3]

Isolation also functioned as a protection for internal industries. A comparison of Japanese agriculture and industry with those of the Western countries clearly shows that Japan then had a comparative advantage in mining and agriculture.[4] It would have been more beneficial for her to specialise in them and exchange their products for foreign manufactured goods than to produce those goods within the country. Therefore, if free trade had been permitted between Japan and the West, Japanese handicraft manufacturing industries might have been wiped out. Thus this isolationist policy prevented the Tokugawa economy from specialising in primary industries and allowed it to maintain manufactur-

---

[3] K. Marx, *Capital* (Progress Publishers, Moscow, 1965), pp. 660–1.
[4] Before the adoption of seclusion Japan had imported from Spain, Portugal, Holland and Britain commodities such as weapons, gunpowder, woollen cloth, carpets, raw silk, silk goods and sugar. In return she had exported such goods as silver, copper, iron, rice, wheat, wheat flour and beans. These commodities show in which industries Japan possessed the comparative advantage at the time.

ing industries, though at a primitive level. The relative ease with
which the Meiji government succeeded in industrialising Japan
was due in part to the Bakufu's possession of workshops for the
manufacture of gunpowder, shipyards and other Western-style
factories during the later years of the Tokugawa period, and the
development of these Western-style factories was in turn due to the
preservation of handicraft skills throughout the Tokugawa period.
In order to protect Japan's craft industries from the West's export
offensive and to prevent Japan's becoming a purely agricultural
country an appropriate protective trade policy had to be implemented, and by following a policy of national seclusion the
Tokugawa Bakufu had, quite unconsciously, implemented a perfect protective trade policy. It was therefore thanks to the isolation
of the Tokugawa period that the Meiji government was able to
enforce its policies in pursuit of national wealth and strong armed
forces so soon after its seizure of power.[5]

Although the Tokugawa Bakufu government was backed by
military power, it promoted Chinese studies, especially Confucianism, as a way to suppress and prohibit the propagation of Western
thoughts. This education policy, which lasted for over 200 years,
had at least three positive effects. Firstly, Confucianism, as a
philosophy rather than a religion, has never been in serious conflict
with Shintoism or Buddhism in Japan, so that Shintoists and
Buddhists and even Christians have been strongly influenced by
Confucianism. The fact that the whole nation was trained in the
Confucianist way of thought throughout this more than 200-year
period of isolation should not be undervalued. In fact, since the
Japanese, though ethical, is nonreligious by nature, we can at once
understand that it was of immense significance. During that
period, the Japanese were brainwashed and moulded into a specific
type of person by their Confucianist education. When the country
was opened at the end of the Tokugawa era, the Japanese
appeared, to the eyes of Western people, to be distinguished by

[5] Seclusion certainly played a role in the protection of Japan's infant industries, but this
does not necessarily mean that without seclusion Japan's craft industries would inevitably
have died out. Iwao, however, in his above-mentioned book, mentions the existence of a
record of Japan exporting large numbers of bullets in 1619. It might well have been the
case, therefore, that provided that some sort of protective trade policy had been
implemented short of complete seclusion, then even in the seventeenth century, as was the
case with the Meiji period, Japan would have had the ability skilfully to transform import
industries into her own export industries.

certain idiosyncratic features; that is to say, they were all gentlemen of the samurai type.

Secondly, it was fortunate for Japan that Confucianism was intellectual and rationalistic. It rejects mysticism, incantation, magic and ghosts. The development of modern science in Europe, however, was slow. Galileo Galilei and Nicolaus Copernicus faced tremendous difficulties, and it was only subsequently that science began at last to be widely accepted. Sir Isaac Newton, the father of modern physics, studied alchemy in addition to performing scientific research. In Japan, however, it was entirely owing to the intellectualism of Confucianism that the Western sciences were able to plant their roots deeply and quickly without great suffering on the part of brave scientists.[6]

Thirdly, Confucianist education, against a background of 200 years of bureaucratic control, had trained the warriors to be efficient bureaucrats by the end of the Tokugawa era. Furthermore, they had equipped themselves with the discipline needed by soldiers of a modern army or workers in a modern factory, thus facilitating the commencement of a modern military organisation and a modern factory system. Without these well-trained samurai Japan could neither have established a modern government nor have carried out the policy of 'rich country with strong army' so soon after the Meiji Revolution. One must not undervalue the role which the Tokugawa period played in the emergence of modern Japan.

As part of their policy to suppress and prohibit Christianity, the Tokugawa Bakufu promoted not just Confucianism but Chinese learning in general. With the establishment of the class system the three productive classes of farmers, artisans and merchants were obliged to provide economic support for the ruling class of warriors. Early in the Tokugawa era the Bakufu believed that Confucianism would serve perfectly well the purpose of persuading them to bear this burden. The government in those days took Confucian-

---

[6] It is true that a number of scholars of Western studies were cruelly punished, persecuted or executed in the Tokugawa period. But these incidents should not be regarded as the suppression of the rationalistic way of thinking demanded by modern science, rather as attacks on these scholars' criticisms of the feudal clan system and the isolationist policy. In Japan there has never been a serious struggle between religion and science, except for the attacks on the rationalist way of thinking by the Shintoist–Taoist ultranationalists in the last years of the Tokugawa era and in the fascist Shōwa period which led to the Second World War.

ism as a philosophy of feudalism, whereas Confucius himself, though born in the period of feudalism looked back upon the ancient golden age of the city–state regime and was always considering how his contemporary system with its subdivisions into warring states could be reorganised into a more advanced, centralised bureaucratic form. In the latter period of the Tokugawa era, however, because of the continued stability of the regime, the warrior class was no longer a group of men prepared for combat; they had been transformed into bureaucrats in the centralised feudal state of the Tokugawa. At the same time, they were the conveyers of scholarship and along with a small minority of farmers and townsmen formed the intelligentsia. Among these farmers and townsmen and the lower grades of warriors who cherished the arts and scholarship there was an interchange which disregarded class differences, and such groups of intellectuals emerged fairly universally and on a considerable scale.[7] Furthermore, the 'alternate attendance' system ensured that there was not too great a cultural disparity between the centre and the provinces.

Along with rejecting Christianity, the Tokugawa government thus encouraged Confucianism in order to reinforce ideological support for the system. However, such a cultural policy not only had the effect of protecting the system, but, conversely, of demolishing the structure at the same time. Firstly, Confucianism is inseparably and intricately related to the 'China as centre of the world' doctrine. This stimulated the national consciousness of the Japanese and resulted in the unexpected birth and upsurge of a scholarship and ideology opposed to it, that is, *kokugaku* (national learning) and *shinkoku shisō* ('land of gods' doctrine). Secondly, when one pursues the concept of *chū* (loyalty), the most important virtue in Japanese Confucianism, one discovers that this concept does not necessarily provide a justification for the Tokugawa structure. Many right-wing intellectuals of the Tokugawa period reasoned, as did Yoshida Shōin at one time, that they owed their loyalty to their feudal lords, feudal lords to the Shōgun, and the Shōgun to the Emperor, and thus they themselves owed only an indirect loyalty to the Emperor. And when the relationship between the Emperor and the Shōgun was no longer amicable the

[7] Watsuji Tetsurō, *Nihon Rinri Shisō Shi* (History of Japanese Ethical Thought), vol. 2 (Iwanami Shoten, Tokyo, 1952), pp. 695–701.

consistency of such a chain of loyalty was disrupted, and one was forced to select between loyalty to the Emperor or to the Shōgun.

Moreover, the growth of the 'land of gods' doctrine resulted in a corresponding increase in the emphasis on the deity of the Emperor. Thus, once the Tokugawa system became involved in political crises, an atmosphere emerged quite readily in which people advocated the transition to a system centring on the Emperor. Even without pressure from the West at the end of the Tokugawa period, such a stage would probably have been reached sooner or later. But the Western warships advancing towards Japan's shores compelled the Japanese to face the technology gap. After some meandering, Western technology and the 'land of gods' doctrine combined in a strange fashion and many Japanese intellectuals began to believe that 'Japanese spirit with Western ability' was the path Japan should take. In this way, in the latter stages of the Tokugawa period, Japan was endowed with an intelligentsia inclined to the right, which was a product of the Tokugawa cultural policy. This intelligentsia emerged on a fairly large scale and was found throughout Japan.

There were other noteworthy changes in the social structure of the Tokugawa period besides the rise of the intelligentsia. Because of her long isolation, Japan was almost completely severed from the international market, but, with the continuation of stability and unification, the internal market expanded and steadily developed. As a result, part of the agricultural sector was transformed from its natural, self-sufficient form to one which produced merchandise, i.e. mercantile agriculture. However, on the other hand, feudal lords had to finance the enormous expenditure which accompanied the 'alternate attendance' system, and, in addition, there was a non-productive ruling class which was disproportionately large in relation to the productive capacity of the day. This meant that the farmers were subject to excessive taxes. As a result, poorer peasants had to part with their land and became even more destitute, while those who had acquired some wealth through the commercialisation of agriculture could annex these lands and conduct their farming on a large-scale commercial basis, becoming even more affluent. As the farmers strengthened their ownership of land the feudal lords' dominion over their territories weakened; and thus the foundation of the feudalistic organisation was shaken. Similarly, with the development of a monetary economy, the amount of capital involved in high-interest money lending increased, and the merchant class also became segmented into a minority of wealthy merchants and a majority of small-scale merchants. At the same time the ruling class became disrupted; poor warriors were not only unable to maintain the standard of living befitting them as members of the ruling class, but needed to engage in some secondary occupation in order merely to live.

Of the segmented classes, it was the intelligentsia, with the low ranking warriors as its nucleus, which was the motivating power behind the Meiji Revolution, and not the affluent classes (rich farmers and merchants) nor the propertyless (tenants and servants). The Tokugawa bourgeoisie, unlike its Western counterpart, was neither militant nor revolutionary. In fact, many of them sided with the Bakufu at the time of the Meiji Revolution. Although impoverished peasants and tenants did resist the Bakufu through peasant uprisings these did not amount to anything more significant. They had neither the will nor the capability to overthrow the Bakufu and establish a new regime. Servants working in the homes of rich merchants and the urban poor were similarly unorganised and incapable of consolidating their power.

As stated previously, the Japanese already knew of the capabilities of Western science and technology, and were fully conscious through their experiences of the warring period that if anyone outside the Bakufu imported such Western products, the dominance of the Bakufu was immediately threatened. Therefore, absolute control of the import of Western technology was vital for the maintenance of the regime. In this sense, although the isolationist policy was passive, it was an effective means of controlling imports over a period of 200 years. If one looks at it in this way, the isolation does not express a disregard for Western culture and technology, but rather fear and admiration of it.

When the merchant and military fleets of Britain, Russia and America began to arrive in Japan and demand the opening of the country towards the end of the Tokugawa period, it became apparent that if isolation was continued the entire country was liable to be besieged by these Western countries. The ruling classes and the intelligentsia realised that the isolationist policy which has been devised for the internal purpose of maintaining the centralised feudal system of the Tokugawa Bakufu was not viable as a foreign policy, and that this policy might, on the contrary, lead to the destruction of Japan.[8] Such a contradiction is not attributable to the autonomous evolution of the economy and productive capacity in Japan, claimed by orthodox Marxists to be the cause of the Meiji Revolution, but to the external pressure created by the technology gap between the West and Japan. Therefore, it was the intelligentsia who displayed the most sensitive reaction to this problem, and a seething desire to know the West arose amongst them.

It is not in the least surprising that national opinion as to how to cope with this technology gap was divided into two camps. Firstly, there was the *jōi* (expel the barbarians) argument which asserted that the Western fleets should be defeated and isolation continued as before. Secondly, there was the *kaikoku* (open the country) argument, which insisted that such a forceful policy would not help to bridge the technology gap, but would instead compel the country to be faced with the gap, exposing her to danger; the country should therefore be opened. In practical terms, the first plan was nothing short of suicidal, but neither was the more realistic second the ultimate solution, as opening the country would not by itself solve the real problem. At that time, nobody could propound the right answer and so events unfolded without anyone having a clear vision of the future. Intrigues and incidental happenings affected the course of events, causing policy to swerve this way and that; matters proceeded by trial and error. In the beginning, quite naturally, the Bakufu and many of the intelligentsia upheld the conservative 'expel the barbarians' argument. When the Bakufu, which was obliged to deal with matters, was converted to the more realistic 'open the country' argument and finally executed this policy, the confrontation between the Bakufu and the anti-foreign intelligentsia, centred on the low ranking warriors, intensified.

There were naturally many versions of the 'expel the barbarians' theory. At one extreme, there were the fanatical and simplistic ultranationalists who regarded the Westerners as foreign barba-

---

[8] For Japan the most serious aspect of the technological gap which existed between her and the West during the last years of the Tokugawa period was shipbuilding technology. Japanese people at the time had a horror of the 'Black Ships' of the Westerners similar to their fear of the atomic bomb in the closing stages of the Pacific War. At the time of the Meiji Revolution Britain is believed to have had about 400 steamships, as well as steam-trains and other vehicles operated by steam; London was equipped with an underground system, and an under-water telegraph cable under the Atlantic Ocean had started operation.

rians. At the other, there were people like Yoshida Shōin (1820–59) who recognised the capacity of the West and gave sufficient thought to the necessity of opening the country, yet asserted the theory because they disapproved of the militaristic and oppressive way in which the West had demanded the opening of the country. (Therefore they agreed that the country should 'expel the barbarians' but only for the time being for the sake of national honour; at a later stage, Japan should open voluntarily.) Despite these various shades of opinion, even the most thoughtful among the 'expel the barbarians' supporters did not have a precise plan as to how to deal with matters if they were defeated by the West after 'repelling the barbarians'. Therefore, this theory itself was reckless and extremely precarious.

When, however, one considers the problem of national defence against the Western countries, the question arises as to the type of political system which would render Japan externally most powerful. Many of the intelligentsia, whether consciously or not, were inevitably led to ponder this question, and as a result became convinced that even if the present Bakufu system could be retained it could not avoid undergoing revision. What needed to be revised? If no amount of revision could be expected to bring about much improvement, should the Bakufu structure be abandoned entirely? And if so, what sort of new system should replace it? The intelligentsia did not have a single lucid answer to these questions, nor the ability to analyse the situation dispassionately.

Such ignorance was the penalty for having suppressed Western scholarship during the long period of isolation; the intelligentsia lacked training in social–scientific thinking. When the Tokugawa structure had been stable Confucianism had filled this void, but once the system began to falter bastard products of Confucianism, such as 'national learning' or the 'Mito school of history' (namely the 'land of gods' doctrine and the 'land of the Emperor' concept which emulated the 'China as centre of the world' doctrine), became the criteria according to which external policies were decided. For instance, Yoshida Shōin, who, as a military strategist, was well aware of the technology gap between Japan and the West but remained a supporter of the 'expel the barbarians' idea because of his nationalistic sentiments, was entirely transformed into a fanatical advocate of the 'land of the Emperor' doctrine under the influence of the Mito school of history in his last days. Since the fanatical 'land of the Emperor' ideology, which acknowledged itself as the only just argument and brandished the standard of loyalty, was combined with the 'expel the barbarians' argument, the result was menacing indeed. Many of the advocates of the latter argument who were under the influence of national learning or the Mito school of history did not maintain any particular political doctrine, apart from vaguely considering that the present system should be exchanged for one centring on the Emperor. They could not view problems of foreign relations and national defence with a dispassionate and analytical eye. Instead, everything was judged from the subjective viewpoint of 'great duty' or 'just argument'. Thus the possibility for this right-wing ideology to lead the country astray was as great as at the time of the Second World War.

In addition the opposing 'open the country' argument was nothing but the reverse of the 'expel the barbarians' one and did not have its own logical base. Just as there were hard and soft-liners among the 'expel the barbarians' supporters, there were a variety of versions of the 'open the country' argument. In contrast to the 'foreign barbarians' faction of the 'expel' school, there was the corresponding 'surrender' faction, who argued that the West was certainly barbarous, but, considering their military might, Japan had no choice but to 'open'. Then, corresponding to the 'expel for now, open later' faction, there was the 'open for now, repel the barbarians later' faction; that is, those who felt that opening was inevitable due to the difference in military strength, but afterwards Japan should endeavour to strengthen herself and, when sufficiently powerful, she should expel the 'barbarians' and return to the good old days of isolationism. In this way, there were innumerable variations among both arguments, and not only was the distinction between the versions obscure, but the line of demarcation between the 'expel' and the 'open' arguments was not all that apparent. Besides, no one was capable of developing a logical argument in defence of a particular faction; they could only appeal to sentiment.

Thus the argument of an individual frequently displayed uncertainty, or else upheld the 'expel' argument in sentiment but asserted 'opening the country' as a practical policy. Since this was the situation with individuals, there was even greater diversity of opinion in such institutions as the clans, the Bakufu, or the imperial court, depending on who their spokesmen were. In one case, a certain clan sent two representatives to two separate conferences that were held at approximately the same time; this resulted in the clan advocating two opposing opinions at the two conferences. Therefore, the drift of national opinion concerning this 'expel' *versus* 'open' issue was totally befogged, and continued on its irregular course, affected by chance happenings.

Under such conditions Ii Naosuke, an advocate of the 'open' policy, became Chief Minister of the Bakufu; he not only concluded commercial treaties without prior imperial sanction, but also placed feudal lords who objected to his measures under house arrest and suppressed the anti-Bakufu movement of the pro-Emperor intelligentsia in the Great Purge of Ansei.[9] This drove the intelligentsia to an even stauncher anti-Bakufu position. As a result, Ii was assassinated in the Sakuradamon Incident of 1860. After this the Bakufu took a more conciliatory line, and the two clans of Chōshū and Satsuma proposed the 'united Court and Bakufu' theory. This asserted that the Tokugawa Bakufu and the Imperial Court in Kyoto should combine to create national unity. There were two factions which differed as to whether the Bakufu or the Emperor was to be the principal partner of the combination, but for both factions the unification argument was nothing but a device to preserve the Tokugawa structure. If matters were solved in this way the anti-Bakufu intelligentsia who advocated the 'honour the Emperor, expel the barbarians' theory would be the losers.

Even while the higher levels were discussing the 'unity of the

[9] The commercial treaties which the Bakufu had concluded with various foreign countries in 1858 were excessively unequal. The terms of the treaties enabled revision in 1872 and the Meiji government opened negotiations for revision that very year; they were eventually successful in getting Britain and the other countries to agree to revision only in 1892. The revised treaties did not come into force until 1899, and it was not until 1911, thirty-nine years after the negotiations for revision had first been initiated, that Japan fully recovered her tariff autonomy. During this time the Japanese were made to feel well aware of the misery of being a weak country. This was the sort of situation behind the Meiji government's attempts to implement their radical 'rich country, strong army' policy. It must not be forgotten that it was experiences such as these in Japan which formed the background for the ideas relating to peace and the world order formulated by Kita Ikki and Konoe Fumimaro which will be described in Chapter 4, ideas which led up to the Pacific War. At all events, since under the unequal treaties Japan's enterprises were compelled to develop the capacity to export, they had in return to receive adequate protection from the state. It was when the treaties were revised – and also as a result of the First World War which broke out shortly afterwards – that the great advance in the Japanese economy began.

Court and Bakufu', the lower segment of the 'expel the barbarians' movement intensified its violence; there occurred a number of acts of terrorism against foreigners and Bakufu constables. This tactic was successful in that finally in 1863 the imperial sanction was granted for the 'Expel the Barbarians Edict'. The Chōshū clan bombarded American merchant vessels, French and Dutch warships, and encountered counter-offensives from the American and French fleets. The Satsuma clan was also fired on by the British fleet over the issue of compensation for a murdered English merchant, Mr Richardson, in the so-called Namamugi Incident (or Richardson Incident). In the following year, the Chōshū clan came under attack from the combined fleets of Britain, France, United States and Holland. As a result of these encounters advocates of the 'expel the barbarians' argument realised its impracticability and became friendly with such British diplomats as Sir Rutherford Alcock and Sir Harry Parkes (the first and second British Ministers to Japan, respectively) and, especially, Ernest M. Satow (the minister's official interpreter, later knighted). From that time, their primary aim became the overthrow of the Bakufu.

III

Immediately after the edict for the expulsion of foreigners had received the Emperor's approval men from Satsuma and Aizu initiated a coup d'état in Kyoto which brought the overthrow of the nobles of the anti-foreign faction. At the time both of these domains were advocates of unity between the Court and the Bakufu, but whereas the Aizu domain envisaged a unity whose central point was the Tokugawa house, that envisaged by Satsuma was a unity whose focal point was an imperial court manipulated by Satsuma. Consequently the aims of these two domains were hardly completely in accord with one another, but they felt a mutual hostility towards Chōshū's anti-Bakufu activity. The year after the coup Chōshū samurai provoked fighting at the Hamaguri Gomon, one of the gates of the Imperial Palace in Kyoto, in an attempt to restore their influence, but in this conflict as well Chōshū was defeated.

The Bakufu immediately carried out a punitive expedition against Chōshū and defeated it, but as a result of this conflict the problems facing the Bakufu ceased to be of the order of 'opening the country' versus 'expulsion' foreign policy disputes and resistance to the Bakufu among the intelligentsia; the problem became civil war on a domain basis. As a result of Chōshū's defeat its *daimyō* made a profession of his allegiance to the Bakufu, but the following year Takasugi Shinsaku, at the head of his volunteer forces, initiated civil war within the domain of Chōshū, and the *daimyō* was once again brought back to the ranks of the Bakufu's opponents. This provoked a second Chōshū expedition by the Bakufu, but this resulted in the defeat of the Bakufu and anti-Bakufu tendencies among the anti-foreign faction flared up sharply.

The position taken by Satsuma underwent a considerable change between the Bakufu's first and second expeditions against Chōshū. Satsuma had at first asserted the 'unity of the Court and Bakufu' plan and schemed to control the Court itself and subordinate the Tokugawa Bakufu and the other clans. In this sense, the clan had been anti-Bakufu from the start, but not to the extent of seeking to remove the Tokugawa structure in its entirety. Initially indecisive, the Satsuma clan had clarified its anti-Bakufu stance by the time of the Bakufu's unsuccessful second expedition against Chōshū, and (according to the Satsuma–Chōshū pact concluded just before the expedition) rejected the Bakufu's command to dispatch troops for the expedition. This, of course, occasioned a great improvement in relations between the Satsuma and Chōshū clans, and it confirmed their mutual aim to overthrow the Bakufu. Such an alliance between Satsuma who had previously advocated the 'open' policy and Chōshū who had asserted the 'expel' argument testifies to the fact that the intellectuals of the 'expel' faction finally realised that the only real solution to the problem of the technology gap between Japan and the West lay not in fighting the West but in defeating the Bakufu and establishing a powerful, unified, modern nation state.

By this time the Bakufu itself was dispatching envoys and students abroad, equipping a Westernised army and navy, appointing men to government service on the basis of talent, constructing a shipyard, iron works, a cannon factory and so forth, and generally endeavouring to modernise the Tokugawa structure. The 'expel' faction also willingly conducted commerce and trade with foreign countries and attempted to assimilate Western science and technology. The question of opening the country or 'expelling the barbarians' was no longer a point of controversy, not only between one anti-Bakufu clan and another, but even between the Bakufu and the 'expel' faction clans. The issue had shifted to that of either preserving the Tokugawa Bakufu structure (in a modernised form) or establishing a truly modern, new unified nation state.

For the intelligentsia of the 'honour the emperor, expel the barbarians' faction, the concept of 'expelling the barbarians' no longer had any meaning beyond that of a slogan; similarly, as time went on, the term 'honour the Emperor' (*sonnō*) was also reduced to being merely their campaign watchword. There was never an accurate blueprint for the Meiji Revolution; the revolutionaries learnt what the issues and solutions were by repeating the process of trial and error and approached the correct ones step by step. They realised that the 'expel' argument was irrelevant to overcoming the technology gap and the answer was the establishment of a modern, unified nation state; thus they united in the cause of overthrowing the Bakufu. But when they came to consider exactly what constituted a modern state, no one had a clear vision. There was only the extremely ambiguous, simplistic and dangerous sentiment that the ancient Japanese political system centring on the Emperor would be ideal for the Japanese.

The upper strata of warriors had supported the 'unity of the Court and Bakufu' argument, as Emperor Kōmei (1831–66) had enthusiastically done. According to this plan, the Emperor would resume his central position in Japanese politics and the Tokugawa Bakufu would remain, though in a modified form. For the low-ranking warriors and intellectuals, such a solution would mean that the source of evil and conflict would not be removed, but since the Emperor himself was an active advocate of this unification plan, the 'honour the Emperor' faction revolutionaries came into conflict with the Emperor. In September 1866, twenty-two anti-Bakufu court nobles, including Iwakura Tomomi, made moves in an attempt to prevent the unity of the Court and Bakufu; the Emperor responded by punishing them resolutely. A month and a half later, the Emperor died suddenly (it was immediately rumoured that he had been killed by loyalists) at the early age of thirty-six, and was succeeded by the sixteen-year-old Emperor Meiji.

It was unfortunate that such an incident occurred between the Emperor and the 'honour the Emperor' faction revolutionaries, but it signifies that for some loyalists the phrase was a slogan without content. That is, they were not loyal guards acting according to the will of the Emperor and executing his wishes, but had their own distinct programme of action (though they themselves were ambiguous about its details), and revealed themselves to be political opponents of the Emperor. In the series of unsuccessful revolutionary events, which occurred frequently in the 1930s, such as the 15 May or the 26 February Incidents, the relationship between the Emperor and the 'honour the Emperor' advocates of the 1860s was reproduced in the relationship between the Emperor and the young right-wing officers who at first attempted to revolutionise the court. In particular at the time of the 26 February uprising in 1936 the Emperor was highly incensed and ordered that 'the rebel soldiers must be suppressed with all haste'. However, in as far as the army utilised army purges in pursuit of inter-factional strife it did not really purge itself, and there was eventually a 'palace revolution' with the Emperor effectively held hostage by right-wing army officers; the momentum gathered pace and Japan was eventually plunged into the Pacific War. At the time of the Meiji Revolution as well, before Satsuma and Chōshū could receive an imperial edict to bring down the Bakufu they had to face resistance from within the court, which ended with the death of Emperor Kōmei.

Following the revolution in the imperial court, it took more than two years to complete the Meiji Revolution. Although the diminishing ruling powers of the shogunate were handed back to the Emperor late in 1867 the war continued between the Bakufu and the Satsuma–Chōshū allied forces. After the battle of Toba-Fushimi, near Kyoto, Edo Castle quickly surrendered and Aizu Castle, the remaining stronghold of Bakufu influence in the Tōhoku (northeast) region, fell. Enomoto Takeaki, the deputy commander of the Bakufu navy, eventually surrendered in Hokkaido in 1869. The fact that the Meiji Revolution started in the western tip of Honshū, the southwestern coast of Kyūshū, and the southern coast of Shikoku, areas which had the greatest opportunities for contact with the West, and concluded in the northeast of Japan where contact was minimal, and also that the victors were the armies of the Satsuma and Chōshū clans who were highly equipped with western armaments, characterises the nature of the Revolution very appropriately. This geographical pattern of the Revolution may also suggest how the balance of political power had shifted away from the Shōgunate.

During the two years of the Revolution, the new government groped for a fresh political structure. The revolutionaries did not have any definite plans on how to treat the Shōgun, who had already returned political power to the Emperor: i.e. whether to demote the Tokugawa to the position of feudal lord, establish a council of feudal lords in place of the Bakufu, and form a united court and Bakufu government; or, alternatively, whether to eradicate the Bakufu system and replace it with a modern structure under direct imperial rule (*hanseki hōkan*, 'surrender of domain registers' and *haihan chiken*, 'abolition of domains and establishment of prefectures'); or, furthermore, what sort of political position would the Emperor occupy in the new system. For example, would he be an absolute or a constitutional emperor? The revolutionaries cogitated in perplexity, modifying their plans as the Revolution progressed, and, in the worst cases, they resolved matters only on an *ad hoc* basis.

Meanwhile the new government made various decisions which they enforced. However, as demonstrated by the correspondence of the principal characters of the new government, such as Kido Kōin, Ōkubo Toshimichi, Sanjō Sanetomi and Iwakura Tomomi, it did not put these policies into practice with confidence but with a sense of crisis that the new government might collapse any day.[10] The government was extremely active and made innumerable decisions, many of which reversed previous decisions, prompting the public to criticise its inconsistency.

But one should not censure this unsystematic approach too severely. It must be remembered that the new government was formed by those people who had originally advocated the 'expel the barbarians' argument as a defence policy against the West, although they began to realise their mistake with the passage of events and finally learnt that the only true defensive policy was the modernisation of Japan. Thus, it is natural that they had not thought through how modernisation could be realised. On this point, one should compare the case of Japan with the Russian Revolution. In Russia the social sciences had attained a high standard and the Revolution was executed only after the revolutionaries had had rational discussions of the potentials for Russian development. In contrast to these Russian revolutionaries, it must

---

[10] Oka Yoshitake *op. cit.*, p. 90 ff.

be said that their Meiji counterparts were totally ignorant. Quite inevitably, therefore, the Meiji government made many mistakes, and with hindsight it may be said to have been in various respects a reactionary government. For instance, the new government inherited the Bakufu policy of banning foreign religions and invited protests from foreign countries by putting up a proclamation prohibiting Christianity. Moreover, the First Article of the five articles of 'Charter Oath' stated: 'An assembly widely convoked shall be established and all matters of the State shall be decided by public discussion.' This, however, did not stipulate the establishment of modern parliamentary politics, but rather a council of feudal lords or something similar.

Despite these imperfections, however, and considering the period in which it occurred, the inauguration of the Meiji system of a modern imperial state with a chief minister advising the Emperor and ultimately power vested in that chief minister must be deemed a success. One should not ignore the influence of Britain which played the leading role among Western nations in relations with Japan in finalising the form of the Meiji Revolution. But we cannot overlook the fact that their experience of the final days of the Bakufu also led the Meiji government to desire a limited rather than an absolute Emperor system. France had aided the Bakufu side to counteract Britain's backing for the anti-Bakufu factions, but neither faction allowed the internal conflict in the years leading up to the change of power to develop into a proxy war between the two major powers. Instead, they dissolved the long standing dual political structure of the Court versus Bakufu in a short period of time. Credit for this must be given to those involved, though Britain and France also had not wanted a prolonged internal conflict.

Some term the Meiji Revolution as described above an aristocratic revolution.[11] Superficially this may be justified, as it is true that the main force behind the Revolution consisted of the low-ranking warriors, who, despite their rank, did belong to the ruling class of the Tokugawa feudal system; furthermore, some feudal lords and noblemen did play important roles. But if the Meiji Revolution is called aristocratic, or a revolution from above, it greatly interferes with the interpretation of succeeding events.

[11] E.g. T. C. Smith, 'Japan's Aristocratic Revolution', *Imperial Japan, 1800–1945* (1973).

Firstly, the revolutionaries did very little to benefit their own class. On the contrary, they endeavoured to remove the privileges of the warrior class, and in 1869 they simplified the complex class system of the Tokugawa period, guaranteeing universal freedom of choice in occupation and marriage, and in 1871 they confiscated the right of dominance of the clan-lords and abolished clan domains. With this last measure, the stipends which the warriors had been receiving from the clan lords were now paid by the central government, though beginning in 1873 these stipends were gradually abolished, and ceased entirely in 1876. With the abolition of stipends, the warriors were issued with bonds; many of them who started enterprises with this as capital failed in their endeavours and eventually became members of the proletariat.

In this way, the feudal economic privileges of the warriors were cancelled. On top of that, in 1873 the conscription edict was promulgated, which meant that the warriors no longer monopolised the obligation and honour of defending the country. The Meiji government's adoption of a modern military system with universal conscription as its principle amounted to a declaration that the Meiji structure was not based on the old ruling class, and it became apparent that the ideology of the Meiji government differed completely from that of the Tokugawa. Thus, it was the warrior class, i.e. the aristocrats, who were most severely affected by the Revolution, and they were fully aware of this. Dissatisfied warriors continued to rebel even after the Revolution, culminating in the Satsuma War of 1877. Such a revolution cannot be designated as aristrocratic. If the progressive reforms which Tokugawa Keiki had been carrying out had been successful and a new structure along the line of the 'unity of the Court and Bakufu' argument had emerged, then it might have been appropriate to call it an aristocratic revolution; but not as the Meiji Revolution actually happened.

Secondly, another theory states that loyalists aimed to restore the imperial reign through the Meiji Revolution. It is true that many of the intelligentsia were advocates of the 'honour the Emperor' theory, and among them were many fanatical revivalists who followed the school of Motoori Norinaga and Hirata Atsutane, and right-wingers influenced by the Mito school of history. Even Yoshida Shōin, the most realistic and progressive among them, became an incorrigible right-wing fanatic a few years prior to his execution. It is clear that these ideologies did not contribute towards modernisation; not only that, they even had destructive effects. Therefore, their advocates were treated in a far from sympathetic manner after the Revolution. It is true that immediately after the Revolution the new government placed the Religious Affairs Minister above the Chief Minister and proclaimed the doctrine of 'Shinto as the national faith'; many scholars of the National Learning (*Kokugaku*) and Shintoists were appointed to the new government. But after the abolition of the clans and establishment of the prefecture system, the Religious Affairs Minister was placed under the Chief Minister. In addition, it became gradually apparent that the conservative nature of Shintoism did not harmonise with that of the new government, and the doctrine of 'Shinto as the national faith' rapidly disappeared.

The dissatisfied right-wing intellectuals who had played a considerable part in the Revolution did not obtain sufficiently important appointments in the new government and they joined with frustrated warriors and started the Saga Uprising, Shinpūren Uprising and the Satsuma War. The surviving extreme right-wing ideology went underground and exploded like a time-bomb sixty years later, eventually leading the country to destruction. It was definitely an error of the Meiji government not to have been more careful and thorough in their counter-measures against right-wing ideologies, but the fact that the Meiji government was able to launch itself as a modern government by eliminating fanatical right-wing elements who had previously been its comrades must be regarded as a great achievement, considering the process of the Revolution.

Moreover, there are those who consider that the Revolution was caused by the final eruption of the economic inconsistencies that had accumulated under the Tokugawa system. They cite the frequency of peasant uprisings in the latter part of the Tokugawa period as supporting evidence. As the Tokugawa regime approached its end the polarisation intensified between the rich and the poor in the strata of peasantry and townspeople. However, I consider that such an accumulation of inconsistencies may form part of the background to a revolution but not be its cause nor its motivation. Since around 1750, there had been frequent peasant uprisings and riots, which had reached a climax in the Revolt of Ōshio Heihachirō in 1837. When one examines the number of such uprisings, the annual average for the Tenpo period (1830–43) is 11, Man'en–Bunkyū period (1860–63) 8.5, Genji–Keiō period (1864–67) 15. But even after the Revolution these uprisings were hardly under control; the average for 1868–70 was 30 and for 1871–73, 25.[12] These figures indicate that the Meiji government was less than genial not only towards the warrior class but also towards the peasants.

In addition, the consciousness of peasants in general at that time had not been sufficiently developed to demand, plan and carry out the downfall of the feudal structure and the establishment of a unified government. Indeed, by the end of the Tokugawa period the preconditions for the creation of a nation state had been fulfilled in the trade and cultural exchange among the provinces, standardisation of the language, and development of the people's awareness of nationality. But this was so only in comparison with Japan prior to that period or with certain underdeveloped countries, and the national consciousness of the masses was not yet very advanced and must not be evaluated too highly. In spite of this standardisation of language which had been brought about by the 'alternate attendance' system, a number of clans (Satsuma, for instance) endeavoured to preserve the uniqueness of their own dialects. Moreover, it was only the warrior class who intermingled as a result of the system; the common people, particularly the peasants, were tied to the land. I regard the level of national consciousness which existed among the masses by the latter part of the Tokugawa period as being just sufficient to accept a nation state, but not adequately developed for them to deliberate and execute a revolution for the purpose of unifying the people.

Certainly, among the volunteer troops organised by Takasugi Shinsaku there were peasants and townsmen, and they had defeated the Bakufu troops in various regions. Also, it is doubtful whether the Meiji government would have enforced the conscription system had it not been for the activities of these peasants and townsmen. Some attach great importance to the role of the masses in the Revolution because of this, but one must also consider the other side of the coin. For example, in the attack on Edo Castle in 1867, twenty-odd clans, including Satsuma and Chōshū, had

---

[12] Tsuchiya Takao, Ono Michio (eds.), *Meiji Shonen Nōmin Sōjō Roku* (Record of Peasant Disturbances in the Early Meiji Years) (Keisō Shobō, 1953); also Sakamoto Tarō *op. cit.*, pp. 404–5.

participated, and in the battles in the northeast and Hokuriku districts over thirty clans fought on the side of the ex-Bakufu. Among clans of both sides, it was Satsuma, Chōshū and Aizu which fought valiantly; the remainder hardly showed any fighting spirit. Satsuma and Chōshū distinguished themselves partly because they were highly equipped with Western armaments, but also because the other clans manifested such low morale. Furthermore, as I have previously stated, it was to the credit of those involved that the Meiji Revolution did not develop into a large-scale civil war or a proxy war between the great powers. Such a development, however, is due to the fact that apart from Satsuma and Chōshū the other clans were relatively unconcerned with the Revolution. If one supposes that many clans had been as highly aware as Satsuma and Chōshū and that there had been as many clans intensely opposed to the Revolution as Aizu, a large-scale civil war would have been unavoidable.

The low level of awareness of the general public is substantiated by the accounts of sailors of the foreign fleets which participated in the bombardment of Shimonoseki and by Sir Ernest Satow, who was also on the scene.[13] Towards the end of the Tokugawa period the class system had begun to disintegrate and cultural exchange between the provinces was well under way. However, class and clan consciousness was still pervasive; thus the majority of the peasants and townspeople of the Chōshū clan regarded the exchange of fire with the foreign fleets as a local battle between the Chōshū *warriors* and the fleets; the people of the Buzen clan across the Shimonoseki Straits also looked upon it as a battle between the *Chōshū* clan and the foreigners.[14] This is representative of the general attitude of the day. It is therefore impossible to consider the Meiji Revolution as being by the people for the people; it should be regarded as a revolution by the elite. After the new government was established it immediately eased the restrictions of the class system and later abolished them, organised the educational structure, and modernised the state system and so forth. These were all measures concerned with long-term national development. Their short-term economic policies were not necessarily successful, which led people to think that the Revolution was not for the people but only for the elite, by the elite. Therefore, for a fairly long time after the

[13] E. M. Satow, *A Diplomat in Japan* (London, 1921).   [14] Oka Yoshitake, *op. cit.*, p. 56.

Revolution, dissatisfied elements continued to rebel, but the Meiji government overcame them and continued with the task of long-term nation building. In this way, after two centuries of isolation, the nation started on a forced march of radical modernisation and Westernisation, with the intelligentsia, who had awoken to the world situation, at the forefront.

I have emphasised above that the Meiji Revolution did not have a clearly defined plan; events developed after many complications and were influenced by chance happenings. Thus, I consider that if either Yoshida Shōin or Emperor Kōmei had not died so young in the midst of the Revolution, the course of events might have evolved differently. For example, Yoshida Shōin, who was extremely diligent and had a flexible mind, might have responded appropriately as events unfolded, but he had become a fanatical advocate of the 'land of the Emperor' doctrine during the last few years of his life. Since his disciples were the main force behind the Meiji Revolution, he could have been expected to assume the highest office in the new government, if he had lived. And if he had continued to support the fanatic 'land of the Emperor' doctrine, one can imagine that the Meiji structure would have been a more right-wing system with absolute imperial rule than it actually became.

As another example, Emperor Kōmei was an enthusiastic supporter of the 'unity of Court and Bakufu' argument, although he had previously been against the Bakufu's policy of opening the country to foreigners. Since Shōgun Tokugawa Keiki was a progressive, if the duration of Kōmei's reign as Emperor and of Keiki's rule as Shōgun had continued (in fact, their terms of office coincided for only four months), they would have broken the deadlock, and a powerful ruling structure with a united Court and Bakufu would have been realised.[15] If a more right-wing absolutist system or a feudal structure of a united Bakufu and Court had been established, Japan would most likely have required a second revolution sooner or later. Particularly in the case of Yoshida, it would have meant that the early Meiji period would have been directly connected to the ultranationalistic years of the early Shōwa period, and Japan might have destroyed herself without attaining

[15] The sudden death of Shimazu Nariakira, who was a firm advocate of unity between the Court and the Shogunate, also had favourable results for the establishment of the Meiji regime.

any sort of positive reputation in the West. Would it be reading too much into events to regard the course of Japanese history as being indebted to the tragic deaths of two outstanding personalities during the Revolution for modernisation and if one were therefore to express gratitude to the two?

IV

If we compare aspects of Japanese history such as have been discussed above with the history of England – and for reasons of length our comparisons can only be made on the basis of considerable simplification – it is clear that there are interesting similarities and points of difference. First of all, Henry VII is perhaps a figure in English history somewhat comparable to Hideyoshi and Ieyasu; in 1485 he defeated Richard III, last king of the House of York and became the first king of the House of Tudor. At the same time he ordered the disbanding of the bodies of retainers of the feudal nobility. Until that time the nobility had kept what were, in effect, private armies, bands of retainers who wore their uniform and carried their crest, but Henry VII forbade all his subjects, regardless of status, rank and position, to maintain retainers; by doing so he monopolised power for himself and initiated an absolute monarchy. This sort of measure taken by Henry corresponds to Hideyoshi's 'Sword Hunt' edict of 1588. Hideyoshi unified the country and made the *daimyō* more or less subject to his will, so he can be regarded as bringing about the establishment of a centralised feudalism with an absolutist monarchic character. In England, however, the feudal character of the state was weakened with the establishment of absolute sovereignty, whereas in Japan from the time of Hideyoshi and through the Tokugawa period government was in the hands of a centralised feudal system headed by a *Kampaku* or a Shōgun with powers akin to those of an absolutist monarch. This means that the period of a centralised ruling system came some hundred years earlier in England than it did in Japan.

Absolute monarchy in England came to an end as the result of the English Civil War (1642–60). In Japan the period of centralised feudalism came to an end with the Meiji Revolution, and the country entered on a period of more modern political structures. Japan's establishment of modern government, therefore, came some 200 years later than it did in Britain.[16] Similarly, from the time of the Tudor monarchy new sea routes and new continents began to be discovered. In 1445 Cape Verde in Africa was discovered, and in 1486 the Cape of Good Hope. Other discoveries included that of America by Columbus in 1492, Vasco da Gama's discovery of the route to India in 1498 and Cabral's discovery of Brazil in 1500; between 1519 and 1522 Magellan circumnavigated the world. These discoveries of new continents were made mostly by men from such countries as Portugal, Spain and the Netherlands, and England was well behind, but from the latter half of the sixteenth century Englishmen as well came to play a positive role in making inroads into these new continents. For example, in 1583 Sir Humphrey Gilbert established a colony in Newfoundland, and in 1584 Sir Walter Raleigh founded the colony of Virginia. Then at the same time England began a more positive involvement in foreign trade; numerous trading companies were established and monopolistic trading rights accrued to nobles and merchants who were in collusion with the royal family. This tendency was further strengthened by the rout of Spain's 'Invincible Armada'. In 1600 the East India Company was established.

In contrast, in Japan contact with Western Europe (mainly Portugal) had flourished before the start of the centralised feudal system of Hideyoshi and the Tokugawa but before long Japan became a society completely closed to foreign contact. The seclusionist policy was enforced in its entirety until about the end of the eighteenth century, but from then on contacts with Western Europe were resumed. Despite the difference in their earlier degree of foreign contact, the absolutism of England and the centralised feudal structure of Japan both began to collapse as interchange with the world at large became keener.

---

[16] One faction of Japanese Marxist historians (the so-called Rōnō faction) regard the Meiji regime as a modern regime, albeit as one tinged with absolutism, and believe that in Japan the period of modern government followed on directly from the feudal period (the Tokugawa period). In contrast the other major faction (the so-called Kōza faction) regards the Meiji government not as a modern (capitalist) regime but as an absolutist monarchy, believing that Japan, like England, shifted to a period of absolutism when feudalism ended. I personally regard the Meiji government as a modern regime and see the Tokugawa period as a feudal era replete with absolutist characteristics. It is true that the Tokugawa Bakufu did not carry on such fervent mercantilist activity as did the English monarchy during the era of absolutism. This must be attributed at least in part to the seclusion policy. Commercial capital tied up with the Shōgun and the feudal lords did grow markedly during the Tokugawa period.

The circumstances of this collapse in Japan and England, however, were absolutely different. In Japan the Tokugawa regime was brought down as a result of foreign pressure attributable to the technological gap which existed; in England the pressure which brought it down was internal. In 1642, when the Civil War began in England, modern science was still only in its infancy. Copernicus had formulated his heliocentric theory a hundred years before (1543) and Galileo had discovered the simultaneity of the pendulum sixty years earlier (1583), but differential and integral calculus were still as yet unknown, as was universal gravitation. Even in those days there were, of course, warships, but they were sailing vessels and the invention of the steam ships which menaced Japan was still 165 years in the future. Unlike Japan, England did not start a revolution to bring down the absolutist system in order to build a strong nation state capable of withstanding foreign pressure; the absolutist structure collapsed of itself from within, in both spiritual and ideological terms.

As mentioned above, from about the time of the confrontation with Spain's 'Invincible Armada' England became actively involved in foreign trade, and as a result the monopolistic traders, who were closely tied up with the absolutist monarchy and held its special trading licences, came into conflict with the general industrial capitalists (wool manufacturers), smaller merchants and yeomen. These controlled parliament (House of Commons) and so there was political conflict between the monopolistic faction and the parliamentary faction. Furthermore, many of the lesser merchants and industrialists and yeomen were Puritans and so the conflict also became one between Puritanism and the established church. Thus, the parliamentary faction with its adherence to Puritanism and advocacy of liberty and popular rights started a revolution against the Royalist faction which had the backing of the established church and inclined to monopoly and despotism. After a lengthy struggle a bourgeois revolution was achieved, which brought about the downfall of the absolutist monarchy and, creating a limited monarchy (constitutional monarchy), firmly established parliamentary politics. In this way the English Revolution was a revolution which resulted from the rise of a new class but was not a revolution aimed at defending the country against threats from abroad, as was the Meiji Revolution.

However, as a result of this sort of revolution modern capitalism began in Britain. But for modern capitalism to be established, two types of human beings must exist, i.e. on the one hand the capitalist who is eager to accumulate capital and on the other the worker who labours unremittingly. Even if there are workers and capitalists, if the workers make no attempt to work, short of the capitalists threatening them with whips or guns, there is no way they can be made to produce any surplus produce. On the other hand, even if the workers have worked in an orderly manner, if the capitalists end up by squandering all the surplus production, accumulation of capital cannot occur. In order to establish modern capitalism, in the sense of a progressive economic system where capital is accumulated and capitalistic production is carried out on a larger scale year by year, both capitalists and workers must be frugal by nature.

Fortunately, Christianity was frugal. In Catholicism, however, the life of the monastery was separate from everyday life and the pursuit of frugality was something carried out by monks in monasteries. In this way in the Catholic world frugal behaviour was something engaged in by the clergy outside the ordinary world and no demands for frugality were made on lay people. In the world in general there was no need to be frugal when engaging in economic activity, and even extreme indulgence was condoned; therefore, modern capitalism, whose mainstay is frugal behaviour, did not thrive under Catholicism. For the rise of modern capitalism, a religious revolution was necessary; that is to say, the liberation of frugal behaviour from the monastery, the removal of the differentiation between the holy and the worldly, and the fusing, in the world at large, of a profitable life with a frugal life.

Puritanism achieved just such a liberation and as a result there was a situation where the worker, 'at least during working hours, is freed from continual calculations of how the customary wage may be earned with a maximum of comfort and a minimum of effort. Labour must, on the contrary, be performed as if it were an absolute end in itself, a calling.'[17] Entrepreneurs also came to consider their own profit-making activity as an occupation which carried out a mission given to them by God. In addition Puritanism's worldly frugality meant opposition to enjoyment and con-

[17] M. Weber (tr. Giddens), *The Protestant Ethic and the Spirit of Capitalism* (George Allen & Unwin, London, 1976), p. 61.

sumption, and luxury consumption especially was completely squeezed out. In this way the formation of capital was carried out through frugality; new capital was then used productively and became a new source of profit. Thus the religious revolution resulting from Protestantism created the modern entrepreneur and capitalist – a new type of person who was the possessor of an earnest faith, and who controlled huge wealth, but nevertheless contented himself with a life of extreme simplicity, striving to accumulate capital.

For modern capitalism to be established in this way a special type of person must already exist and for this a religious revolution had to come first. Even Marx, who called religion an opium and denounced it in extreme terms, recognised this fact (although he obviously did not approve of its religious basis), when he said 'Accumulate, accumulate! That is Moses and the Prophets!' If we put Marx's words differently, in the fashion of Weber, we have 'Be frugal, be frugal! That is Calvin and the Prophets!' It means that capitalism cannot be established where there is no spirit of abstinence. The year 1642, when the bourgeois revolution began in England, was about a century after the death of Luther, some 80 years after the death of Calvin and some 20 years after the voyage of the Mayflower to North America. On the other hand this year was also the year of Galileo's death and of Newton's birth. In terms of historical order, there was first the religious revolution; then a revolution to achieve modern capitalism was carried out, and then finally, modern science was established. Afterwards, various powerful machines were invented and the industrial revolution occurred. One can see that from 1780–1800 in England productive power increased by leaps and bounds; it was over a century after the English Revolution had ended in 1660 that English capitalism really took off. It had taken about a hundred years to create the conditions for take-off.

In this way the spread of Protestantism (Puritanism) and the rise of the bourgeoisie were prerequisites for the establishment of modern capitalism in England, but the Meiji Revolution in Japan did not happen as a result of the same preconditions being fulfilled. Firstly, Japan was not a Protestant country, of course. Secondly, in the later years of Tokugawa rule a bourgeois class had emerged to a certain extent, but it was not yet that strong and it was not militant like the English bourgeoisie. Many of them supported the absolutist regime of the Tokugawa. During the eighteenth century, in fact, men such as Ishida Baigan (1685–1744) had appeared who expounded a doctrine of commercial morality. They asserted that moneymaking activities as well as savings activities aimed at accumulating capital by frugality were by no means morally base; they spoke in defence of efforts aimed at the pursuit of profit and encouraged the merchants. However, the fact that the Tokugawa commerce developed in this way remained throughout a domestic commerce operating under the circumstances of seclusion meant that the merchants possessed neither the courage nor the spirit of adventure which was usually found among merchants of foreign trade. It was quite natural that Japanese merchants should show docility towards the Tokugawa government and support the existing order, because in order for internal commerce to prosper on a national scale the domestic status quo had to be maintained, and even during the last days of the Tokugawa regime the eyes of Japan's merchants were still scarcely opened to the possibilities of foreign trade.

This was the situation when Japan came face to face with the amazing techniques born of modern science. The most important thing for the Japanese was to protect Japan from technology of this kind and to preserve Japan's independence; the acquisition of personal profit through the use of such techniques had not yet become a matter of primary concern. The question which arose was the manner in which Japan's political structure should be reformed if Japan as a country was to obtain the mastery of modern technology and become a nation as powerful as those of Western Europe. The Meiji Revolution was thus carried through by lower-ranking samurai and members of the intelligentsia who had some feeling of national consciousness, and it was only natural that the Japanese bourgeois class, which was concerned with little but personal profits from internal trade, should be very much outstripped in such a revolution as this. As a result even after it the capitalist class, the driving force behind capitalism, remained weak in Japan.

The British government and parliamentary system was produced as a compromise between royal authority and the bourgeoisie. The English capitalist class had an energy which gave an inbuilt momentum to its development, but the Japanese capitalist class was small in scale and had no power. Therefore the Meiji government itself was forced to construct modern factories, either with money raised as taxes from the peasantry or with funds obtained by printing paper currency. Before very long, however, the government could no longer cope with the management of this sort of state capitalism, inflation was provoked, and a state of bankruptcy followed. So the government was forced to sell off its modern factories at cheap prices, but as a quite unexpected result of this rather desperate policy a more hopeful prospect was revealed. That is to say, the men who had purchased these modern factories from the government very cheaply had, at one step, become large capitalists, and one of the prerequisites for capitalism, the existence of powerful capitalists, had been fulfilled in Japan as well. Moreover, they were not strong-willed capitalists who were opposed to government; since many of the Meiji capitalists had owed their existence to government favour, they continually sought government patronage and remained loyal and cooperative towards the government.

However, if the Japanese had not adopted the belief of frugality, which was another of the prerequisites of capitalism, then modern capitalism could certainly not have been achieved in Japan. In Japan in those days Buddhism and Shinto, the traditional religions, did not have that great an influence on the everyday life of the Japanese people. However, as has already been pointed out, as a result of the Tokugawa Bakufu's cultural policy, Confucianism had spread widely and deeply among the Japanese people. Confucianism was understood in Japan as an ethical system rather than a religion, and it directly (or rather indirectly through the medium of *Bushidō* or chivalry) taught the Japanese people that frugal behaviour was noble behaviour. Therefore Japan, at the end of the Meiji Revolution, had already fulfilled the second prerequisite for capitalism, but since the frugality advocated by Protestantism and that advocated by Confucianism are different, quite naturally the capitalist spirit is not the same in Japan as in England.

Confucianism in Japan stresses (1) loyalty to the state (or lord), (2) filial piety to one's parents, (3) faith towards friends, and (4) respect towards one's elders. Therefore, according to the Confucian ideology it was quite natural that a nationalist–capitalist economy should develop based on a seniority system and lifetime employment. (Moreover, many of the Meiji capitalists owed their existence to government favour and for that reason alone cooperated with the government.) Confucianism was always concerned with the mutual relationships between people and gave little thought to evaluating the conduct of the individual according to any absolute yardstick such as 'God', and so in the Confucian world individualism was suffocated. Nevertheless, Confucianism was intellectual and rational, and compatible with modern science. Immediately after the Meiji Revolution, Japan succeeded in assimilating and absorbing the science of Western Europe with amazing speed, and in the period from 1878 to 1900 the Meiji government successfully achieved 'take-off' in the Japanese economy. Thus a capitalist economy which was managed in an entirely different spirit from English capitalism – an economy combining Japanese soul and Western technology – was set up in Japan.

Finally, it should be noted that, in Confucian political thought, those who play the most important role in the society are bureaucrats, who are strictly and competitively selected. Having been deeply influenced by that thought, the feudal age of Tokugawa was an era of bureaucratic rule, during which a samurai was a civil as well as a military officer. The Meiji government was an advanced modern bureaucracy from the outset. It is therefore not at all surprising that Japanese capitalism started as state capitalism – an economy guided and driven by bureaucrats.

CHAPTER THREE
The Japanese empire (I)

I

Following the Meiji Revolution the new government embarked on the building of a 'modern state'. In search of a model for their modern state the government sent many missions to Europe and America. Not just after the revolution, but even before it, both Bakufu and the governments of the larger fiefs had in secret dispatched missions to the advanced nations. Since they realised that the problem was not whether to maintain seclusion or whether to open the country, they were groping for what sort of modern, unified state to create, and how to create it. At that time all foreign travel was formally prohibited, and when these missions encountered each other in such places as London or Paris they smiled sardonically at each other.

These men brought back with them a wealth of new knowledge and information concerning the modern state. The Meiji government compared and examined all this information to judge which country was the most outstanding and the most advanced in each sphere, for example which country was best in terms of its education system, which country for the navy, and which for the army. In each country they investigated the conditions of such things as the police, industry and finance. On the basis of the information relating to these subjects obtained from the missions the government made its decision as to which sphere should be patterned on which country. For example, the education system promulgated in 1872 was patterned on the French system of school districts. The Imperial Japanese Navy was a copy of the Royal Navy, but the army was very greatly influenced by the French army. The telegraph and the railways followed the British example, universities the American. The Meiji Constitution and the

Civil Code were of German origin, but the Criminal Code was of French origin.

In this way the Meiji state was a hotchpotch of Britain, the United States, France and Germany. It is true that because at the time the Japanese regarded Britain as preeminent in many spheres, British influence was outstanding; but there could also be seen in Japan a synthesis of statist ideas of the German kind, the concept of 'a rich country and a strong army', a French type legal system and business along American and British lines. It was not to be expected that such a synthesis would be free of discord and free of contradictions. Nor could it be expected that a French army and a British navy could happily coexist. Therefore, internally there were confrontations and wrangles between different spheres, and Japan presented the appearance of a region which was, as it were, a cultural settlement of the advanced nations. Nevertheless, Japanese at the time believed that adoption of the best in each sphere would result in the best collection possible.

There was also the problem of whether or not the imported systems and culture would become established in Japan as being more suitable to the Japanese than their traditionally accepted indigenous counterparts. For this reason a certain degree of concession and compromise was inevitable; at any rate some Japanisation or amendment along Japanese lines was imperative and could not be avoided. Moreover, conditions in Japan immediately following the Meiji Revolution were obviously quite different from those in Britain following the English Civil War in the seventeenth century. Therefore it was quite impossible for Japan to carry out an industrial revolution and become a powerful country by the same historical process as Britain had done. Japan was fated to follow a different path from the very beginning.

This difference is tied up with the fundamental nature of the Meiji Revolution. As we mentioned before this was not a revolution by the bourgeoisie; it was a revolution brought about by lower samurai and the intelligentsia in order to build a modern state. They deemed the feudal system to be an obstacle to the modernisation of Japan; the new government returned to the Emperor the lands and people hitherto under daimyō control; they carried out the abolition of the domains and establishment of prefectures. The caste system was also abolished. However, the industrialists, those who had to bear the burden of the new era, did not make their appearance from among members of the farming, artisan or merchant classes. Such men made few demands for freedom to engage in business, and lacked courage to carry out innovations. Following the English Civil War which had arisen because of resistance from the middle class, the English government had had no need to undertake the task of creating industrialists, but in the case of Japan the fostering of industrialists was something which had to be undertaken immediately. While private industrialists were weak the government itself had to play the role of industrialist. Had the Meiji Revolution come a little later Japan might well have become a socialist state, or a national socialist state. At that time, however, socialism was no more than a theoretical programme. Japan made her start as a country run on the lines of state capitalism.

The Meiji government founded state-operated industrial enterprises which they regarded as important from the point of view of nation-building. Since the government had been formed by members of the intelligentsia (mostly former warriors), who had awakened to an awareness of the new era, management of the state-operated enterprises was also in the hands of the same sort of people. And since the ideology of these sort of men was Confucianism the ideology of industrialists was also Confucianism. These enterprises were all large-scale factories and required the organisation and disciplined work of large numbers of workers. Since the existing farmer, artisan and merchant classes had little disposition to adhere to this sort of discipline, initially the workers as well were naturally chosen mainly from the warrior class (for example, in the case of silk mills the first operatives were the daughters of the warrior class). This kind of government factory was the most advanced model factory in Japan at the time. That is to say Japanese capitalism started off with a nucleus of model factories run according to a Confucian ideology. Japan was fated to develop along a totally different path from English capitalism which had advanced under the slogans of individualism and liberalism, guided by 'the invisible hand of God'.

Out of the various virtues stressed by Chinese Confucianism, such as benevolence, righteousness, gratitude, wisdom, faith, loyalty and filial piety, Japanese Confucianism, almost consistently since Shōtoku Taishi, had paid little attention to benevolence and righteousness, and emphasised loyalty, filial piety and wisdom.

(Indeed, in Japan the word *jingi* (lit. benevolence and righteousness) is used also to mean a certain kind of moral code which
prevails in gangster society.) Consequently, Japanese had no
understanding of Western individualism and liking for liberalism.
Especially in the years of the Meiji period, and subsequently, when
there was an upsurge of nationalist ideas, the Japanese had special
praise for 'law and order', and regarded individualism and liberalism as obstacles to 'law and order'. Successful businessmen in the
period when state capitalism flourished were regarded as having
done valuable service to the state, while the successful businessmen
of the period when the domination of state capitalism had
weakened and a free system was flourishing were regarded as lucky
scoundrels who had made money under the guidance of the
invisible hand of an evil spirit. In America money-making was one
of the most effective methods of achieving social respectability, but
in Japan money-making was in no way a sufficient condition for
achieving the respect of society. Not just that, allowing for greater
or smaller differences depending on the social atmosphere of each
period, money-making was often even a condition for social
censure. In Japan people were well aware of the trade-off
relationship between money-making and social respect. Therefore
businessmen were aware that, apart from making money, they
must do 'something' for society and for the country and thought
that in order to achieve this 'something' they must withhold to a
certain extent from the act of making money.

This sort of spirit which pervaded state capitalism from the
beginning of the Meiji period was quite consistent with the view of
the acquisition of wealth held by the merchants of the Tokugawa
period. In the early Tokugawa period these merchants were of low
status, and they held no particular ethical responsibility; it was
therefore regarded as unimportant if they acted shrewdly to gain
themselves a profit. But in the middle and later Tokugawa period
when the merchant houses had become large, producing formal
master–servant relationships within the merchant houses, they
themselves came to be bound by Confucian ethics, and they ceased
to regard the acquisition of wealth and the material well-being of
themselves alone as the ultimate goal of their lives. To be moved
only by the motivation of one's own interests was 'base' and it was
important even for a merchant to sacrifice himself for his town and
for his lord. Loyalty to the family business, and, through the family

business, service to the people, service to the lord and service to one's village, all these were emphasised for merchants as well.

However, the Meiji government did not entrust industry to this kind of Tokugawa period merchant. These traditional merchants were certainly not usurious men, and had a considerable sense of service to 'society', but the society they conceived of was not a large society such as could be found in a modern state. They did not think of devoting themselves to anything more than a much smaller society, for example to their feudal lord, to the town, and to their own house. They had no sense of an obligation to make Japan a modern state by founding in Japan such businesses as railways, telegraphs, shipbuilding and steel manufacturing; and, moreover, the capital they could find was too insignificant to be used for building this sort of large business. Inevitably the state had to establish this kind of business using the power of the state itself. Although the country had been fully opened following the advent of the Meiji period this applied only to the field of trade, and the Japanese government did not yet feel inclined to open the country to the extent of importing foreign capital. Consequently the government had to use its own powers to create the capital for these businesses. A large proportion of the government's income at that time was supplied by the land tax, so the government levied land tax at a very high rate, and used this sort of government income and domestic saving to start various businesses. Thus even after the beginning of the Meiji period the burden borne by the peasantry was just as heavy as it had been in the feudal period.

A further source of capital for industry was cash from feudal stipends. At the time of the abolition of the domains the government had taken over the stipends formerly paid by each domain; in the years 1873–74 the government gave those former feudal lords and warriors who renounced their stipends cash and government bonds to the value of 4–6 years of the old stipend. In this way the warriors found themselves possessing money, and the former lords and upper-ranking warriors especially became at a stroke very wealthy; they invested this wealth in industry. These men's criteria for investment were, quite unlike those of the merchants, not economic; they made their investment decisions using as their yardstick national necessity and national interest. Many of them possessed a strong national consciousness and had a comparatively clear perception of what was in the national interest, but they had no idea of the profitability of individual industries – especially considered in the short term. It was indeed an amateurish, samurai way of business.

The important posts within the central government were held mainly by samurai, and able samurai were treated favourably by the government, and yet on the other hand the government abolished the caste system according to the guiding principle that the Meiji state should not be a feudal state. Because of this last, there were numerous discontented elements within the warrior class. Especially in the case of the lower samurai, even when they had received four years' worth of stipend in the form of cash or government bonds the amount was negligible and they could no longer parade their status as samurai. Apart from the stipend the status of samurai had brought with it various fringe benefits, and they had lost the whole lot. These discontented elements not infrequently started revolts.[1] The government investigated the possibility of a foreign expedition to divert the attention of such discontented samurai. The plan for the attack on Korea proposed by Saigō Takamori was rejected, but there was an expedition to Taiwan (1874).[2] Following this rejection of his proposal, Saigō, a figure of most distinguished service in the Meiji Revolution, resigned from the government. These discontented warriors regarded him as their commander and they eventually rose up against the government in 1877 in the Satsuma Rebellion. Within a decade of its establishment the weak Meiji government had (1) issued large amounts of cash and government bonds to cope with the former samurai, (2) carried out one foreign expedition, and (3) experienced one major civil war, several insurrections and numerous peasant uprisings. Inflation was to be expected under these circumstances, and by 1880 the government's financial policy was virtually bankrupt.

[1] The implementation of a system of conscription was one thing which contributed to the discontent of samurai.

[2] The crisis in the Meiji government produced by the split between the pro-invasion and anti-invasion factions is more or less comparable with the crisis situation later faced by the government at the time of the 26 Feburary uprising (the Shōwa coup d'état) in 1936. In terms of ideas there is not that much difference between Itagaki Taisuke, who called for a Japanese invasion of Korea, parted company with the government as a result of the dispute, and subsequently founded the Freedom and People's Rights movement, conducting anti-government activity, and Kita Ikki, who was regarded as the ideological leader of the young army officers who took part in the rebellion of 26 February. Furthermore, many of the various right wing factions in Japan from the Meiji period (e.g. the Genyōsha, the Kokuryūkai, etc.) were derived from the remnants of the Satsuma pro-invasion faction.

The government had no option but to dispose of the state-operated enterprises, and they were sold off as one of a series of deflationary measures. From the founding of the Meiji government, merchants were to be found within close reach of the government who acted as government purveyors and who at all times pursued it in the hope of obtaining concessions and privileges. It was merchants such as these who had taken charge of government procurements at the times of the Taiwan expedition and Satsuma Rebellion, making huge profits. At the time of the sale of government mines and government factories (shipbuilding, cement, glass, textiles, etc.) the government made over the enterprises at very low prices to this sort of 'political merchant' or to former high officials in the government. There is no doubt that many of these enterprises were of low profitability; so the fact that some enterprises were sold at prices so low that they were virtually given away was perhaps not as scandalous as is often claimed. At the time, however, state enterprises paid far higher wages than did private enterprises, which contributed to low profitability within those enterprises. When those enterprises became private and wage rates were normalised they all became economically sound enterprises. In this way many of the so-called 'political merchants' into whose hands the government enterprises fell became at a stroke large industrial capitalists. They included such firms as Mitsui, Mitsubishi, Furukawa, Kuhara and Asano. As well as affording them official protection the government assisted them by assigning to them able individuals. In this way the government had succeeded in creating a nucleus of industrial capitalists which had been won over to the government, and which would therefore listen attentively to what was said by the government.

Kawasaki Masayoshi, for example, was Vice-President of the Japan Postal Steamship Company, and came from a Satsuma domain warrior family. In 1878 he rented land owned by the government to start the Kawasaki Shipbuilding Yard. In 1884 the business was bordering on bankruptcy, but was saved by government assistance. In 1886 he was able to purchase the government-run Hyōgo Shipyard at an outrageously low price, and taking over the equipment and personnel at one stroke he had gained control of a major shipyard. From then until the beginning of the Pacific War, even during times of depression he was always able to keep his yards full with orders placed by the navy.

II

The creation in this way of what one might call 'the friendly industrial capitalist' was carried out once again by the military in the 1930s. The *zaibatsu* fostered by the Meiji government had always cooperated with the government. In the Shōwa period (1926–   ), however, there started a period of a kind of dual government. Although the new duality was not as explicit as that of the Tokugawa period, when the imperial court had been the government in name only and the military government of the Tokugawa Shogunate had been the effective government, in the 1930s the influence of the government became weaker, and the military came to wield most of the real power in politics. In collusion with one group of younger bureaucrats – the so-called renovationist bureaucrats – the army tried to contain the power of the Emperor, senior statesmen, political parties and conservative bureaucrats. In the early Shōwa period the military became the first rank government, and the government had to resign itself to being a second rank government.

The *zaibatsu* created by the Meiji government were from the first loyal to the government and had grown to vast size under the protection of the government. When they had become big and strong the *zaibatsu* in their turn came to control the government through the political parties. The military hated the *zaibatsu* which had become identified with the conservative government. The *zaibatsu* were criticised by the right wing and the military, and Dan Takuma, the managing director of the Mitsui Partnership, was assassinated by the right wing in 1932. Consequently the members of the *zaibatsu* as well had a thorough dislike of the military.

It was necessary for the military to create industrial capitalists – new *zaibatsu* – who would be loyal to the military itself. The military had to cultivate powerful businessmen of the kind that would cooperate with its development of Manchuria. Moreover, this sort of businessman was needed in new fields such as the heavy chemical industry, the electrical industry and industries connected with the production of armaments. In this way such companies as Nissan, Nihon Chisso (Japan Nitrogen), Nihon Sōda (Japan Soda), Shōwa Denkō (Shōwa Electrical), boomed under the protection of the military. The capital for their enterprises was raised from the public on the open capital market. Through their

close connections with the military they gained various concessions, and were therefore loyal to the military.

Armed with the loyalty of the new *zaibatsu* the military enforced
their policy of 'rich country, strong army', so the government and
the older *zaibatsu* had to run along behind.[3] In this stage the new
and old *zaibatsu* did not merely supply the goods demanded by the
government and the military; they always had to keep a close
watch on them and make sure that their own enterprises corre-
sponded to the national interest. Failing this the names of their own
enterprises would probably be excluded from the list of those
patronised by the government. In this way the demands of the
government and the demands of the military were largely filled by
the *zaibatsu*, new or old. This resulted in a derived demand for
goods and services by the *zaibatsu*, and the derived demand had
repercussions on each industry. Therefore, all industries whatsoever had some sort of government connection.

Moreover, over the 77 year period between 1868 and 1945 Japan
was involved in 10 major wars (Taiwan Expedition 1874, Satsuma
Rebellion 1877, Sino–Japanese War 1894–95, Russo–Japanese War
1904–5, First World War 1914–18, Siberian Expedition 1918–25,
Shantung Expeditions 1927–28, Manchurian Incident 1931–33,
China Incident 1937–41, and the Second World War 1941–45),
extending in toto over some 30 years. At the beginning of this
period Japan had virtually no military capability, but during it she
became the world's third largest naval power and the world's fifth
largest military power. Moreover Japan did not just control Korea
and the Manchurian region; in the final stage she succeeded in
bringing a large part of Asia within her sphere of influence. In
addition during this period Japan's G.N.P. grew at an astonishing
rate. This economic growth was certainly not achieved through
using the mechanism of free operation of the economy; it was the
result of the government or the military, with their loyal following
of capitalists, manipulating and influencing the economy in order

[3] In 1937 Nissan (Nihon Sangyō) moved into Manchuria and changed its name to the
Manchurian Heavy Industries Company. The extremely preferential treatment given to
Nissan at the time of this move aroused the jealousy of the other *zaibatsu*. At the time
Nissan was subject to financial difficulties and gained a new lease of life by the move to
Manchuria. Subsequently all the *zaibatsu* cooperated with the military and the government
in making advances into the occupied territory during the war with China. They
established two huge organisations aimed at carrying out public policy, the North China
Development Company and the Central China Promotion Company.

to realise national aims. In the final stage this kind of state capitalism was eventually transformed into a controlled economy; since the leaders of private enterprise had from the outset shown a dependence on the government they submitted easily – or at least with relatively little resistance – to a control of industry which depended on administrative guidance by the government.

Under a free enterprise system where entrepreneurs possess a strong character of autonomy and independence it is probably not possible to achieve this sort of long-term economic development on the basis of government guidance. But in an economy whose creed was the Confucian ethic, which always had the country in mind and where the major enterprises were managed by samurai-type businessmen who were loyal to the government, this sort of development was indeed possible. In this sort of economy the price mechanism scarcely played an important role, and the questions of importance were how to raise the capital to meet government demand, to which industries to direct government demand and the nature of the demand generated from the enterprises at the receiving end of a government demand – all of them related to Keynes' principle of effective demand. Enterprises which had been in receipt of government favour grew huge, producing a situation of monopoly or oligopoly. These enterprises did not carry on fierce competition which could have been advantageous to economic efficiency, although by using different means they carried on a non-economic competition to obtain for themselves government demand. The market mechanism did not work well and resources were not allocated in a satisfactory way. In spite of all this it is true that Japan succeeded in establishing in a fairly short time a large monopoly sector and *zaibatsu* sector as the nucleus of her economy.

Thus the Japanese government had a special partiality for a limited group of enterprises. To other enterprises it showed an unequalled heartlessness. But this sort of favouritism was more or less inevitable, and indeed it was even a rational means whereby the government could realise its aims. The consistent aim of successive governments from the Meiji Revolution onwards was to build Japan into a strong country with a top class military capability and a top class industry – a country which could not be defeated by the advanced nations of Europe and America. There were two formulas by which this could be achieved. One was the formula of going ahead with modernisation uniformly over the whole country, making no distinctions. The other formula was that of forming representative teams in the Japanese industrial world, raising them to the first rank by dint of special training and then enlarging the scale of the team. Under the first formula it would take a huge amount of time before first class enterprises would appear in Japan, enterprises which Japan would not have been ashamed of when they were exposed to the world, but under the second formula it was possible to create within Japan in a fairly short time the small nucleus of a 'modern sector' which had attained to world levels. Then subsequently the government could press on with modernisation over the country as a whole by enlarging this nucleus.

The Japanese government adopted the second formula as its policy for growth, on the basis of its judgement that a situation where some sections in Japan were at the same level as England but others still as far behind as ever was preferable to a degree of development where in all sections of the economy the disparity between the two countries had been reduced, say, by only one tenth. As a result the government came to show partiality in its dealings with enterprises, and this policy was supported not only by the enterprises which received favourable treatment, but also by those which did not. That is to say there was a national consensus in favour of having a strong team of representative enterprises. Just in the same way as when representative participants have been chosen for the Olympics they alone receive favourable treatment, and those not selected do not normally complain, neither did those enterprises which had not been selected voice any complaint. The establishment of this kind of national consensus was not that difficult in a society governed by Confucian ethics. Those who had not been chosen were, as it were, 'resigned to their lot'.

And then, in order to bestow privileged treatment on representative players an added measure of exploitation for some others was inevitable. Needless to say the ones who suffered were the farmers, and they too were resigned to their role. It was to be expected that at the last moment resistance, rebellion and peasant rioting would come from one section of the farming population but these have to be regarded as exceptions. The farmers endured their role and suffered their heavy exploitation. However, it was impossible to achieve the development of the country merely on the basis of an unrestricted exploitation of agriculture and unlimited sacrifice by

Table 1. *Wages of indigenous workers compared with wages of Japanese workers in major cities of the Japanese colonies (1922)* (*Japanese wage = 100*)

	Carpenter	Plasterer	Tiler	Blacksmith	Stevedore	Printer	Picture framer	Rickshaw puller
Koreans (Seoul)	54.9	64.6	60.7	—	—	—	62.6	93.6
Taiwanese (Taipei)	51.4	50.0	44.4	52.0	71.4	—	—	—
Chinese (Talien)	38.2	39.0	41.2	42.2	—	31.3	—	—

Source: Meiji–Taishō Kokusei Sōran (General survey of the state of affairs in Meiji–Taishō Japan), Tōyō Keizai Shinpōsha, Tokyo, 1927.

farmers; the government had to look elsewhere for an alternative source to exploit before very long. With her victory in the Russo–Japanese War Japan had established a firm foothold in Manchuria, and her privileged position there was recognised not only by the powers but also by China herself. Furthermore in 1910 Japan annexed Korea. Japan had thus become a colonial empire, and gained vast new areas for exploitation. The people of Korea were compelled to cooperate without much benefit in the great task of building in Japan the nucleus of a 'modern state' which could stand up to the West and in increasing the size of this nucleus year by year. Both in Korea and in Taiwan the racial discrimination which was carried on was harsh; over the period 1910–25 the wages paid to Korean or Taiwanese natives were only 60% of those paid in each district to Japanese doing the same work, and in some cases the figure frequently fell below 50% (see Table 1).

Japanese enterprises made tremendous advances in these colonies because they could depend on this kind of disparity in wages. The Japanese furthermore carried out large-scale land survey operations in Korea and many Koreans were dispossessed of their land. Korean rice was bought up cheaply and shipped to Japan proper. Korean workers who migrated to Japan suffered from harsh discrimination both in terms of wages and in terms of living in the Japanese community. Subsequently at the time of the great Kantō earthquake in 1923 false rumours circulated to the effect that Koreans were trying to utilise the opportunity to provoke rioting and 6000 innocent Koreans resident in the Tokyo area were arrested and massacred. This included some Japanese who were killed because they were suspected of being Koreans. The Meiji government had abolished the caste structure of the feudal system, but by its victories in imperialist wars it created a new structure of discrimination whereby people were ruthlessly forced into classes according to their race. Sustained in this fashion by a new area of exploitation the government step by step realised what it regarded as 'the national interest'; until 1920, at least, the mechanism worked fairly smoothly.

From the Meiji period the everyday life of the Japanese people underwent a marked Westernisation in the name of 'civilization and enlightenment'. For a time in the 1880s the government as well encouraged a policy of extreme Westernisation both of consumption habits and of culture in general, but on becoming aware that a

Westernised lifestyle of this kind might bring about the demise of the 'spirit' of the Japanese people it subsequently encouraged the preservation of the traditional Japanese way of life. In conjunction with this the people as well resisted any total Westernisation of their way of life, and individual Japanese came to lead what might be called a double life, whereby they adopted a Western lifestyle in all aspects of such things as clothing, food and housing, while at the same time continuing to live in the traditional Japanese manner as well. A Western lifestyle was gradually adopted while the traditional mode of living was also preserved. This kind of dual lifestyle necessitated two sets of goods – suits and kimono, tableware for use with Western food and tableware geared to Japanese food, furniture for Western style rooms and furniture for Japanese style rooms – and also made living expenses high, but the Japanese preferred such a dual lifestyle to one which was either purely Western or purely Japanese. The Western lifestyle symbolised progressiveness; the Japanese one was proof of a continuing awareness that they were Japanese. Therefore given that the government's slogan was 'Japanese spirit and Western learning' this dual lifestyle was an entirely natural mode of life for the Japanese.

This sort of duality of lifestyle, however, serves to explain certain elements of the dualism which has developed in industry. Since the Japanese had not developed the techniques for the large-scale production of the consumer goods traditional to the Japanese way of life such goods were all produced by small enterprises, and productivity was extremely low. Even among the consumer goods integral to the Western way of life, however, there were some with production not necessarily restricted to large factories, and where the optimal scale of the producing enterprise was small. Matches, for example, were initially produced by a large enterprise purely because they were a Western good, but when it was realised that the optimal scale of production of matches was small the enterprise was split up into smaller ones.

Let us now call the small enterprises manufacturing traditional commodities Type A, and those which produce Western style consumer goods, but which for reasons of economy of scale are small, Type B. Out of the A type some found their Western counterparts in large enterprises, and it is unlikely that such small enterprises would have existed were it not for the duality existing in the consumption habits and lifestyle of the Japanese. The simultaneous production of the same good, or of goods with the same use, both in large enterprises and in medium and small scale enterprises with differing productivity is what one might call dualism (duality) of production; it is seen in Japan that duality of consumption serves to exacerbate the degree of duality of production. Thus dualism in production was also in part the result of the policy of 'Japanese spirit and Western skills'.

However there developed a further third type of medium and small enterprise which we can call Type C. This was the subcontractor for the large-scale manufacturing enterprise, and it existed in such fields as machine manufacture, shipbuilding, vehicles and electrical goods. These enterprises carried on production in accordance with orders placed by the large enterprises. In most cases the large enterprises had connections with the government, while the subcontractors were completely independent companies despite receiving technical guidance and financial assistance from the parent company. On rare occasions a C type enterprise which through its own abilities was successful in invention and innovation grew into a large enterprise, while the majority had to resign themselves to playing the role of cushioning the gap between demand in times of prosperity and that in times of depression. If the scale of a large enterprise was geared to the level of demand at a time of prosperity then it would be forced to curtail sharply its number of employees at a time of recession; consequently management adapted the scale of production to the level of demand existing in a time of depression, or something close to it. This would normally mean the existence of a certain demand that could not be fulfilled by the large enterprise, and it was this demand that was filled by orders to the subcontractors. The subcontractor did well in times of prosperity, but in times of depression he bore the full brunt of the recession and was on the verge of bankruptcy. In contrast the operation of the large enterprise rested on an extremely stable and sound basis. The large enterprise supervised the subcontractor not only in technological and financial matters, but also in terms of personnel involvement. Employees of the large enterprise who were transferred to the management of the subcontractor were like commanding officers sent to the front line; there was a high probability of death in battle, but it was also possible to return to a high position at headquarters if one distinguished oneself in the fighting.

These three types of small and medium enterprise had recipro-
cally to engage in fierce competition with other enterprises. The
goods were sold cheaply, the profit margin small, and wages low.
Here was a world quite different from the *zaibatsu* sector. Furthermore, in the background, behind the industrial sector, there was
the agricultural sector. The industrial sector expanded through
using the agricultural sector as its source of labour supply; as
industry expanded, agriculture contracted, at least in a relative
sense. In 1904 64% of all Japanese households were engaged in
agriculture but twenty years later (1925) the figure had fallen to
49%. Within the agricultural sector the percentage of owner
farmers shrank,[4] and along with this the proportion of tenant
farmers or owner–tenant farmers increased. Marginal owner farmers became tenants, and those unable to engage in tenant farming
migrated to the towns to become labourers. Industry thus expanded at the expense of agriculture, and within industry the
relative weight of large enterprises steadily became larger. It has
been the aspiration and the achievement of the Japanese to create
by this sort of mechanism a military force (before the war) and
large companies (especially after the war) which could be favourably compared with those of the leading countries of the West. The
products of their modern sector have afforded the Japanese great
satisfaction – even when they were non-consumer goods such as
zero fighters or the mammoth battleship 'Yamato'. They meant
that the armed forces and the large enterprise sector were able to
stand in competition with those of the West, and because of this the
mass of the people were content to be exploited by these two
groups, and gave every encouragement to their development.

III

When the Meiji government, intent on building a modern state,
realised that there were too few entrepreneurs with the ability to
manage modern enterprises, it also realised that the supply of lower
level employees and operatives was insufficient. As we have said, it
was warriors who had become unemployed as a result of the

---

[4] For example, it fell from 35.4% in 1899 to 33.4% in 1910, to 31.1% in 1925 and to 30.9%
in 1935.

abolition of the domains who became this kind of employee. In cases where it was necessary to have female workers they were hired mainly from among the daughters of lower samurai. Therefore it was not merely the capital for the government enterprises of the early Meiji period that was supplied by the state; the employees too were very much samurai and therefore possessed a lively national consciousness. They regarded themselves as engaging in the work of production both for themselves and for the sake of the nation. Many of the state-operated enterprises subsequently either became the parent organisation of a *zaibatsu* or became affiliated to one. Those individuals who desired to promote the construction of a new Japan gathered in the *zaibatsu* sector, while it was in the other, traditional sectors that the members of the farmers, artisan and merchant classes of the feudal period collected. The former warriors and their daughters possessed a relatively high level of education, and thought very highly of themselves.

Nevertheless, workers who had acquired both discipline and skill were an extremely rare commodity at that time. Consequently the two main problems for the managers of modern enterprises were: (1) how to obtain in larger numbers this kind of worker for their own enterprise and (2) how, once they found such workers, to have them work for a long period for their own enterprise without losing them to another one. For the government the problem was how to produce this kind of a labour force in large quantities. It was for this reason that from the very beginning the government concentrated its efforts on the provision of an education system.

The government embarked on the provision of a modern school system with the issue of the *Gakusei* (Education Law) in 1872. This provided for the division of the country into roughly 50,000 primary school districts on a basis of each area covering 600 people, and for the implementation of nationwide compulsory education through the building of one primary school in each of these areas. In addition these primary schools were to be standardised, without regard to status, pedigree or sex.[5] In 1873 only 28% of the total school age population was attending primary school, but by 1882 it was 50%, in 1885 67%, and by 1904 it had reached 98%. Figures such as these show the remarkable rate at which

---

[5] Note that it was only two years after the implementation of the Education Act in Britain and seven years after the abolition of slavery in the United States that Japan embarked on this kind of progressive compulsory education.

compulsory education spread, suggesting that the people strongly supported the government's plans for the building of a modern nation state. However, it was impossible for the effects of this education to have an impact within a very short space of time, so during the Meiji period the supply of skilled and educated workers was totally inadequate.

Until the middle of the Meiji period private enterprises recruited their supply of labour by traditional methods. Labour bosses kept a number of workers, anything up to several hundred. The enterprise contracted the whole operation to the labour boss, paying him a fixed sum, and the allocation of work and distribution to the workers of the money which had been paid was entrusted to the labour boss. The workers who worked for the labour boss were collected from poor families in the farming villages. Since such workers possessed a very low level of skill, however, enterprises were placed in difficulties by a shortage of skilled labour. Consequently from the late nineteenth century and into the early twentieth century companies not infrequently 'poached' the labour force of other companies. A 'spirit of loyalty' to the company was therefore emphasised in an attempt to secure 'regular employees' over a long period. The Imperial Injunction to Soldiers and Sailors and the Imperial Rescript on Education were issued by the Emperor in 1882 and 1890, respectively, and Confucian morality, above all loyalty to the state, was impressed upon the people by the government. It was therefore easy to conceive of a 'spirit of loyalty' to the company as something which was analogous to this. As a result of compulsory education it was not only samurai who now received a Confucian education but the whole population, but even so a spirit of loyalty was still a fairly rare commodity, and to that extent a company had to make special payments with a view to procuring it. Thus the seniority wage structure was introduced.

It was to be expected that the seniority wage system would begin with the white-collar employees of large companies. It was the large companies which possessed an appearance of dignity which could claim a spirit of loyalty from the company's employees, and it was the white-collar workers who were the new samurai. Of course, given that there were strong relics of feudal society in Japan a certain spirit of loyalty vis-à-vis the head of the enterprise existed also among employees of medium and small enterprises; but since the heads of such enterprises did not have the financial power to purchase a spirit of loyalty the seniority wage system and the lifetime employment system were not introduced in the medium and small enterprise sector. In the large enterprise sector, while companies purchased feelings of loyalty through the seniority system, they asked in return for a lifetime's work. Where an employee left an enterprise to go to another without the full agreement of his employer, he was regarded as someone who had left the company 'not under harmonious circumstances' and was branded as a 'traitor'. Other large enterprises were reluctant to give work to this sort of 'traitor' since if they broke ranks by making such an offer this would initiate a full-scale war between large enterprises bent on stealing each other's labour, and others would retaliate in a manner extremely injurious to them.

Therefore the so-called 'traitors' had no alternative but to seek employment in the medium and small enterprise sector. There was no longer a place for them in the splendid large enterprises which produced modern commodities and vied for superiority with enterprises from the advanced countries of the West, in the team representing Japanese industry which struggled for the sake of the country, and on which rested all the aspirations of the Japanese people. The likelihood of 'traitors' making an appearance was therefore small, and most people, once they had become employed in a large enterprise, would, notwithstanding a few causes of discontent, keep a tight grasp on that sector for the rest of their lives. The labour market for the medium and small enterprises was a permanently open one, but the chance of entering the large enterprise sector came only once in a whole lifetime, on graduation from school or college. In this sense the elite of the Japanese industrial world – the employees of the large enterprises – had, and have, no freedom of choice of employment. In just the same way as their fathers had worked for the domain lord (*daimyō*), they dedicate their whole lives to the new domain lord, the enterprise.

While the countries of Europe were squandering their energies on mutual slaughter during the First World War the Japanese economy made inroads into the Chinese and other markets and achieved a remarkable development. How to ensure the supply of skilled workers became a major problem in large enterprises from this time; the lifetime employment system and the seniority wage system, which had been applied only to white-collar workers, came to be extended to blue-collar workers. However the seniority system was an uneconomic wage structure. High wages were paid to older employees only for the reason that they were older; the expenditure on wages was unnecessarily high. To make up for this starting wages had to be lowered, but if enterprises did this they might then lose young people to other companies, so they could not engage in any great reduction in starting salaries. Yet if they started from a high starting salary then older employees would have to be paid a wage in excess of their contribution to production.

In order to remove this kind of weakness from the seniority system the enterprise had to strengthen training at the workplace and carry out the kind of on-the-job training which would result in increasing age being accompanied by an increase in skills and ability. In a Confucian society, where it was considered that age should be respected but also that in return older people had a duty to acquire virtues which were worthy of respect, the groundwork had already been laid for the workers to obtain on-the-job training in skills. In addition, if the enterprise was going to use older workers then it would have to use them in a non-manual labour capacity; so it was the norm under the lifetime employment system for workers who had been engaged in manual labour to end up either in non-manual work or in the middle or lower grades of management. Within the enterprise there was no clear division between the manual workers and the non-manual workers; there was considerable movement between the two groups. In such a situation workers lost any deep awareness of particular occupations, and instead their awareness of being a member of a particular company became stronger.

This system whereby workers spent their whole life in one company and the disposition of workers was decided by the order of the company meant that workers devoted their whole lives to the company; they did not devote their whole lives to their trade (work). Since during their lives workers had to experience various different types of work which they themselves had not chosen, they had few feelings of loyalty towards the work itself. Loyalty to the company was far stronger. The labour movement was weak. (Even where labour unions have been formed in the postwar period most of them are not unions organised on the basis of trade; they are employee unions, formed on the basis of company.) Moreover, management was especially skilful in its handling of relations with older workers, and through them successfully strengthened discipline among the workforce. Labour disputes were few, and a strong 'paternalistic', 'familial', 'comradely' atmosphere pervaded the company.

With employees changing their job on the order of the company the education and training (vocational training) necessary for this altering distribution of the workforce was carried on mainly within the company and all the necessary expense was naturally borne by the company. Some large enterprises even came to possess their own schools, which were used exclusively for the training of their own workforce. From the beginning of the twentieth century large companies such as Mitsubishi Shipyards and Mitsui Mining built their own trade schools; by about 1920 a system of education and training within large enterprises was virtually complete.

Of course there existed outside these companies regular middle schools which concentrated on vocational education – commercial schools, industrial schools and agricultural schools – but over the period 1868–1945 the number who graduated from such schools was small; the majority of workers had to start work in the factory immediately after leaving elementary school, with no vocational education. In the medium and small enterprises there was no systematic training. Workers there had to acquire skills by following the example of the older workers. However the large enterprises, even where they did not have a proper training school, carried out technical education in a more or less systematic fashion. As a result, even where they used the same skill the large enterprise mastered it more perfectly than the medium or small enterprise; its productivity was consequently higher.

Where vocational training is the responsibility of the individual worker and conducted outside the enterprise both large and small enterprises have more or less the same quality of worker; so far as they utilise the same skill there is no great productivity difference between enterprises. However, as has been seen, the large enterprises in Japan adopted the life-time employment system and seniority wage system and provided education within the company, while the medium and small enterprises were not powerful enough to offer their workers lifetime employment and had no reserves to train them within the enterprise; consequently there appeared a difference in labour productivity between enterprises, which in turn produced wage differentials.

Table 2A. *Wage disparities (wage per worker in plants of 1000 or more =
100)*

Scale of plant (number of workers)	1909			1914			Britain 1949
	Male	Female	Total	Male	Female	Total	Total
5–9	80.0	75.7	99.6	72.7	72.3	91.8	—
10–29	85.8	78.6	96.7	77.1	75.2	85.9	84
30–49	88.9	85.5	92.1	78.8	81.0	80.2	83
50–99	91.9	93.2	94.1	82.6	87.4	81.9	84
100–499	94.1	94.4	96.6	85.4	89.7	83.1	86
500–999	92.2	103.2	98.6	87.6	100.9	91.2	89
1000–	100	100	100	100	100	100	100

Source: Archive of Secretariat of Minister of Agriculture and Commerce: *Kōgyō
Tōkei Hyō* (Statistical tables of factories) for 1909 and 1914. British figures are
obtained from S. Broadbridge, *Industrial Dualism in Japan* (Frank Cass and Co. Ltd,
1966), p. 51.

Pieces of quantitative evidence can be provided to trace this
movement. While it can be seen from Table 2A that wage
differentials between large and small enterprises were greater in
1914 than they had been in 1909, the difference was not, however,
very great over these years. In fact, if by a large enterprise we mean
one with over a thousand employees, then the level of wages in
enterprises of all sizes expressed as a percentage of the wage level in
'large enterprises' was high in the period around 1909–14; the wage
disparity in these years was not very different from that of Britain
in 1949. However Table 2B shows that by 1932 a quite considerable wage differential already existed, though it must be noted
that, while Table 2A shows the scale of the enterprise measured in
terms of the number of employees, Table 2B, in contrast, measures
scale in terms of the amount of capital, so that the two tables
should be compared carefully. In 1932 the wages of the smallest
scale enterprises amount to no more than 26% of those of the
largest enterprises. This kind of typical 'Japanese' wage difference
emerged around 1920,[6] and subsequently the disparity got pro-

[6] With the exception of 1909 and 1914 there are no statistics for wages measured according
to scale of enterprise for prewar Japan. The figures given in Table 2B are those estimated
by Umemura Mataji from a survey of industry of the five cities of Ōsaka, Kyōto, Nagoya,
Yokohama and Kōbe and the Metropolitan area of Tokyo carried out in 1932. However,
Japanese economists now believe that wage differences on a large scale developed from
about 1920. Until then labour bosses of a very traditional Japanese type controlled the
labour supply; so ironically it was totally 'un-Japanese', undifferentiated wages which
prevailed.

gressively larger until Japan was thrust into war. When the postwar period of confusion came to an end the large differential again prevailed. As will be seen in Chapter 5, during the period of rapid economic growth between 1963 and 1973, when available labour was insufficient, medium and small enterprises offered high wages in order to attract labour. As a result wage differences decreased greatly but even now a considerable gap remains.

It was from the 1920s that a disparity in wages between large and medium/small enterprises developed in the private sector in this way, but prior to this there had been a considerable disparity in the wages of government-owned and private enterprises. In 1909 the wages of male workers in private enterprises with over 1000 employees amounted to no more than 1.13 the average male wage in all private enterprises; the wages of male workers in government-owned enterprises amounted to 1.43 of this same average.[7] For women the corresponding figures were 1.10 and 1.22 respectively, suggesting that the disparity in wages between government-owned and private enterprises was not as great for women as for men. However this kind of disparity as well was decreasing rapidly at the time and by 1914, in the cases of both men and women, the wages of operatives in government enterprises were lower than those in private enterprises with over 1000 workers. In Japan, government enterprises originally started off with very high wages and failed to make any profits, so the government sold them off. Wages in the remaining government enterprises still remained excessively high, but high wages of this kind did not correspond to the productivity of the worker. They were the result of non-economic considerations such as the fact that many operatives were members of the old samurai class, or an attempt to demonstrate the dignity of the government. A little while after wage disparities of this kind had disappeared wage disparities between large enterprises and medium or small enterprises in the private sector began to appear. It was quite natural that it was first government, and then private enterprise, which demanded loyalty from their workers and paid high wages in return for it.

The wage disparity between large and small enterprises developed into a chronic illness of the Japanese economy. Able young people wanted to enter the large enterprises, and the medium and

---

[7] See *Meiji–Taishō Kokusei Sōran* (General survey of the state of affairs in Meiji–Taishō Japan), edited by Tōyō-Keizai Shimpōsha, Tokyo, 1927, pp. 540–1.

Table 2B. *Wage disparities 1932 (wage per worker in plants of 5 m yen or more = 100)*

	Scale of plant (amount of capital in thousand yen)									
	0–1	1–5	5–10	10–20	20–50	50–100	100–500	500–1000	1000–5000	5000–
wage differential	25.9	30.1	33.2	38.3	45.3	54.1	67.5	78.1	84.4	100

Source: Y. Andō (ed.), *Kindai Nippon Keizai Yōran* (Survey of the economic history of modern Japan) (Tokyo University Press, 1975), p. 119.

small enterprises had to take those who were left over. Therefore the large enterprises were able to recruit workers who were already outstanding when they entered the company. This contributed to a widening of productivity differentials which already existed. As wage rate differentials became even greater profit differentials also increased and large enterprises could accumulate capital more rapidly than the medium and small enterprises. The large enterprises had sufficient capital to take up the best technology, and the technological difference which was thus produced brought with it further increases in productivity and, therefore, in wage differences. In this way a vicious circle came into being with the difference in wages between medium and small enterprises and large enterprises becoming greater and greater.

Table 3 shows changes in productivity differentials over the period 1929–42, measuring the size of the enterprise in terms of its number of employees. Since the slump of the early 1930s first of all hit small enterprises (1930), subsequently affected large enterprises (1931) and it was these large enterprises which recovered first (1932), productivity differentials over the period 1929–32 were somewhat variable. In 1933 the range of difference increased considerably and it was only under the quasi-wartime structure of the years after 1940 that this considerable range of difference was reduced. From 1940 the effects of the forced consolidation of enterprises became apparent, and a marked reduction in the range of difference of productivity can be seen;[8] but since this was a time of price control it is difficult to say whether or not the level of production attributed to each individual worker measured in terms of official prices in fact shows the real level of labour productivity.

This kind of productivity range did not just give rise to a wide range of wages. It also occasioned a wide difference in the welfare and health facilities made available to employees. Those who were employed by the large enterprises were, as we have seen, the labour aristocracy, the 'samurai' of the labour force. The large enterprises

---

[8] Economic control was strengthened from 1940. Factories in industries which were not absolutely indispensable for pursuit of the war effort and medium and small enterprises with low productivity became unable to secure raw materials and personnel; they either ceased to exist or were taken over and absorbed by large enterprises. This kind of weeding out raised the productivity of medium and small enterprises. On the other hand, since there were some large enterprises which had grown only superficially by encompassing inferior enterprises, productivity differences between large enterprises and medium/small enterprises were reduced.

Table 3. *Productivity differentials (gross output per man in plants of 1000 or more = 100)*

Scale of plant (number of workers)	1929	1930	1931	1932	1933	1934	1935	1936	1937	1938	1939	1940	1941	1942
5–9	75	63	74	65	46	42	41	43	45	49	48	60	61	69
10–29	84	71	86	75	56	51	51	48	54	59	58	69	69	79
30–49	95	82	97	87	70	62	61	62	66	63	71	85	81	91
50–99	109	91	101	95	75	66	65	70	74	80	83	92	94	99
100–499	124	95	107	102	86	81	82	85	90	90	90	98	106	102
500–999	104	100	109	105	88	82	89	91	96	91	87	96	92	114
1000–	100	100	100	100	100	100	100	100	100	100	100	100	100	100

Source: Research and Statistics Division, Minister's Secretariat, Ministry of International Trade and Industry, *Kōgyō Tōkei 50 Nen-shi* (Jubilee history of the census of manufacturers (for 1909–58)), 1962.

did not just provide technical training within the enterprise; their
efforts extended as far as character training, cultural education
and the inculcation of leadership qualities. As a result literary
clubs, sports clubs, tea ceremony and flower arrangement clubs,
and other such facilities, were established within the enterprise
and the enterprise became something of a school. This is especially true of the postwar period. Furthermore, employees were
able to deposit their savings with the enterprise, for which they
received a higher interest than that payable by the banks; this not
only encouraged workers to save, but also provided the company
with an extra source of capital. Mutual aid associations and
cooperative associations were also formed within the company,
and under its guidance. When the company celebrated the anniversary of its founding parties, athletics meetings and excursions
took place. All these things enhanced the workers' feelings of
unity with the company and served to support the lifetime employment system.

IV

This kind of company was quite different from the English type of
company where company–employee relations were characterised
by acquisition of skill by the individual, and the subsequent
purchase by the company of that skill, which combined with other
factors of production to make a product which the company then
sold; where a worker would leave his company if he considered that
he could sell his skill more profitably to another company; where a
company dismissed a worker when it was dissatisfied with his skill;
where a worker would himself study to acquire another trade when
he considered that the acquisition of another skill would increase
his income and provide him with greater job satisfaction; and
where a worker could enter the labour market for a second time
offering a quite different skill. In Japan, both for the company and
for the individual, employment was a lifetime commitment similar
to marriage; therefore, when assessing an individual's suitability
for employment a person's character, sense of loyalty and his
potential ability to contribute to the company over the long term
were regarded as more important than his immediate labour
productivity and skill. In just the same way as when taking on an

adopted son, when taking on an individual as a company employee careful consideration was paid to any harm or any contribution he might or might not make to the company. Times of depression in particular gave rise to tendencies such as new company employees being limited to those with personal connections, or only workers from specific areas being taken on.

The company was paternalistic. Among the employees themselves and between employees and management there prevailed what one might call a kindred feeling of solidarity; the company was, in fact, one large family. We have seen that the company valued the continuing employment of a worker more highly than his contribution to production in the short term, and with a view to such continuing employment provided remuneration which increased as a result of years of service and was stable over the long term. The workers, too, did not waste their efforts in a short-term sprint, as it were, but maintained sufficient stamina to do their best to contribute to the company over the long term. To continue the analogy, in a sprint the runner is concerned with overtaking those who are running in front of him; in a long-distance race he is concerned with not being left behind by the others. To assist a runner who falters in a short-distance race means dropping out oneself, but in a long-distance race it is easy for a competent runner to extend a helping hand to another athlete. In the case of a company, assisting colleagues serves to enhance appreciation of a worker and therefore boosts his long-term rating. In the long-term competition one's fellow runner is also at the same time a comrade-in-arms whom it is one's duty to assist. This is particularly true when the company as a whole is considered to comprise one team and faces the other companies as a single entity.

The view of society which was held in prewar Japan, that society was not the scene for individualist competition, but rather a place for collective struggles, where one team competed with another, was something which the samurai of Japan had grown used to during the course of the Tokugawa period. The economic competition which went on within the Japanese company was certainly not fierce; due to the emphasis on collaboration over the long term, there was little competition between one individual and another. Once the decision to enter the company had been taken the employee just rode along on the escalator of the seniority system, so one can call it something of a 'plodding' society.⁹ However, just as an engineering corps might have a higher productive capacity than a construction company, it is possible to say that Japanese companies have maintained an extremely high productive efficiency not through competition between individual members of the workforce, but through the employees' mutual cooperation, assistance and encouragement. Employment in a Japanese company was, and is, probably rather more like being in the police or the army than is the case in an English company.

Employees experience considerable job satisfaction when they believe that they have made a special demonstration of their loyalty to the company; they achieve a greater degree of job satisfaction by working overtime than by their work during regular hours. Since the management side is not infrequently absent during overtime hours, overtime can be something like voluntary club activity. Colleagues are no longer competitors at all, they are classmates or comrades-in-arms. A few examples of this sort of family-type firm have existed in Britain and America, but they have not lasted very long, and have never become the norm. In Japan, however, the system requires of the worker not merely the stipulated work, but also that he devote the whole of his waking hours to the company. For example, suppose the company plans an athletics meeting at the weekend for its employees, and that each individual is at liberty to decide whether or not he will attend. In England many employees would be reluctant to be tied to the company at the weekends as well as during the week; many of them would not attend. The company would fail in its attempt to hold a successful athletics meeting and would probably abandon the whole idea. In Japan, a worker's attendance at the athletics meeting would mean that he is particularly approved of and remembered by the company as a loyal worker who cares for the company; and the matter of whether or not to attend the athletics meeting is no longer the free decision of each individual employee. In this way, an employee's life becomes tied to the company even outside working

---

⁹ This does not mean that there was no competition between employees. Competition to be regarded as loyal employees was especially fierce. Within this kind of non-economic competition there were a large number of nonsensical elements which apparently had no bearing on the productivity of the company, such as competing to make a deeper bow to senior officials or to be present at parties or athletics meetings held by the company. However, the fact that as a result of this 'competition to be loyal' the company at all times preserved strict order has been of considerable advantage to Japanese enterprises.

hours. In spite of this psychology, however, English employees would probably reject such paternalistic management methods in the name of freedom.

In a Confucian society, however, each individual must strive to demonstrate his loyalty to the society to which he belongs. The extent of his loyalty is measured in terms of the degree to which he is prepared to sacrifice himself. Therefore if he participates in the athletics meeting, abandoning any plans he may have had to enjoy the weekend with his family, this is regarded as a certain proof of his feelings of loyalty. Even if the company lets it be known that attendance at the meeting is up to each individual to decide, it does not make any difference. The company says on the surface that it is a matter of choice, but any loyal worker will take into consideration the manager's deep desire to hold a successful athletics meeting to display the solidarity which exists in the company. Once a worker has grasped the real intention of the company, and puts everything else aside in order to participate, then he is a 'virtuous' employee. The company values highly his loyal service; loyal employees are either given good posts in the future, or are paid high bonuses. In a Confucian capitalist society devoted service is the most important virtue in both ethical and materialistic terms. So when most people do attend the athletics meeting the small number of 'libertarians' who do not are frowned upon by the others as disturbing the 'harmony' of society. In this sort of society the freedom of the individual is often regarded as treachery or a challenge to society or to the majority, and anyone who dares to assert his freedom will probably become completely isolated.

In this sort of society, therefore, there can be little concept of the labour contract in the Western sense. Labour is not regarded as a high-class commodity; it is the spirit of loyalty which is prized. The 'loyalty' market is opened only once in a lifetime to each individual, when he graduates from school or college. It is in this market that those who are able to provide loyalty meet those who are looking for it, their 'lords'. Before the Meiji Revolution it was decided by birth which lord one should be in service to, but since then a man has been able to choose. But to freely leave and enter this market-place in loyal feelings and to choose a different lord several times over contradicts any definition of a spirit of loyalty, unless there is any particular reason. A 'samurai' who has the misfortune to be dissatisfied with his first lord must look for a new lord as a masterless samurai in the mercenary market-place. In this way labour is not considered just as labour, but as an act of loyal service to society, and in this sort of Confucian society the labour market has inevitably developed a dual composition. That is to say the market for loyalty is made available just once to every individual; if at any time subsequently the lifetime employment decided here for any reason ends in disaster then a worker has no alternative but to look for a new employer on the second, mercenary market. The wages which are decided on this second market are appreciably lower than the wages in the large enterprises decided on the first market.[10]

Since large enterprises can recruit only loyal workers in the first market there are virtually no 'mercenary' workers among their regular employees. (However, casual labour is of course mercenary.) In contrast the medium and small enterprises hire a large number of 'mercenary' workers. Even those employees they hire on the first market-place receive wages little removed from purely mercenary wages; they feel little compulsion to discharge their duties in any particularly zealous manner. Indeed, if they presented themselves on the market on a purely mercenary basis they would be able to find another employer at very much the same wages. Consequently a considerable wage difference, and a difference in social status exists between large and medium/small enterprises. Moreover, this kind of difference also produces moral and ideological differences.

During the Tokugawa period there existed four classes, warriors, farmers, artisans and merchants; and the morality of the samurai class was quite different from that of the farmer, artisan and merchant classes. This affected also their concept of loyal service, which was required of a warrior but not of the other three classes. A warrior possessed high status, and in return was not to work for his own personal pleasure. Farmer, artisans and merchants possessed low social status, but in return they were permitted to work according to the dictates of profit. In effect the two groups were directed by totally different moral standards. In the same way large enterprises have been guided by totally different moral standards from those existing in medium or small enterprises. If the employee

[10] Our 'loyal labour' and 'mercenary labour' bear very strong resemblances to Hicks' 'slavery' and 'free labour' respectively. See John Hicks, *A Theory of Economic History* (Clarendon Press, Oxford, 1969), pp. 122–40.

of a large enterprise attempts to move to another large enterprise in the hope of obtaining still higher wages, then this implies an absence of the ideal of loyal service required of the employee of a large enterprise. It is an act whereby the employee signs his own death warrant. However, the low level of wages in the medium/small enterprises has meant that workers can move freely from one enterprise to another. Outstanding workers collected in the larger enterprises have been expected to devote themselves to the interest of their companies, while workers of the smaller enterprises, though poorly paid, have been able to enjoy their personal freedom.

In this way a dual structure similar to that found during the Tokugawa period continued to exist even after the Meiji Revolution, both in economic life and social position, and also in correspondingly different social consciousness, or ideologies. During the Tokugawa period the question of whether one belonged to the ruling group, or to the ruled, was decided by birth, but since the Meiji period it has been decided by the company entrance examinations which are open only once to each individual, on his graduation from school or college. In this sense post-Meiji Japan became a society where individual competed with individual, but it was on this occasion alone that individual competition did take place. As mentioned earlier, once a worker had entered a large company he rose through the grades according to the seniority system. Thus, on the surface at least there was little fierce competition between individual company employees. In the medium and small enterprises real ability certainly counted for something, but, since these enterprises were after all what one might call the 'downstairs', even if one did prove to be outstanding it was not much of a triumph when looked at from the point of view of the 'upstairs'.

Thus competition between individuals was extremely limited, whereas competition between employee groups of different companies was fierce. In order to be successful as a leader a man had to be able to bring together his colleagues within the company and lead them to victory in the inter-company war, either raising the status of his company within the large enterprise sector, or promoting his company from 'medium/small enterprise' to 'large enterprise' status. In Western society, competition has been based upon the individual; individuals are forced to compete for entry into a company, and those who are incompetent have been excluded by the company. Conversely companies have been forced to compete for individuals and bad companies deserted by their employees for another. This kind of competition has not operated in Japan. In Japan the employees of a company have formed a team which has acted as a united body to compete with the teams from other companies; successful companies have then distributed the profit gained to all members of the team in the form of a bonus, more-or-less according to the principle of the seniority system.

Such competition conducted on a team basis can bring tragedy for some unfortunate individuals. On occasions a man might possess ability but have the misfortune to be surrounded by incompetent colleagues; he therefore has no choice but to resign himself to a life with no prospect of advancement. Even if someone in this situation was to try and move to a stronger team and demonstrate his abilities such a move would be regarded as an act of disloyalty, and except in very exceptional circumstances no other company would take such a 'traitor' on. So unless he becomes a mercenary he is unable to move to another company.

Such limitations on the freedom of movement amount to limitations on free choice of association. Any free society must guarantee certain freedoms, such as freedom of choice of consumer goods, freedom of thought and expression and freedom of religion, but the most important of these freedoms is freedom of choice of association. In fact, where there is no freedom of choice of association there is likely to be virtually no freedom of thought, expression or religion either. Within one economy and society there are various groupings (associations) and the pattern of the life of an individual is built up by his selection of these various associations. A person's life is changed by which associations he chooses. The life of an individual who has chosen company A, hobby club B and evening school C will be different from one who has chosen company A', hobby club B' and evening school C'. But in Japan even now an individual can choose a company only once in a lifetime (assuming it's a large company), and the hobby club that he belongs to will be the one organised by the company; similarly for the school. The company is not just a profit-making organisation; it is a complete society in itself, and frequently it is so all-embracing that all the activities of the daily lives of the company's employees can take place within the company framework. Because the company is so huge that it swallows the whole life of its employees and because an individual cannot change his company, he does not have the freedom to reconstruct his own life. Like soldiers, therefore, employees of the same company are all of the same type.

In 1932, at a ceremony to commemorate the fifteenth anniversary of the founding of the Matsushita Electrical Company the employees' representative formally replied to an address made by Matsushita Kōnosuke, head of the company, as follows:[11]

> Nothing gives us greater pleasure than to be here today at this ceremony of commemoration on the occasion of the anniversary of the founding of the company. I believe that we employees must admit to our shame that it is entirely due to our own inadequacies that we are today unable to repay our president for the cordial guidance which he has given to us over this long period. However the address with which he has honoured us today is an alarm bell aimed at waking us from our indolence and we pledge ourselves to bear carefully in mind its implications, to be increasingly aware of the mission of our company, Matsushita Electrical, and to try and fulfil our duty at the risk of our lives.

Clearly these employees were pledging themselves to live and die within Matsushita; so for them there was no question of asserting their freedom to change their job. This kind of spirit of selfless devotion to the company shown by employees, the state of mind which regards the company as the place where they will die, still prevails in Japanese companies even in the postwar period, although not at such an extreme level as that of prewar Matsushita.

As we mentioned, unlike Chinese Confucianism, in which the supreme virtue was benevolence, the Confucianism found in Japan attached special emphasis to the concepts of loyalty and harmony; under Shōtoku Taishi weight was given to harmony, and under the Meiji Emperor loyalty and filial piety were emphasised. Of all the imperial rescripts at that time the Imperial Injunction to Soldiers and Sailors of 1882 and the Imperial Rescript on Education of 1890 were the most influential; and since the latter was repeatedly read out in schools something like the Bible it can be regarded as the

---

[11] Chō, Y. (ed.), *Jitsugyō no Shisō* (Business Thought in Japan) (Chikumashobō, Tokyo, 1964), p. 371.

most widely circulated Confucian scripture in Japan. This imperial rescript enjoined its readers to 'pursue learning and cultivate the arts, and thereby develop intellectual faculties and perfect moral power', but the aim of cultivating such individual qualities was to assist in times of national contingency. It said: 'should emergency arise, offer yourselves courageously to the state; and thus guard and maintain the prosperity of our Imperial Throne coeval with heaven and earth'. This kind of emphasis on loyalty meant that loyalty to the president of a company from within that company was regarded as entirely appropriate, and although companies might compete with each other the company itself was required to profess allegiance towards the state. Consequently this rendered impossible the completely ruthless pursuit of profits in the name of competition; in the final analysis they had to restrict their pursuit of profit in accordance with considerations of public interests and the aims of the state.

The role of the large companies as the team chosen to represent Japan in the achievement of the national aim of building a strong country able to compete with the West meant that more than any others it was they who had to be conscious of this national purpose, keep in mind the views of the government and at all times support the government. With this understanding for some fifty years following the Meiji Revolution Japan strove as a united country to build a modern state. Japan's victories in the Sino–Japanese and Russo–Japanese wars, not to mention her undreamed-of achievement of the status of one of the world's five great powers in the years after the First World War, sent the Japanese people into complete ecstacy. The conceit which resulted among the people from these successes gave rise to a situation of discord and this conceit brought about the revival of one part of the anti-foreign faction which had said 'we have now been forced to open the country, but before very long we will have made ourselves strong enough to expel the barbarians'. As a finishing touch to the policy of 'rich country and strong army' which it had pursued through the Meiji period, in 1917 the government published the draft of its powerful new plan for national defence, the 'proposal for 25 divisions and an eight-battleship–eight-cruiser squadron', but with the conclusion of the Washington Naval Treaty in 1922 they had to abandon the plan for the eight–eight-squadron. This was taken by the Japanese as a move by America and Britain to keep them down, and completely changed the national situation. Within the Japanese people as a whole there was a shift to the right and increasing hatred of Britain and America. At the same time both the industrial and financial worlds had to reform themselves to comply with the new demands of the country, the new trend of public opinion.

CHAPTER FOUR

The Japanese empire (II)

I

In his novel *Kokoro* Natsume Sōseki wrote the following:

> Then at the height of the summer Emperor Meiji passed
> away. I felt as though the spirit of the Meiji era had
> begun with the Emperor and had ended with him. I was
> overcome with the feeling that I and the others, who had
> been brought up in that era, were now left behind to live
> as anachronisms. I told my wife so. She laughed and
> refused to take me seriously. Then she said a curious
> thing, albeit in jest: 'Well then, you should commit self
> immolation and follow the Emperor to his grave.'[1]

During the first half of the Taishō period (1912–26) which followed
on from the Meiji period some of the momentum of this period
remained but in the latter half the gulf between rich and poor grew
deeper. Socialists maintained that this was the result of capitalism.
Those on the right wing believed that it was because the Emperor
was surrounded by statesmen who were both cunning and evil.
They wanted to carry out a court revolution and subsequently
realise an ideal society where an Emperor presided over a nation all
of whose members were equal before him (the concept of 'one lord
whole people'). On the other hand the despotism of the militarists
became more and more dominant. During the Tokugawa period
any farmer or merchant who showed discourtesy towards a member of the warrior class could be reprimanded even to the extent of

---

[1] Translated by E. McClellan. The last part of the passage is altered because I disagree with
his interpretation; cf. Natsume Soseki, *Kokoro*, translated by Edwin McClellan (Peter
Owen, London), 1968, p. 245.

being killed by him; the military came to adopt the same sort of attitude towards both the government and the people at large. Their watchword was a martial spirit.

The Meiji regime did not bring equality to the people, but they did experience a feeling of unity under that regime. A common saying at the time was 'As long as he's a university graduate we'll let our daughter marry him'; there were considerable differences in earnings between white collar and blue collar workers within an enterprise. The elite stratum of government officers and *zaibatsu* earned particularly high salaries. On top of this at the level of operatives as well in 1909 the wages of male operatives in factories directly owned by the government were equivalent to 1.27 times the average wage of male employees in large manufacturing enterprises with over 1000 employees. However, in Japan, a country where traditionally government had always been put above the people – and in addition under the Meiji government which had been consolidated by men of distinguished service in the revolution – while such a difference in wages and salaries between government and private enterprises may have excited envy, people nevertheless accepted it as an entirely natural difference.

At the time, differences in income among the people at large were not very great. In the labour market in general there was as yet no division between the large enterprises and the medium and small enterprises; since workers were hired through a labour boss in the big enterprises as well there was no large wage differential based on the size of the enterprise such as appeared later (for example in the 1930s or the 1950s). If we look at manufacturing industry as a whole, in 1909 wages in enterprises of 5–9 employees amounted to no more than 80% of wages in enterprises with over 1000 employees. (This figure was for men; for women it was 76%.) In 1914 the figure was 73% for men and 72% for women. However in these years the majority of male workers (90% in 1909 and 85% in 1914) worked in medium or small enterprises with fewer than 1000 employees, so male workers employed in factories with over 1000 employees can be regarded as the exception. If we recalculate the indices of wage differentials in Table 2A with the level of wages in factories of 500–999 employees as 100 then the result is as in Table 4, and it becomes clear that there was virtually no differentiation in wages based on the scale of the enterprise for male workers during these years.

In contrast to this the majority of women workers (74% in 1909 and 79% in 1914) worked in enterprises with over 30 employees. If we consider that the wages of female operatives in enterprises of 30–49 employees were in 1909 86% of wages in large enterprises (over 1000 employees), and in 1914 81%, then we must conclude that for women as well there was essentially no great difference in wages during these years. But there were considerable differences between the wages of men and women. The wages of female employees were about half those of men and the female operatives led miserable lives.[2] However, in Japan at that time women had been granted neither the right to vote nor the right to be elected, and the Confucian ethic which asserted the dominance of men over women prevailed; wage differences resulting from sex differences did not become a major labour problem.

Table 4. *Wage differentials for male workers*
(wage per worker in plants of 500–999 = 100)

	1909	1914
5–9	87	83
10–29	92	88
30–49	96	90
50–99	100	94
100–499	102	97
500–999	100	100

Source: *Kōjō Tōkei Hyō* (Statistical tables of factories).

The structure of Japanese industry changed considerably during the First World War. As early as August 1914, immediately following the outbreak of fighting in late July, Japan entered the war and successfully eradicated German influence in China and the Pacific area. Since it was Europe which had become the real battlefield, European exports to Asia dried up and Japan and

[2] The famous *Jokō Aishi* (Pitiful History of Women Workers) which described the harsh lives of female operatives at that time was published in 1925. Both in 1909 and 1914 women workers constituted a high proportion of all workers in the large enterprise sector, and men a high proportion in the small enterprises, therefore for men and women workers as a whole it is almost impossible to perceive any difference in wages based on the scale of the enterprise. The loose wage differentiation according to the scale of the enterprise which existed within male workers or female workers respectively was almost completely cancelled out by differences resulting from sex – this was especially true of 1909. (See Table 2A)

America between them came to monopolise markets in the East. Japanese commodities made great inroads into all parts of Asia. Not just that, but since Japan was now deprived of her supplies of drugs, fertilisers and dyestuffs, which had hitherto been imported from Germany, Japan's chemical industry experienced considerable expansion. The number of employees engaged in the spinning industry rose by 65% between 1914 and 1919, and Japan replaced Britain as the world's largest spinning nation.

In addition, over the same years the firm foundations were laid for Japan's heavy and chemical industries. Looking merely at large enterprises with over 500 employees, in 1914 the spinning industry accounted for 74% of the total number of all employees, while the heavy and chemical industries (machinery and machine tools, metals and chemicals) accounted for no more than 20%. By 1919 the latter sector had succeeded in reducing the spinning industry's share to 65%, having itself expanded to account for 31% of all employees in enterprises of over 500 employees.

Whereas the spinning industry was very much a women's industry the heavy and chemical industries were the province of men. In 1914 the number of women workers employed in the manufacturing industry sector was over $1\frac{1}{2}$ times the number of male workers, but by 1919 the numbers of male and female workers were approximately equal. Since it was in large enterprises that the move into heavy and chemical industries was strongest, it was these enterprises which became male-dominated. The enterprises had no expectations of long-term employment from their female employees, while they expected their male employees to stay with them for their whole working lives. Especially at a time such as this, when Japan's industry was expanding rapidly and the supply of workers was inadequate, an enterprise had no wish to relinquish a male employee once it had hired him, unless, of course, he was particularly defective in one way or another. As we have seen, enterprises increasingly came to require feelings of loyalty from their workers, and apart from the normal labour market there was also formed, as it were, the 'first-class' labour market premised on a tacit understanding of loyalty over a lifetime; it was here that the large enterprises hired students newly graduated from school and college. Each year only those who had graduated in that particular year could present themselves on this market. Only dealings concerning work in receipt of low wages were carried out on the regular labour market which anyone could enter, the one which I referred to earlier as the 'mercenary' labour market. It was at this time that a two-tiered labour market became an integral part of the Japanese economy.

In this way the dual structure of the Japanese economy was inextricably linked to the increasing predominance of men in the manufacturing industries and the shift to heavy and chemical industries. The shift to heavy and chemical industries was subject to recurrent misfortunes in the form of naval arms limitation resulting from the Washington Conference (1922), the great Tokyo earthquake (1923), the 1927 financial crisis following misuse of government bonds issued for reconstruction after the earthquake, and the world depression which started in 1930. Such industries consequently expanded slowly during the 1920s. However, Japan in 1931 started the Manchurian Incident, the following year declared the independence of Manchukuo and made considerable advances into Manchuria; this contributed to Japan's recovering more quickly than any other of the world's industrial nations from the great depression. Subsequently over the ten-year period 1933–1942 the development of the heavy and chemical industries was carried out at a phenomenal speed.

The development of heavy and chemical industries was carried out in parallel with Japan's aggressive war against China. The Kwantung Army, the unit of the Japanese army which was stationed in Manchuria, had plans to manipulate Chang Tso-lin, the leader of the North China military clique, and secure the independence of Manchuria from the rest of mainland China. Chang Tso-lin, however, did not prove amenable to the wishes of the Kwantung Army, which assassinated him in 1928 by blowing up his train as he was returning from Peking to Shenyang (Mukden). This so-called 'certain serious incident in Manchuria' proved a turning point in the chain of events which eventually led to the outbreak of the Manchurian Incident in 1931, and to the establishment by the military the following year of the puppet state of Manchukuo in the north-eastern part of China. In 1933 a cease-fire agreement was reached between Japan and China and for a time peace returned; the Chinese were forced to recognise the *fait accompli* imposed upon them. Japan made great efforts to build up Manchukuo, but, as might have been expected, anti-Japanese feeling among the Chinese people ran extremely high, and, al-

Table 5. *Employment distribution in manufacturing in Japan* (%)

| Year | 1934 | | | | 1942 | | | |
Size of enterprise (no. of employees) \ Industry	Heavy chemical industries	Textile industry	Other manufacturing industries	Total	Heavy chemical industries	Textile industry	Other manufacturing industries	Total
Small (5–99)	25	40	35	100	44	21	35	100
Medium (100–499)	25	60	15	100	61	27	13	100
Large (over 500)	30	67	3	100	88	10	2	100

Source: *Kōgyō Tōkei 50 Nen-shi* (Jubilee history of the census of manufacturers), 1962.

though for a while Chiang K'ai-shek called for Sino-Japanese cooperation, boycotts of Japanese goods and anti-Japanese movements spread throughout China. Finally in 1937 units of the Kwantung Army stationed near Peking were fired on by units of the Chinese Army while on exercises, and this incident led to full-scale war between the two countries, which continued for 9 years until the end of the Second World War in 1945.

Such a war as this could not be carried on without the support of a large and powerful economy. When the Manchurian Incident began only 25–30% of all workers employed in the manufacturing industry in medium (those with 100–499 employees) and large (over 500) enterprises worked in the heavy and chemical industry sector, with 60–67% in the sphere of textiles. Clearly an economy such as this (see Table 5) did not have the economic ability to support this kind of war. While trying to promote the expansion of heavy and chemical industries by the old *zaibatsu* such as Mitsui, Mitsubishi and Sumitomo, the military and the government also provided assistance to newly established concerns mentioned previously, such as Nissan, helping them to develop into new *zaibatsu*.

The old-established *zaibatsu* at first resisted the changes in the economic structure aimed at producing a quasi-wartime economy, but after the assassinations in 1932 of former Finance Minister Inoue Junnosuke and of Dan Takuma, President of the Mitsui Company, by members of the so-called Blood League who were followers of the right-wing ideologists Inoue Nisshō, these older *zaibatsu* had little choice but to cooperate with the quasi-wartime economic structure. The government passed a series of laws to this end: in 1931 the Vital Industries Control Law, in 1934 the Oil Industry Law, in 1937 the three laws for wartime control (Munitions Industry Mobilization Law, Emergency Provisions relating to Imports and Exports, Law for the Emergency Procurement of Capital) and the Factory Workplace Administration Ordinance, in 1938 the National General Mobilization Law and the Electrical Power Administration Law, and in 1939 ordinances to control such items as prices. The cabinet resolved upon *An Outline Plan to Increase Productive Power* and *Outline for the Establishment of the New Economic Structure* in 1939 and 1940 respectively. In addition, in 1940 the Wage Control Ordinance was enacted. In this way by 1940 the government and the army had taken a complete hold over the Japanese economy. Parallel to the 'militarisation' of the economy in this fashion the shift to heavy and chemical industries was pushed ahead at a remarkable pace, so that within a year of the outbreak of the Second World War, i.e. in 1942, development had reached a level where 88% of employees of large manufacturing enterprises (61% in medium enterprises) were working in the heavy and chemical sector. Backed up by this sort of industrial power the Japanese militarists carried out their decisive attack on Pearl Harbour.

However, perhaps one should not assess this kind of industrialisation purely at face value. It is true that they succeeded in concentrating the labour force in the heavy and chemical industries sector, and in 1942 91% of total production of large manufacturing enterprises was of heavy and chemical industrial goods. But nevertheless, as was mentioned above, over the years 1940–42, at the end of the period when heavy and chemical industries were developing, there was a marked decrease in the productivity differences which existed between different scales of enterprise (see Table 3 above). This suggests that during this period the productivity of large enterprises had not increased as much as the productivity of small enterprises, although it is extremely difficult to establish to what degree this apparent sluggishness of productivity, when measured in terms of value, reflects the existence of price control, and also whether the physical productivity of the large enterprises was ever really sluggish at the time.

In addition, many heavy and chemical industrial enterprises, starting with Nissan, had extended operations to Manchukuo and China, so the industrial strength which Japan was able to mobilise can be considered far greater than that indicated by statistics for Japan alone. Against a background of military aggression in China the Japanese governments of the time were achieving the 'rich country and strong army' which had been the aim of the Meiji Revolution; and when the dream was at last becoming reality Japan's energies had run berserk to a degree where she could no longer keep them under control. The military was no longer the strong guard of a wealthy country; it was the economy which had to sacrifice itself completely for the sake of providing a strong army. However, the enforcement, the forced march, as it were, of such a huge industrial transformation to comply with the requirements of such a national policy was not totally meaningless for Japan. From this great experiment the Japanese government, industrialists and workers all learnt how to achieve industrial change. One of the greatest strengths of the Japanese economy in the postwar period has been the high degree of flexibility which it has shown in speedily adapting to all manner of drastic changes in external conditions, and this sort of ability to adapt may well have been acquired at the time of the 'forced march' of the 1930s imposed upon it by the military.

II

Not just the enterprises but the military as well welcomed low wages. The existence of enlisted men able to endure hardship and officers exuding loyalty was what the army considered to be most important. Working on very much the same concept, Hitler also believed that it was necessary to preserve the peasantry in order to strengthen the army. Similarly, the Japanese army – although there were men, such as the young officers among the rebels in the 26 February 1936 uprising, who were deeply concerned at the worsening impoverishment of the farming villages – did not on the whole rejoice at any rise in the standard of living of farmers and workers, which they regarded as productive of weakness. Both the government and the army extolled the virtues of poverty. In order to curb inflation during the war, wages were controlled and extravagant patterns of consumption prohibited. Not only that, but pursuit of a Western lifestyle was regarded as an offence, and in many aspects of the life of the people the dual lifestyle – Western and Japanese – ceased to exist. Life as a whole was very much simplified. The military also encouraged enterprises in their use of the seniority and lifetime employment systems. That a worker should be attached to a single enterprise was not a *sine qua non* for the planned management of the national economy, but it was nevertheless a condition whose fulfilment was extremely desirable for this purpose.[3] Consequently, the lifetime employment system was also encouraged from the standpoint of planning production geared to pursuit of the war. In addition the cultivation of a desire

[3] In order to prevent workers being lured from one enterprise to another, and to restrict movement, in 1939 the government issued the Ordinance to Limit the Hiring of Employees. As a result experienced workers in heavy industries and mining were no longer able to move to other enterprises without official permission.

to devote a lifetime of loyal service to one enterprise, and the acceptance within the company through the seniority system of the custom of not trying to get ahead of one's seniors, can be regarded both as a rehearsal for and a simulation of the life a worker would lead once he had been recruited into the army – a life of loyal service to his country, of following the orders of officers, and of obedience to longer serving soldiers.

Consequently under the quasi-wartime system and during the war itself the ethos of the Japanese employment system and its two main pillars, the lifetime employment system and the seniority system, were widely inculcated, and the system itself spread. At the time there was an acute shortage of labour, and employees never knew when they might be conscripted into the army. All enterprises, even the medium- and small-sized ones, had no wish to lose workers once they had taken them on. Since the labour market was hard pressed at the time it was impossible to work on a purely 'mercenary' basis. Many medium and small enterprises also adopted the lifetime employment system, gave an employee leave for the period during which he was called up by the army, and awaited his return.

I pointed out earlier that the ethic which had ruled the large enterprises was quite different from that prevailing in the medium and small enterprises, but this kind of dual ethical structure based on the scale of the enterprise was lessening during the period of the quasi-wartime economy and the war itself. Since the country as a whole had undergone a process of militarisation it was to be expected that a militarist ethic would prevail not just in the large enterprises but in the small and medium ones as well. Furthermore, since wages were regulated under the Wage Control Ordinance, it was likely that in principle the difference in wages which existed between enterprises of different sizes would diminish at that time.[4] However, since many of the large enterprises were integral parts of the munitions industry they were in receipt of distributions of raw materials and foodstuffs. Consequently there did develop a gap between enterprises involved in the production of munitions and those involved in the production of goods for civilian use. The gap in nominal wages was not so great due to such factors as wage

[4] Under the Emergency Wages Provisions Ordinance issued in 1939 wages were frozen and this edict was absorbed into the Wage Control Ordinance of the following year. Under this regulation wages were laid down, detailed according to age, years of experience, region and type of work, and the total amount of loans was also limited.

control, but workers in munitions industries received considerable fringe benefits in the form of extra rations of foodstuffs and other similar advantages. The gap which existed then between enterprises was essentially a military–civilian difference, and not a difference based on the scale of enterprise.

Given that at the time Japan was on hostile terms with almost all other countries of the world, with the exception of Germany and Italy, it was not possible for Japan to strengthen her military capacity by relying on foreign technology; the Japanese therefore had to make scientific progress themselves and develop new techniques within the country. As we have seen, the Meiji Revolution had from the first been a revolution by the intelligentsia, and the Meiji government had advocated a policy of a 'rich country and a strong army'; the acquisition of education and scientific expertise was from the outset regarded as being of crucial importance. The implementation of compulsory education throughout the country, the provision of a higher education system equipped with several imperial universities, and the implanting in Japan of science and technology imported from the West, these were the main aims of the cultural policy of the Meiji government.

As we have said above, in importing such skills the government carefully surveyed each country, made an assessment as to which country was the most outstanding in each field, and in each field absorbed knowledge from that country – and from that country only – which it judged had most to offer. For example, if we look at the places of employment of those foreigners employed in Tokyo by the government over the years 1871–76 we find they were as follows: at the Navy Ministry (including the Waterways Board and the Naval Academy) 87 Britons, 1 American, 2 Dutchmen and 1 Portuguese; at the Army Ministry (including the Military Academy and the Military Preparatory School) 46 Frenchmen; at the Board of Engineering (including the College of Technology) 16 Britons, 3 Italians; at the Railways Board and the Telegraph Board 59 Britons; at the Board of Construction 6 Dutchmen; at the Medical College 11 Germans; at the Kaisei Gakkō (afterwards Tokyo University, then reorganised as the Tokyo Imperial University and still existing as the present Tokyo University) 5 Britons, 6 Americans, 4 Germans, 5 Frenchmen and 1 Chinese.[5]

[5] Nakayama Shigeru 'Kokuei Kagaku' (State Science) in Sugimoto Isao (ed.), *Kagaku Shi* (History of Science) (Yamakawa Shuppansha, 1967), p. 368.

This meant that the culture imported by the Meiji government was not a general, unplanned import of Western culture equally from all countries. Its elements were selected following a careful analysis of their potential contribution to the economy and defence of the nation; these various imports were fused together to produce a Western culture unique to Japan. The government also sent large numbers of students abroad each year to study in the countries of Europe and in America to acquire information on Western culture, and to provide for future needs. Unlike China, where control was firmly in the hands of an officialdom committed to bureaucratism and to agriculture, the core of the Meiji government consisted of members of the former samurai class, who were acutely aware of the military threat posed by the nations of the West. Consequently there was in Japan a considerable desire to learn and master Western natural science and technology which could provide a basis for military strength. The first students graduated from Tokyo University in 1880 and 90% of these graduated in physics or chemistry. It was only from the middle of the Meiji period (1895) that arts students reached the level of 50% of all students.

Having profited from the fighting of others during the First World War, Japan became one of the world's five greatest powers in the postwar period. The government was at first inclined to try and equip Japan with a military capability and education befitting her new status, but following the arms limitation agreed under the Washington Treaty of 1922 the government concentrated its energies on the completion of the education system. In 1918 there were in Japan only 5 universities and 104 high schools and colleges, but a decade later, in 1928, these figures had risen to 40 and 184 respectively, and by 1945 to 48 and 342. In 1942 a second engineering faculty concentrating on the application of science to warfare was started at Tokyo Imperial University. Both the military and the government were well aware that they were involved in total war, and in a total war scientific and engineering ability play a crucial role. Both during the quasi-wartime period and during the war itself desperate attempts were made to perfect Japan's higher education, especially those aspects which appertained to science and engineering. As the war progressed it was arts and social science students who were conscripted into the army, while the science and engineering students were kept until last. Japan's technology had attained a level where she could make the

Zero fighter and the 'Yamato', the world's largest warship, and had a high-speed express train, the 'Asia', operating in Manchuria; quantitatively, however, her technology was still pretty thin on the ground. Graduates from the science and engineering departments of universities and colleges which had been expanded to meet the requirements of the war came too late to assist the war, but after the war these graduates played an important role in Japan's high rate of economic growth.

For nearly thirty years, half of the 60-year period from 1886 to 1945, Japan was involved in a number of wars, either declared or undeclared. Not surprisingly military expenditure reached huge proportions. Annual military expenditure as a proportion of GNP averaged over 10% over this 60-year period, and the average over the last thirty years was in excess of 12%. Moreover, to come into conflict simultaneously with America, the British Commonwealth, Holland and China on the basis of an industrial strength which had only just at long last managed to develop the heavy and chemical industries – even given that for a late developer like Japan this was a splendid and praiseworthy achievement – was nothing short of madness. Nevertheless, until the last, dark decade, for a period of over fifty years following the Meiji Revolution the policy of 'a rich country and a strong army' had been attended by success.

It is true that the successful outcome of wars had meant the acquisition of vast indemnities, of new territories, huge economic interests or enormous new markets, leading the Japanese people to regard war as a profitable venture; it is, however, extraordinary and unbelievable that this kind of warmongering set-up could continue for such a long period in view of large numbers of war victims and vast amounts of money disbursed. But the people – the property-owning class, managers and workers – always bore in mind the designs of the government and showed a splendid degree of cooperation. It is true that there was certainly at one point friction between the old *zaibatsu* and the military; there was also resistance from workers who had associations with the Communist Party. There was subsequently also the appearance of the black market which was an expression of the unspoken feelings of resistance of the Japanese people. But nevertheless enterprises were appropriately equipped; a controlled economy was achieved; advances were made by capital into Manchuria in the manner required by the military and the government; the people yielded to thought control. Finally in 1938 the National General Mobilisation Law was passed, and the people gave their approval to the establishment of a 'fascist' state. Nishio Suehiro of the Shakai Taishūtō (Social Masses' Party), who postwar became a founder of the Democratic Socialist Party, said in a speech arguing for the approval of the National General Mobilization Law in a session in the House of Representatives (Lower House) of the Diet, that Prime Minister Konoe 'should be a leader full of conviction like Hitler, like Mussolini, like Stalin'. Nishio was struck off as a member of the Diet on the grounds that 'Stalin should not be one of our heroes', but Japan had clearly already been transformed into a totalitarian state.

The Japanese found it easy to uphold the idea of a totalitarian state. Shōtoku Taishi's Seventeen Article Constitution had also called for harmony (*wa*) in the attitude of the individual towards the majority. Early in the Shōwa era, a 'majority faction' had been formed whose centre was the military, but which also contained the new bureaucrats, the new *zaibatsu* and right-wing intellectuals, and the Emperor was made to play the role of their symbol. The Japanese people were sensitive to where 'the will of the majority' lay, and in which direction it was tending; they catered to the wishes of the 'fascists' in as far as they followed the principle of maintaining harmony (*wa*). Moreover, since the 'fascists' had made the Emperor into their own symbol it needed a considerable amount of courage on the part of any of the Japanese people at large to express a different opinion. This was because after the Meiji period the people had been taught through the medium of compulsory education that the ultimate virtues were loyalty to the Emperor and filial piety towards one's parents. For an individual to fail to demonstrate the appropriate loyalty was to cause distress to his parents and consequently also to demonstrate lack of filial piety.

Up to the final stage where totalitarianism brought about self-destruction the Japanese people had shown a remarkable cooperation in productive activity as well. Following the attack on Pearl Harbour, during the period of three years and nine months up until the surrender in August 1945 Japan's shipyards completed 15 aircraft carriers, 6 cruisers, 126 submarines, 63 destroyers, 70 transport ships, 168 coastal defence ships, and others up to a total of 682 naval vessels. Apart from that 720 cargo ships and 271 oil tankers were built. During the same period production of military aircraft was in the region of 60,000. Such levels of production bore no comparison to American achievements during the same period but at the time it was a world record level of production exceeded only by America. It was not surprising that a country like the U.S.A., whose factories had suffered no damage through bombing and which had no trouble in getting hold of raw materials, was producing vast numbers of aeroplanes.

If we recall these sorts of achievement during the period of the war, then Japan's success in the shipbuilding industry and in the automobile industry in the postwar period becomes somewhat less surprising. Unlike the textile industry, industries such as these cannot rely entirely on women workers, and without a shift to male labour in the manufacturing industries the development of the heavy and chemical industries is impossible. During the years of the First World War, Japanese manufacturing industries showed a marked shift towards the use of male workers; male workers as a proportion of all manual workers in industry was 40% in 1914 and rose to 49% in 1922. However the proportion of male operatives failed to increase subsequently and was still 49% in 1932. In 1937 though, it had reached 59% and by 1942 69%. Moreover it was not just that the proportion of male operatives had risen, the total number of male operatives in 1942 was 3.2 times the figure for 1937.

The extraction of such a large supply of male labour necessitated a considerable change in the structure of society. Since at the time a large number of young men were called up into the army it was difficult enough to find extra reinforcements just for these men from agriculture or other industries. Purely by appealing to the people's awareness of national crisis, by enforcing the reorganisation of enterprises and by setting in motion the National General Mobilisation Law the massive upheaval which was required was possible within the space of a very short time. In a peacetime situation male workers could not have been attracted without the inducement of extremely high wages, but payment of such high wages would have meant that the business could not pay its way. In time of peace, therefore, the speed of development of the heavy and chemical industries in Japan would probably have been far slower. In the name of the war male workers were assembled forcibly, and made to learn their skills whether they wanted to or not. This was the key which made such a major transformation possible. The demands which the military and the government made of the people were harsh ones and the sacrifice and damage were immense; but despite that in Japan it was far more easy to secure the cooperation of the people than would have been the case in the countries of the West.

Either way during the war a huge shift within society was carried out, and while many workers did return to farming after the war the relative proportion of male workers within manufacturing industry started from a level of 67% in 1947. To revert to being a country whose economy rested on agriculture and spinning was already impossible for Japan without what would be, in effect, a big social U-turn. The foundations for Japan's postwar success were laid during the war.

III

Although it was made under the wartime or quasi-wartime regime, this kind of radical transformation in the organisation of the economy would have been impossible without ideological support from the people. The Japanese economy completely lost its liberal-istic character, and after 1937 became, at the best, a planned economy, or a controlled economy, and, at the worst, a 'fascist' economy. Such an economic structure, therefore, was quite com-mensurate with the extremely right-wing ideology of the people at the time.

Following the Meiji Revolution the Japanese right-wing was well controlled for a while, but from the latter half of the 1920s it re-emerged into vigorous activity. Of course even before then right-wing ideology was not entirely dormant; it never sat and watched the world go by. During the late Tokugawa period, when pro-Emperor and anti-foreign sentiments were rampant, right-wing ideas were widely held by members of the intelligentsia, and the contribution made to the Meiji Revolution by right-wing ideol-ogists cannot be disregarded. They therefore resented the Meiji government's unkind treatment of them all the more, and this discontent did explode into the open from time to time. The most serious incident of this was probably the Satsuma Rebellion of 1877, when samurai from Satsuma, commanded by Saigo Takamori, started a rebellion against the Meiji government. Following the Sino-Japanese war, when Russia, Germany and France intervened to put pressure on Japan to amend the terms of the peace treaty which had been concluded between China and Japan, and also in 1905, when the terms of the peace treaty at the end of the Russo-Japanese war did not come up to their expectations, the people were quite naturally in a ferment of right-wing ideas. In addition compulsory education and military education served to spread the concepts of loyalty and filial piety among the populace as a whole, and by the closing years of the Meiji period the people's national consciousness had been raised to a level incomparably higher than that which had existed at the beginning of the period. Furthermore, many people did not take too kindly to the abrupt Westernisation of their life style which had occurred during the Meiji period; when people indicated an attachment for the traditional lifestyle of their ancestors they were at the same time cultivating a deeper sympathy and interest for ultra-patriotic thought and Eastern culture. Despite this sort of right-wing activity and the rightist inclinations of the people, until about 1910 the government maintained a tight control over the right, which on occasions even acted as refreshing stimulus for the government.

But from the latter half of the 1920s the dualism which existed in Japan's society and economy became quite overt. Wage differences between large enterprises and medium/small enterprises became conspicuous and the gap between rich and poor increased markedly. Faced by this sort of situation the left-wing movement in Japan grew more intense, but neither did the right-wing remain a passive spectator. In Japan there existed the concept of 'one lord and the whole people' and since the time of Shōtoku Taishi it had been held that all people ought to be equal, apart from the Emperor. As previously mentioned, the division of the Japanese people into rich and poor was regarded by the left as the result of capitalism, and by the right as due to the Emperor's being surrounded by evil men – elder and senior statesmen (*genrō* and *jūshin*), leading members of the government and of the political parties, and the *zaibatsu*. Such people as these were regarded by the right-wing as the corrupt elements at the Court, but most right-wing thinkers did not have any clear idea of what sort of system they would build once they had cleared the court of such undesirable influences.

An exception to this was Kita Ikki, and he considered that the most suitable system of organisation for Japan was one of national socialism headed by the Emperor. Many right-wing ideologists had little argument with the ideas of Kita. At the time of a confrontation in the late 1960s between a group of radical left-wing students and the right-wing author Mishima Yukio it was said that their views were completely in agreement, except on one point, how to deal with the problem of the Emperor. In the late Taishō (1912–26) and early Shōwa (1926–   ) periods relations between the left-wing and the right-wing in Japan were very similar to this; both groups supported a kind of socialism.

Kita Ikki was far and away the most outstanding right-wing ideologist in Japan. He had gone to China, where he had been involved with Sun Yeat-sen and the Chinese Revolution of 1911, and this experience taught him the importance of the military in any revolution, especially younger low ranking officers and enlisted men. In Japan there was increasing political awareness among such men. At the same time as Kita was writing, young officers as well were concerned at the impoverishment of the agricultural and fishing villages from which came their own soldiers. In addition young naval officers believed that the Washington and London treaties were extremely disadvantageous to the Japanese Navy, and felt considerable bitterness towards the Genrō and leading members of the government – the corrupt elements at the court – who had submitted to this sort of treaty. Thus it was not difficult for right-wing thinkers and young officers to form links with each other, but even in this period, ending with 1937 when Konoe Fumimaro held the premiership, the Japanese right-wing had not been forceful enough to influence Japan's external policies. In this period the right-wing was still thinking purely in terms of a rebuilding of the Japanese state so the problem of the right-wing was nothing more than a domestic matter for Japan alone.

However, the third stage of the shift to the right brought the increasing prominence of a different kind of right-wing. Earlier on in discussing the Meiji Revolution I indicated that there was a whole spectrum of different groups making up the anti-foreign faction and the faction which favoured opening Japan to the West. Among these was a faction which favoured opening Japan in the short term, but expelling foreigners in the long term, who proposed, as a compromise, that 'while the country is weak we should agree to open the country to foreign intercourse, but as soon as we are successful in increasing Japan's strength we should resolutely turn to an anti-foreign policy'. When Japan became one of the world's five great powers after the First World War, she expanded her markets in China and the other countries of Asia; such success boosted the confidence of Japan's upper classes – the nobility, the middle and upper ranks of government and the military, professors and students of the Imperial Universities. They came to feel sympathy for the nations of Asia, while at the same time despising them; increasingly they harboured a sense of obligation that Japan must take up arms against Britain, America and other world powers in order to assist these Asian nations. These men classified the countries of the world into three groups – the forerunner advanced countries, the late-starter advanced countries and the developing nations. Japan was regarded as a late-starter advanced nation, in conjunction with Germany, Italy and Russia. Once this kind of right-wing came to the fore it was no longer addressing itself to internal problems; the main aim of the right-wing had become 'world liberation'. To embark on a succession of foreign wars and to be victorious in them was its main task, and the internal system had to be reformed in a manner most appropriate for pursuit of foreign war. They had ceased to recognise any particular significance as being attached to the internal reform itself.

One of the exemplars of this 'third stage' right-wing can be found in the person of Prince Konoe Fumimaro. Konoe was a descendant of Nakatomi (later Fujiwara) no Kamatari, who had played such a major part in the Taika Reforms, and it would therefore not be an exaggeration to say that he was born into a family so illustrious that it was second only to the imperial family. Konoe graduated from Kyoto Imperial University in 1917, and was subsequently employed at the Ministry of Home Affairs. In 1919 he attended the Paris Peace Conference as a member of the Japanese delegation. Prior to this in 1917 he had already published an article in the journal 'Japan and the Japanese' (*Nihon oyobi Nihonjin*) entitled 'A rejection of pacifism along the lines laid down by Britain and America.' In this article he argued that Britain and America's advocacy of democracy and humanitarianism was due to this being the best way to preserve their own interests, and what these countries regarded as peace was not a true peace which would find satisfaction with all other countries. It was, argued Konoe, nothing but an attempt to have other countries recognise the existing situation of British and American supremacy, and to cooperate in support of this status quo. The forerunner advanced countries desired to preserve the status quo as regards the way in which the world was divided up, but the late-starter advanced nations could never be on a par with their forerunners unless they could break down the existing state of affairs. Consequently, merely to advocate peace and disavow militarism amounted to a recognition of the uneven distribution of natural resources which resulted from the economic imperialism of the past; it was not necessarily in accordance with the demands of justice and humanity. Konoe therefore argued that a prerequisite to the elimination of militarism was, first and foremost, the removal of economic imperialism and racial discrimination between the white and yellow races.

Some of these ideas have a considerable amount in common with Hitler's *Mein Kampf*, and Konoe continued to adhere to this way of thinking for almost his whole life. When he subsequently became Prime Minister and took over the responsibility for handling the war between China and Japan it was from this standpoint that he regarded the so-called China Incident. He believed that the war was not Japan's war against China, it was a war of liberation aimed at ridding China of British and American influence. It was therefore a war fought to achieve justice, a holy war. In the same way the Pacific War was also a holy war, fought to release Asia from the clutches of the British and American imperialists. Such a view of Britain and America was not peculiar to Konoe alone; it was an idea which was shared by many right-wing ideologists, socialists and communists. Konoe was therefore able to talk on friendly terms not only with members of the right-wing but also leftist intellectuals; as a result of his pedigree he could also talk readily and freely with members of the nobility and the Emperor, as well as capitalists and senior government officials.[6]

[6] On the occasion of the Washington Treaty the navy split into the Treaty Faction and the Fleet Faction. By the 1930s a clear split could also be seen in the army between the Tōsei (Control) Faction and the Kōdō (Imperial Way) Faction. The Control Faction cooperated with the Fleet Faction and the so-called new bureaucrats, and, attended by the new *zaibatsu*, called for a managed economy. The Imperial Way Faction, along with young army officers and the right-wing, called for state socialism. The government, the *zaibatsu* and the navy's Treaty Faction supported the free enterprise system and desired cooperation with Britain and America. There was in addition the illegal Communist Party. Hopes were high of Konoe, as someone who could show understanding of the whole range of this broad spectrum; he worked for the unity of the country in as far as he was able, but he was able to achieve almost nothing. Japan's tragedy was that people's estimation of Konoe was too high, and Konoe himself had a high opinion of himself and was given to excessive self-conceit.

Over the period from 1933 until the establishment of the Imperial Rule Assistance Association in 1940, Konoe convened regular meetings of a group which assembled to discuss current issues. This was the Shōwa Study Group (*Shōwa Kenkyūkai*). Many leading figures from the worlds of politics and finance, the bureaucracy, academia and journalism were assembled here in a group which was, in effect, Konoe's brains trust. Up and coming economists of the time, such as Nakayama Ichiro and Tobata Seiichi participated in the group, and other members included Miki Kiyoshi (left-wing philosopher who afterwards died in prison), Ozaki Hotsumi (reporter for the *Asahi Shinbun*, subsequently executed following the Sorge–Ozaki spying case), Shimizu Ikutarō (sociologist, regarded postwar as a 'leftist, progressive intellectual' and more recently one of the leaders of the 'New Right'). The following extract embodies what Konoe called 'conclusions which I have recently reached after careful consideration, and on the basis of ten years' friendship with people in a multitude of spheres on both the left and the right, both military and bureaucrats'.

> Even though it may be assumed that those within the military who are calling for reform do not necessarily aim at bringing about a communist revolution, the group of bureaucrats and civilian sympathisers which surrounds them can equally well be called right-wing or left-wing – the so-called right-wing is nothing more than communists wearing the garb of the *kokutai* (national polity) – and consciously entertains plans to take things as far as a communist revolution. It would be safe to assume that ignorant, simple soldiers are manipulated by such bureaucrats and civilians. (Part of Konoe's 'Memorial' to the Emperor)

It was this Konoe who, on three occasions during the four years immediately prior to the Pacific War, was Prime Minister and in charge of the political situation. Following the formation of his first cabinet Konoe announced at a press conference the creation of a system of organisation of 'national unity', in order to 'bring about true peace on a basis of international justice'. Only a month after the formation of the Konoe cabinet the war with China had broken out. Some Japanese expected Konoe to take action to curb these arbitrary moves by the army, but Konoe, who 'had many friendly

defeat in the Second World War reforms made under the guidance of the General Headquarters of the Allied Forces achieved all those things for which Kita had argued – abolition of the peerage system; removal of the *Genrō* (senior statesmen) and Privy Council (Kita's so-called 'obstacles' between Emperor and people); abolition of the House of Peers; and reform of the election laws. In some cases the reforms were more radical than those proposed by Kita. Also if we consider that in 1919 the average amount of G.N.P. per individual in Japan was ¥260, that the average value of private property per person was ¥1,337 (including land) and that on average each individual possessed ¥593 worth of private land, then the limits suggested by Kita for the holding of property, with the exception of those on land ownership, were, in fact, extremely high. Kita's plans for the reorganisation of the state can therefore be regarded in economic terms essentially as a proposal for land reform, and land reform too was carried out under the directions of the occupying forces after the war. It is generally considered that there were a considerable number of people among the staff of the occupying forces immediately after the war who had left-wing affiliations, and Kita was no more radical than they were.

The end of Kita's life was something of a tragedy; he was implicated in the 26 February 1936 uprising and sentenced to death. Nevertheless, if one asks whether it was Kita or the ruling elite of the time who held mistaken views concerning the points mentioned above, then one is forced to conclude that Kita was somewhat ahead of his times.[8]

IV

However, Kita's ideas as to the method by which the reconstruction of the nation should be achieved were somewhat extreme. As has been pointed out earlier, from his experiences in the Chinese Revolution of 1911 he believed that it was the military who were the main force of revolution. Moreover, since the army was bound

---

[8] In his later years Kita received large sums of money from Mitsui. Consequently, rather than his being a ringleader in the 26 February Rising, we are inevitably led to suspect whether he might not have acted as a double agent or spy vis-à-vis both sides, the group of radical young army officers and the Mitsui *zaibatsu*. Whatever the case we can be sure that he did not wish to provoke the 26 February Rising.

to be corrupt in any country where a revolution was necessary, Kita also believed that generals and higher ranking officers could not be relied on, so the revolution in Japan must be brought about by an army coup d'état led by younger officers and enlisted men. Following the success of such a coup d'état, maintained Kita, the Emperor should proclaim martial law to last for a period of three years, disband both houses of the Diet and during that time lay a firm foundation for the rebuilding of the state. During the imposition of martial law army reservists should come under the direct control of the cabinet and should be entrusted with the task of maintaining public order. At the same time reservists should carry out a survey of the assets possessed by wealthy people in each locality, and confiscate any surplus where total assets were in excess of the stated limits on private property.

There exists the view that it is the civilians who are the main force behind a revolution: there is also the view that it is the military which is more important. A revolution may only be the process or the step whereby certain goals are achieved, but whether it is the civilians or the military who are regarded as playing the major role in the revolution implies a fundamental difference in the kind of society a person hopes for after that revolution has occurred. Following a revolution whose main force has been the civilians it is possible for a government based on the principles of bourgeois democracy and internationalism to come into being, but in a revolution where the principal part has been played by the army an ultra-patriotic, ultra-nationalist, fascist state may well follow. Japan, where Kita sought to apply his own formula for revolution, had already become thoroughly nationalistic in the years following the Meiji Revolution; so when a country of this kind underwent a revolution along the lines suggested by Kita the inevitable result was an ultra-fascist state where there was no possibility of the moderate, true socialism envisaged by Kita being realised. Kita was guilty of the error of trying to achieve his aims by a method which was totally at odds with those aims.

When a country's nationalism is closely identified with the self-interest of that country, exposure of such selfishness by another country will cause its nationalism to waver. However, it is when nationalism is closely allied with a conviction of its own absolute justice that it becomes extremely dangerous. In much the same way as Konoe Fumimaro envisaged the establishment of a new world order based on justice, Kita as well thought about the same thing, but in a much more systematic fashion. 'On just the same grounds as we call for fair distribution in terms of the people's standard of living within the country, we should call for internationally fair distribution of all that affects a country's standard of living.'[9] That is to say 'the building of revolutionary Japan' and 'the liberation of the peoples of Asia' were, for Kita, twin propositions both of which stemmed from the same axiom of 'justice'.

Furthermore, Kita believed that both in the international situation and in the domestic situation this justice must be achieved by force. In Kita's words,

> The vast wealth of Britain extends over the whole world, Russia owns vast tracts of land in the northern hemisphere. Does not Japan, which in international terms has very much the status of a have-not, have the right to fight in the name of justice to break these monopolies? The socialists of Europe and America who, while recognising the domestic struggles of the proletarian class, believe that war when waged by what one might call the international proletariat amounts to aggression and militarism, are completely contradicting themselves . . . That Japan, a proletariat in international terms . . . has had recourse to war to correct the injustices in international territorial boundaries is something to which people ought to give their unconditional approval.[10]
>
> If Japan had fought in concert with Germany during the present great war [i.e. First World War] the armies could have subdued Russia at a stroke, and while the German navy crushed the British fleet in Europe the Japanese navy could have routed it in India and Australia. By this means Japan could quite easily have built a huge empire stretching from Russia in the north to Australia in the south.[11]

It can come as no great surprise that such a *Mein Kampf* of Kita's became, as it were, the Bible of impetuous young army officers. In

---

[9] Kita Ikki, *Shina Kakumei Gaishi* (An unofficial history of the Chinese Revolution), 1921, p. 6.

[10] Kita Ikki, *Nippon Kaizō Hōan Taikō* (An outline plan for the reconstruction of Japan), 1919.

[11] Kita, op. cit.

addition, this kind of concept of the reordering of the world on a basis of 'justice' conformed with the view of the world held by Konoe of whom, through the 1930s, the army, the financial world, the intelligentsia and the people in general had high hopes, hailing him as the 'new star' of the political world. After Kita's death, as a result of the actions of Konoe and his colleagues, history took very much the course that Kita had predicted, and the great empire stretching from Manchuria in the north to New Guinea in the south rose and fell within the space of the Second World War.

Kita's works contained ideas which appealed to a large number of Japanese. However, it was unlikely for that reason alone that the people of Japan would have embarked on an act of folly such as would within the space of a few years tragically end in the destruction of the great Meiji state built up by their own fathers. At the end of the First World War the Meiji state – a state which was ideologically Confucian nationalist, politically a constitutional monarchy, economically capitalist, at least on the surface, and which diplomatically followed a course of cooperation with the countries of the West – found itself in a situation where things did not seem to run quite as smoothly as they had done previously.

First of all there was discontent among the military. In the two previous great wars, the Sino-Japanese War and the Russo-Japanese War, the generals and high ranking officers had emerged as heroes. The people were full of gratitude towards them and they received an appropriate share of rewards. However, in the First World War it was the capitalists who profited; the forces who had actually attacked Tsingtao (the German-owned city in China), who had chased round after the German cruisers and submarines in the Pacific and been on convoy duty in the Mediterranean had no share in the rewards. This discrimination they regarded as unjust. The capitalists, who during the war had monopolised the China market and even exported goods to Western Europe, in the postwar years became *nouveau riche* millionaires, sometimes several times over. But what awaited soldiers after the war was arms limitation and the mass discharge which accompanied it. What is more, in the closing stages of the war the Japanese army had invaded deep into the heart of Siberia, and even after the end of the war troops remained in Siberia, to be eventually withdrawn in October 1922, having gained nothing at all. (The withdrawal from North Sakhalin did not take place until 1925.) The army's and the navy's feelings of frustration were immense.

Japan had undertaken the Siberian expedition in response to requests from France and Britain. These countries requested Japan and the U.S. to send troops into Siberia because they saw that if, following the Russian Revolution, the Bolshevik regime concluded a separate peace with Germany this would free German troops from the Eastern front, enabling her to throw all her forces into the Western front, which could cause considerable difficulties for them. They regarded it as necessary to try and pin down large numbers of German soldiers in the east by rebuilding a 'new Eastern front'. The Japanese government eventually agreed to send troops in concert with the United States, but even before the request came from France and Britain the Japanese army had completed its own plan to dispatch troops into Russia's Far Eastern territories. The nominal aim of the army's plan was the protection of Japanese residents in the area, but it was in reality an autonomous expedition aimed at bolstering up a regime opposed to the Bolsheviks and intervening to halt the revolution. There were also hard-line elements within the government which called for an independent expedition, whereas the majority view within the government was in favour of a joint expedition in support of Britain and France aimed at bringing an end to the world war.

Consequently, even after the Siberian Expedition cooperation between the government and the army was lacking, and the military asserted the independence of the rights of the supreme command, refusing to allow government interference in military matters. During both the Sino-Japanese and the Russo-Japanese Wars the armed forces had fought brilliantly under the guidance of the government, but this same army began to get out of control with the Siberian Expedition; all military matters, including such concerns as the reinforcement of the expeditionary forces and enlargement of the area to which troops should be dispatched, came to be decided exclusively by the military.

With this the Japanese military became deaf to all other voices, but the Japanese people did not necessarily regard such behaviour by Japan's fighting forces as anything abnormal. The end of the First World War came in 1918, precisely fifty years after the Meiji

Revolution. Prior to that there had been in Japan a period of three centuries of rule by the samurai houses of Oda (Nobunaga), Toyotomi (Hideyoshi) and the Tokugawa. A very clear recollection of the memory of the Bakufu – the military government – remained in the minds of the Japanese. For many of the Japanese people such concepts as civilian control of the military were, if anything, a frightening prospect: of course there were among politicians those who tried to resist this unchecked behaviour by the army, but the members of the army for their part were reassured to find that such resistance was minimal. The military became increasingly high-handed, had its own way against the government, and imposed its own plans. As a result Japan entered a period of dual government and dual diplomacy again. As the political power of the army grew stronger, factional struggles aimed at seizing the initiative within the army itself became fiercer.

Despite the strict prohibition of military intervention in politics contained in the Imperial Injunction to Soldiers and Sailors (1882), members of the armed forces, especially the army, joined forces with right-wing politicians and right-wing thinkers to interfere in political matters, and conspired with the right-wing's so-called 'China *rōnin* (masterless samurai)' to cause trouble in Manchuria. In 1927–28, at the time of the Northern Expedition by the army of the Nationalist government, led by Chiang Kai-shek, the Japanese government dispatched troops to Shantung Province in China under the pretext of protecting Japanese residents. The government of the time was led by Prime Minister Tanaka Giichi, a general who concurrently served as Foreign Minister, so the Cabinet was little more than a branch of the army. The government had drawn up a secret plan to cut off Manchuria and Mongolia from the rest of mainland China and intended that Japan should take over the maintenance of law and order in these regions. When it became apparent that Chang Tso-lin, the strongman of Manchuria, was unlikely to do exactly as he was told, the Kwantung Army assassinated him. In addition to this in 1931 the army caused a second explosion on the South Manchurian Railway, which was owned by Japan, and then, claiming that the explosion was the work of the Chinese army, initiated an attack on the Chinese troops. Thus started the Manchuria Incident. There was no such thing as any effective military discipline.

While there were on the one hand people who had made vast profits out of the First World War, on the other, as has been seen before, there had been a marked increase in wage disparities between large and medium/small enterprises. In addition a succession of bad harvests had brought impoverishment to farming villages. The distressed farmers of the northeast of the country were forced to engage in the sale of their daughters in order that they might continue to exist themselves. Quite naturally not just members of the right- and left-wings but also many of the people at large harboured resentment against the *zaibatsu* and cursed the whole capitalist system. On top of this those who led the main body of the army, blinded by a desire for glory and advancement, conspired to initiate war and better the position of the army. In addition Kita and his followers worked to increase contacts with younger officers in an attempt to realise Kita's plan for national reconstruction, and it was not difficult for these naive young officers who had been made amply aware of the extremes of rich and poor which existed in Japan to feel a deep sympathy with the ideas of Kita.

In 1921 Yasuda Zenjirō, the head of the Yasuda *zaibatsu*, was assassinated by a member of the right-wing. Then in 1930 Prime Minister Hamaguchi Osachi was shot, and died subsequently of the wound. In 1931 certain leading army officers plotted two coups d'état, while other field officers sparked off the Manchurian Incident. Both of these coups were discovered before they took place, so were complete failures; the ringleaders got off very lightly. The country was already involved in the Manchurian Incident and as a whole was tending toward the right; these ringleaders were considered more as patriots than traitors. In 1932 former Finance Minister Inoue Junnosuke and Dan Takuma, top executive of the Mitsui *zaibatsu*, were both assassinated by members of the right-wing. Following this a group of young naval officers attacked the Prime Minister's residence and the Police Headquarters, killing Prime Minister Inukai Tsuyoshi, in what was known as the 15 May Incident. In 1935, as a result of factional disputes within the army, one of the leading figures of the Control faction (*Tōsei-ha*), Lt General Nagata Tetsuzan, Head of the Bureau of Military Affairs at the War Ministry, was assassinated in broad daylight at the War Ministry by an officer belonging to the Imperial Way faction (*Kōdō-ha*). Needless to say the Japanese people abhorred this kind of right-wing terrorism, but they nevertheless felt a considerable debt towards this uncontrollable army which had enabled Japan to establish the 'Manchurian Empire' (Manchukuo), a Japanese puppet regime which controlled huge areas of territory in the North-eastern part of mainland China. As a result balanced criticism of the military was not widespread among the Japanese people. Most of the people had been educated to a belief that the nation should come first; so there was already not that much difference between them and the military.

Manchukuo was a strange country. Its stated policy was that of harmony between its five races (Chinese, Japanese, Koreans, Manchurians, and Mongolians) but in fact it was the Japanese who ruled and exploited the other four races. The composition of the Japanese population in Manchuria was, if anything, more varied than that of Japan itself. Students who had been arrested or punished by their colleges for participating in the left-wing students' movement and right-wing terrorists released from prison worked side by side. For example in the Research Department of the South Manchurian Railway Company (which was in effect the general headquarters for Japan's administration of Manchuria) men ranging from Ōkawa Shūmei, who was arrested as a war criminal at the end of the Second World War, to Ozaki Hotsumi, who was executed as a Russian spy during the war, cooperated in the work of research. Some worked in Tokyo. Others, many of whom had been failures in Japan itself became the top elite in Manchuria and enjoyed privileged treatment.

Eventually, on 26 February 1936, the famous 26 February Incident (which I think of as the Shōwa coup d'état) occurred. Twenty-two young army officers led something over 1400 non-commissioned officers and enlisted men in attacks on the Prime Minister's residence, the Grand Chamberlain's residence and the city's Police Headquarters, and for a time they even occupied part of the Imperial Palace. The slogan of the insurgents was 'Reverence for the Emperor and the Overthrow of Evil'. The attacks ended with the assassination of only three men – Finance Minister Takahashi Korekiyo, Lord Keeper of the Privy Seal Saitō Makoto and General Watanabe Jōtarō – but the original plan was to include in those killed not only all the nation's senior statesmen and members of the cabinet, but also many of the army's top commanders. Quite clearly the coup d'état was also connected to the factional struggle within the army. As a result the punishments meted out following the failure of the coup were extremely severe.

Since the young officers who had planned the coup were members of the Imperial Way faction within the army the Control faction undertook a total purge of its opponents following the incident. The Imperial Way faction had advocated the removal of the evil elements surrounding the Emperor and an internal rebuilding of the country, but the Control faction's aim was to strengthen by legal means the political influence of the military, to establish a state geared to total war with the acquiescence of Japan's statesmen, bureaucrats and businessmen, and to bring the economy under the control of the state.

It is true that the young officers who carried out the attempted coup were influenced by the ideas of Kita Ikki, but the active role played by Kita himself in the incident was minimal. He believed that under existing circumstances it was more important for Japan to make adjustments in her relations with China and the United States. He consequently did not fundamentally approve of the coup and never gave more than tacit approval to the young officers' uprising. He was nevertheless arrested as one of the ringleaders of the incident and executed on 19 August 1937. Nishida Mitsugu, who was regarded in the same way as Kita as a ringleader, was executed at the same time. When Nishida said to Kita 'Let us end by giving three cheers for His Majesty the Emperor' Kita refused, saying 'I don't wish to.' His younger brother, who came to talk to him immediately prior to the death sentence being carried out, reports Kita as saying: 'I had nothing to do with this rising. However, because the group who perpetrated it were admirers of my writings then if people are to be called to account I shall be honoured to be among them.'

In as far as his position permitted him the Emperor attempted to resist this drift to the right. This has become apparent from various materials which have been made public since the Second World War; but at the time nobody among the people was aware of the Emperor's opinions. At the time of the 26 February Incident Japan had already withdrawn from the League of Nations, and during the period of 17 months which ensued from then up until Kita's execution the Anti-Comintern Pact was concluded with Germany and fighting with China broke out again. The Japanese state was already very much one of dual government, with an apparent government which was weak, and behind the scenes a powerful military government. The two governments had separate diplomatic policies; the nominal government subscribed to non-escalation of the war with China and a desire to seek a peaceful solution, but the government behind the scenes made one move after another to escalate the conflict, which deprived the nominal government of any credibility it retained abroad. However, during this process the government lost its ability to make any independent statement concerning foreign policy and was completely led by the military. To voice a different opinion from that of the military and the right-wing at that time could, not only for the mass of the people of course, but also for senior statesmen and perhaps even for the Emperor, mean death. Moreover under the terms of the constitution the Emperor was obliged to be politically neutral. Because the Emperor was a living god he had to discard his own political opinions; as a result of this concept of a manifest god the Emperor was from the first deprived of almost all his freedom. The Emperor and the country's leading statesmen had virtually been taken over by the military and the right-wing; their statements were already no more than whispers and even these were not communicated to the people.

In 1938 the National General Mobilisation Law came into existence, and two years later the Tripartite Military Pact was concluded between Japan, Germany and Italy. All the factions of the right-wing had united and the country was whipped up into a ferment of nationalism, Emperor worship, ultra-patriotism and militarism. Not only did the Japanese people, with their Confucian education and their longstanding worship for any form of warrior, not attempt any fierce resistance to the new system, they themselves were completely intoxicated, as it were, by this saké which was old and yet new. Both Konoe and Tōjō may have been too weak to be dictators, but the country as a whole was by that time already jingoistic enough. Japan had united herself and launched out more and more into her attempt to gain 'A Redistribution of the World on the Basis of Justice' as Kita and Konoe had called it.

Japan had become very much like the Nazi state, but without Hitler. Japan in this period was not fascist in the sense that one dictator disregarded the will of the people and enforced ultra-nationalist and militarist policies, but, as a result of military and right-wing agitation, the compulsory education they had received, and the ethical concepts, view of the state and view of the Emperor which they had traditionally held, the vast majority of the Japanese people called for ultra-nationalist and militarist policies. Japan had therefore become what might be termed a 'democratic' fascist state in the sense of one where the government as well had no choice but to adopt an equally strong line. In this sort of situation even if the government chosen was a moderate one, not only the military and the right-wing, but the people as well, would have been unlikely to permit the government to adopt a conciliatory approach towards America. The thing which needed to be done before anything else was to cool down the jingoistic feelings of the arrogant and conceited Japanese people and ironically this could be achieved only by those who supported the war.

The Emperor himself reached this conclusion by examining the situation. From the time of the Kwantung Army's assassination of Chang Tso-lin (1928) he continued to work for the maintenance of peace within the limits permitted by his status; when Tōjō Hideki, a fervent advocate of war, was eventually recommended as Prime Minister he gave his approval to the plan to make Tōjō Prime Minister with the comment 'It's a case of nothing venture, nothing win, I suppose.' That the Emperor gave his agreement to this sort of sink or swim policy can be criticised as a failure on his part, but under this 'democratic fascist system' even if anyone else apart from Tōjō had become Prime Minister in October 1941, we can assume that it would have been extremely difficult for him to prevent war.

In 1945, by which time Tokyo and almost all the other major towns and cities were in ashes, at long last moves to end the war became possible in Japan; the figures at the centre of these moves were two admirals who had managed to escape during the 26 February Rising. At the time of the incident Okada Keisuke was Prime Minister; as his younger brother-in-law, who worked as his personal secretary, closely resembled Okada, the brother-in-law deceived the insurgent officers by his claim that he was the Prime Minister, and was killed instead of him. Suzuki Kantarō was shot by the rebels and seriously wounded, but his wife had pleaded with Captain Andō, the commander of the insurgents, not to fire the final shot. As a result Suzuki had survived. With the assistance of Okada, Suzuki, the Premier in 1945, was able to restrain the faction which wished to continue the resistance, and eventually obtain Japan's acceptance of the Potsdam Declaration. The Shōwa coup d'état had spurred Japan into war with America, but those whom the rebels had failed to kill were those who brought peace back to Japan.

CHAPTER FIVE

The San Francisco regime

I

Over a long period the Japanese were forced to lead a harsh life under the despotism of the military, living always apprehensively aware of the eyes of the secret police on them; many of the people, at the very latest in the closing stages of the war, became clearly aware of the fact that their real enemy was not Britain and America, but the Japanese military itself. A short while after the surrender, when the Japanese people realised that the Allied Occupation was nowhere near as hard as they had imagined it would be, they ceased to fear the allied forces. What is more they even felt grateful towards them, regarding them as the army of liberation for which they had themselves been waiting. It is a fact that among those soldiers of the occupation army sent to Japan at first morale was high and military discipline strict. There was virtually no trouble between these soldiers and the Japanese and it was, in effect, a model occupation.

In the initial stages the object of occupation policy was to reform Japan, which hitherto had been full of vitality but militaristic and aggressive, into a country which might be somewhat more restrained but peaceful and democratic and based on the free enterprise system. In November 1945, General MacArthur, the Supreme Commander of the Allied Forces, issued a directive to Prime Minister Shidehara, laying down five major reforms; these were female suffrage, the right of labour to organise, liberal education, abolition of autocratic government and democratisation of the economy. On the basis of these the election laws were amended, labour unions were formed and the education system reformed. Furthermore, in order to bring an end to absolutist politics, the peerage was abolished, the House of Peers reconstituted as the House of Councillors (*Sangiin*) and the so-called 'Third Chamber', the Privy Council, was abolished. Subsequently a new constitution was enacted which clearly laid down a system where the Emperor should be no more than a symbol, as well as providing for the sovereignty of the people, fundamental human rights, regional autonomy, division of the three powers of the administration, legislation and judiciary, and the renunciation of war. In pursuit of economic democratisation the *zaibatsu* were broken up and a stiff property tax was levied. The property of the Imperial family was no exception to this democratisation; with very few exceptions the very considerable amount of land owned by the Imperial family through-out the country and the imperial villas were all disposed of. In addition a thoroughgoing land reform was carried out.

This kind of 'new Japan' resembles very closely that in Kita Ikki's plan for reconstructing Japan. When he was writing his 'Outline Plan for the Reconstruction of Japan' (1919) owner farmers on the verge of destitution were being reduced to tenants; rural villages were being reduced to the two extremes of a few large landlords on the one hand and numerous tenant farmers on the other. In this plan for reform Kita advocated an exhaustive land reform, and stated that the Emperor should take the lead in handing over to the nation all the land, forests, stocks, etc., owned by the imperial family. This situation dreamt of by Kita was clearly realised after the war under the guidance of the Headquarters of the Occupation Forces, in very much the same way as Kita had suggested. Just as Kita had wished, the Emperor ceased to be 'an Emperor of the period when, as head of state, he possessed the two basic elements of the state, the land and the people'; as a result of the land reform in 1947 owner farmers who had hitherto been 36.5% of all farmers, rose to 54.1% of the total, and the percentage of tenants fell from 26.6% to 7.9%. In addition, needless to say, the property tax considerably reduced the difference between rich and poor. Although, with the exception of the holding companies, all the *zaibatsu* affiliated companies which had been divided into their component parts by the order of the MacArthur Headquarters revived and expanded subsequently, the *zaibatsu* families were unable to recover the vast economic power they had possessed previously.

This kind of situation was eventually brought about 13 years after the Shōwa coup d'état (the 26 February Rising) which was carried out by young army officers who believed in Kita's plans for renovation, but which ultimately ended in failure. However, Kita aimed at world reconstruction – the liberation of Asia from the imperialist influences of America, Britain and France – following national reconstruction, so that even if the Shōwa coup d'état had been successful and resulted in 1937 in a Japan such as that of 1947, sooner or later Kita's Japan would have started a reckless war which it regarded as a war for the liberation of the world. One must therefore conclude that the defeat of 1945 and the occupation which followed were, in effect, unavoidable. They were unavoidable in as far as the Japanese people failed to suppress the ultra-nationalistic ideology characterised by such concepts as 'Revere the Emperor and expel the barbarian', 'Japanese spirit and Western learning', 'Rich country and a strong army', 'Loyalty and patriotism' and 'Pan-Asianism with Japan at the centre'.

The years 1945–47 were a period of extreme shortage of food-stuffs, but it can be considered that there had never really previously been a period when the Japanese felt such a sense of liberation. It is true that immediately following the Meiji Revolution when the old status system was abolished there was also a great liberation of the people, but at that time education was still not that widespread, and only a few people were able to make an assessment of the significance of the reform. However, following the Second World War, eighty years after the revolution, there were a large number of people who, even if only in the abstract, were aware that liberty was important. During the long years of the war the Japanese people had been starved of knowledge. On the one hand they would form queues in order to purchase foodstuffs, on the other they would also form long queues to purchase books and journals.

All units of the army and navy were disbanded by the occupation troops, but the bureaucratic structure of the government was retained virtually untouched. Japan was now placed under the military administration of the allied forces, and as far as important matters were concerned the government had to abide by the directives issued by the Allied Forces Headquarters. However, over a long period up to 1945 the Japanese bureaucracy had consistently played the role of a 'second' government under the Japanese military; the circumstances of the occupation, where the bureaucracy's role vis-à-vis the Allied G.H.Q. was very similar, in no way presented the bureaucracy with a new set of conditions of which it had no experience. On the contrary, if the Japanese government had been given its independence immediately after the war it is more likely that it would have been at a complete loss as to what to do. The Japanese bureaucracy had become experienced as competent administrators working under the military, and, although the upper echelons of the ruling structure might have been changed, the Japanese army being replaced by the Allied Forces G.H.Q., the bureaucracy remained just as loyal and competent as it had been before, and continued to work in an efficient manner. Throughout the years of the occupation the Japanese government showed no resistance to the Allied Headquarters, nor operated any go-slows at work whatsoever.

Needless to say there were numerous difficulties. Inflation soared, the number of unemployed exceeded five million and there was a rush of strikes. All Japanese were prepared for heavy reparations; they believed that any revival of Japan as a strong military nation would be foolish and that for the people's standard of living to regain even its prewar level was clearly no more than a dream for the distant future. However, by 1948 a rapid change was taking place in the international political situation in Asia, and this could not but affect Japan. During this year in mainland China the army of Chiang Kai-shek was being defeated throughout the country by the forces of the communists, and in the Korean peninsula the Republic of Korea was founded in the southern half while in the northern half the Korean People's Democratic Republic was established. Then in the following year, 1949, the People's Republic of China came into existence and finally in 1950 the Korean War broke out; relations between the Soviet Union and China on the one hand and the United States on the other deteriorated to a very low point.

Forced by this sort of new situation the American government was driven by necessity to rebuild Japan as a bastion against the Soviet Union and China. Furthermore, such a bastion had to be created extremely rapidly. The Allied G.H.Q. carried out a major shift in occupation policy. Abandoning the original policy aim of building a democratic country based on the free enterprise system, whose actions would be restrained and peaceloving, there was a shift to measures such as would rebuild Japan into a powerful country equipped with the military and economic strength appropriate to an advance base of the 'free' (anti-communist) camp. As a result of this shift Japanese capitalism re-emerged like a phoenix in a form almost identical to that of the prewar period.

By this time the army and the navy had already been disbanded and the dissolution of the *zaibatsu* was in progress. Furthermore, former members of the armed services had been purged from public office and leading businessmen gone into forced retirement. However the moment disturbances broke out in Korea, G.H.Q. directed the Japanese government to organise a Police Reserve Force (later the Self Defence Force) and to increase considerably the number of personnel in the Maritime Safety Agency; following this some former army men were depurged and permitted to hold public office. Of these, one group immediately entered the National Police Reserve and were responsible for the defence of Japan following the despatch of American troops to Korea. In addition to this, former naval officers and men were sent to the seas around Korea as members of the Maritime Safety Agency. They there engaged in minesweeping operations.[1] The Police Reserve started recruitment only three years and three months after the new Japanese constitution came into effect, a constitution whose 9th clause clearly stated 'Land, sea and air forces and other war potential shall not be maintained. The right of belligerency of the state shall not be recognised.'

From the very beginning of the outbreak of the Korean War the American forces (United Nations forces) placed numerous orders with Japanese enterprises for weapons, vehicle components and other military commodities. America was forced to undertake the urgent revival of the Japanese economy, and to assist this the policies for the demilitarisation of the Japanese economy which were being carried out at the time were rapidly suspended. At the same time economic cooperation between Japan and America was essential. The concept which had prevailed up to then of rebuilding Japan as a free, peaceful, medium-sized economic unit was cast aside and in its place Japan was expected to assume a role in checking the advance of communism in Southeast Asia.

---

[1] Yoshida Shigeru, Prime Minister at the time when the draft of the constitution was being discussed, said of the matter: 'The stipulation in this draft relating to the renunciation of war is not a direct denial of the right of self-defence, but, as a result of the statement in the 2nd clause of the 9th article that no military potential and right of belligerency of the state will be recognised, even a war which is no more than an invoking of the right to self-defence is also embraced by this renunciation of the right of belligerency.'

The new aim in the rebuilding of Japan consequently became the creation of an economy which could assume the duty of developing the economy of Southeast Asia and which would at the same time provide the sort of reserves which could meet the urgent demand for the supply of goods made by the United States. This was a complete U-turn in occupation policy. Under the measures initially taken towards her, Japan was not permitted a standard of living higher than those of the other countries of Asia toward which she had shown such aggression, and as a result all commodities and equipment – with the exception of necessary commodities and capital equipment – were handed over as reparations either to the allies or to those countries which had suffered from Japanese aggression. In 1949 such reparations plans were shelved. Eventually under the 1951 San Francisco Peace Treaty – by which Japan became a member of the 'free' camp – Japan's responsibility for reparations was recognised, but many of the countries which were a party to the peace waived their right to demand reparations and only the few countries of Philippines, Indonesia, Burma and South Vietnam did in fact demand them.

At the time of the U-turn, policies were adopted almost identical to those adopted by former Japanese governments. An economy revived which once again had as its nucleus large enterprises. Over the five year period starting in 1950, Japanese enterprises were enriched by the huge demand for military commodities to be used in the Korean War by American forces. Over the first two years the chief items in demand included trucks, vehicle components, cotton cloth and coal, but in 1952 the G.H.Q. permitted the manufacture of armaments and these then became the largest item in demand. In very much the same way as damage to the Japanese economy from the depression of the 1930s had been minimised by the 'Special Procurements for Manchuria' made by the Kwantung Army, so now the Japanese economy climbed back from the depths it had reached following defeat with the aid of the 'Special Procurements for Korea' placed by the American army. From 1950 the iron and steel industry geared itself to increased production and in 1951 not just in the iron and steel industry, but in the spinning, coalmining and machine tool industries as well levels of production easily exceeded prewar records. However, it was only large enterprises which profited from this kind of increased economic cooperation with the United States; medium and small enterprises failed to share in the benefits made available by these 'special procurements'.

This was not all. During the 1950s many of the giant army and navy facilities, including former arsenals, were sold off to private enterprise. These arrangements included, for example, the disposal of the navy's fuel depot at Yokkaichi to the Shōwa Oil Company and the Mitsubishi Petrochemical Company, of the army's fuel depot at Iwakuni to the Mitsui Petrochemical Company and the Japan Mining Company, and of the Harima workshop belonging to the army's arsenal in Osaka to the Kobe Steelworks. The sale of government enterprises in the Meiji period had determined the structure of the Meiji industrial world and the 'sale of former military assets' after the war played a similarly decisive role in the subsequent development of the Japanese economy. Many of the conglomerates which acted as bases for Japan's high rate of economic growth had succeeded to army or navy facilities; former naval arsenals were revived as shipyards and steelworks, and prospered.

For the Japanese this kind of development was extremely fortunate. In fact when the Korean war broke out and the special procurements boom started both businessmen and politicians were delighted, and claimed that 'the kamikaze [divine wind] has at last begun to blow in our favour'. The economic distress of the postwar period was far less than had initially been predicted, but in exchange for this the characteristics of the Japanese economy which became firmly established in the postwar years were almost identical to those of the prewar period. The concept of a free competition economy which might be poor but which was nevertheless democratic and rested on a basis of equality – such as had been hoped for immediately after the end of the war – went out like a dream. There was rebuilt an economy such as had existed before the war, one in which government leadership was fundamental, and where, consequently, those who were clever enough profited from ingratiating themselves with the government. On the one hand many companies moved their head offices to Tokyo, and large numbers of people gathered in the capital in search of employment and university education; parallel with this there was, on the other hand, a hatred of all new militaristic elements among the Japanese people.

Many of Japan's intellectuals and student population regarded the overthrow of the militarists in Japan as the one and only fruit of the Pacific War, so were highly sensitive to the matter of re-

armament and the increasing monopoly of large enterprises, react-
ing with the strongest disapproval. They voiced especially strong
criticism of the U-turn in American policy towards Japan, de-
nouncing America's selfishness in first imposing demilitarisation
on Japan, then, when the situation changed, changing completely
and ordering the establishment of a Police Reserve (which in effect
was nothing other than a military force), resuscitating the munitions industry and making Japan into a supply base for the
American army. At one time even members of the Communist
Party had expressed their gratitude towards the American Army as
an army of liberation, but many Japanese, not just communists,
now despaired of the United States. As a result up until the
mid-1960s anti-American feelings were strongly rooted among
certain sectors of the intelligentsia, students and workers. At the
time of ratification of the revised U.S.–Japan Security Treaty in
1960 anti-American feelings reached a peak. Tokyo was enveloped
in an atmosphere as tense as at any time since the 26 February
Rising in 1936.[2] So this was the manner in which Japan compen-
sated for being built into 'the free-world's great factory in Asia'.

II

Immediately after the war was a time of crisis for the traditional
culture and morality of Japan. People in general lost confidence in
traditional culture and life style, and even hated them. Despite this,
Western individualism and liberalism did not become firmly rooted
in Japan. The labour unions, which had been encouraged by the
occupation forces after the war as part of the liberalisation policy,
eventually turned into very 'Japanese' 'Enterprise Unions', and as
regards enterprise management as well very 'Japanese' management methods, which spread very widely, were established
under the doctrine of what one might call 'enterprise-ism'.

There had been labour unions before the war, but by the time
the war ended there were few people who had any knowledge of the

---

[2] At the end of the war one group of army officers showed their resistance by attempting to
obstruct the radio broadcast in which the Emperor announced Japan's acceptance of the
Potsdam Declaration, but by and large the citizens of Tokyo showed great equanimity.
They assembled at the square in front of the imperial palace and wept, but not one person
attempted to rebel against the decision.

pre-war labour union movement. When Japan entered the period
of the quasi-wartime regime the union movement was banned;
instead of unions each enterprise formed a 'patriotic industrial
association', headed by the company president and the factory
manager. The occupation forces had regarded the labour
movement as important; it had been as important as the land
reform and the emancipation of women in their entire occupation
policies. They had, however, no programme, no perspective and
no knowledge as to how to implant an equitable labour
movement in Japan, which was virtually virgin soil as far as such
a movement was concerned. All they did at first was to stir up the
workers.

Quite naturally it was the champions of the prewar labour
movement who grasped the leadership. Many of these men were
communists, among them many people with a great deal of
personal charm; but most of them had been imprisoned for a
number of years (some for nearly twenty years). Japanese society
had undergone a great upheaval; consequently these men had been
separated from society at the very time when they had most to
learn as participants in the social movement. Furthermore in the
world of communists there prevailed the illusion that the longer the
period spent in prison the greater the communist. This in effect
meant that the less knowledge a man had of the world the higher
his position among the leadership of the labour movement. One
must admit that it was quite natural that the Japanese labour
movement should become a base for communism, and a text-book
communism detached from reality at that.

These men mistook the labour movement for a revolution. At the
time the occupation forces were carrying out reforms of Japanese
society, so any group whatsoever, whether of the right or of the left,
which was attempting to bring about revolution with intentions
which were incompatible with the occupation programmes was in
effect an enemy of theirs. Furthermore, throughout mainland
China the army of Chiang Kai-shek, who had been backed by the
Americans, was suffering one defeat after another at the hands of
the communist forces. Relations between the occupying forces and
Japanese communists took a sharp turn for the worse; at first,
despite the fact that the occupation forces had disliked the communists, there had been a love–hate relationship with the communists hailing the occupation forces as an army of liberation. Now,

however, G.H.Q. prohibited the general strike planned for February 1947, which might have enabled a large number of labour unions allied with the Communist Party and the Socialist Party to realise their joint aim of bringing down the cabinet. Subsequently, in July 1950, the so-called 'Red Purge' was begun, and communists, or anyone regarded as such, were purged from public enterprises, educational institutions, and newspaper companies and other media. This was a month prior to the establishment of the Police Reserve, and four months before the depurging of former professional soldiers was commenced.

Following this the Japanese labour union movement quietened down appreciably. At first the activists of Japan's labour union movement believed that unions should initially be formed at enterprise level, and that these local unions must then be further organised according to industry; the industrial unions formed in this manner should then be brought together under the Japan Industrial Labour Unions Congress. This 'congress' was modelled on the organisation of the American Congress of Industrial Organisations but it was a radical organisation whose leadership was controlled by communists. From a peak of 56% in 1949 the unionisation rate of industrial workers decreased annually, and in 1978 no more than 32% of all employees belonged to a union. In 1950, when the Korean War began and occupation policy towards Japan had clearly started its U-turn, there was founded the General Council of Trade Unions of Japan (Sōhyō) which held a far more realistic attitude than the Industrial Labour Unions Congress, which was eventually disbanded in 1958.

With the quietening down and increasing moderation of the labour union movement the focus of the labour movement became enterprise unions. As we shall see later the lifetime employment system and the seniority system spread more and more in the postwar period, and under this sort of system the union began to think of company matters as their main preoccupation, while management as well often felt sympathy with the labour union of their own company. As management and union leaders were engaged in negotiations of wage increases on repeated occasions management became able to assess the ability of union leaders to control their membership while the leaders of the union as well came to have a clear understanding of the circumstances faced by the company's management. There thus grew up between the two sides a mutual awareness of belonging to the same enterprise, and the position of president of the union, or other posts among the union's leadership, even came to be regarded as important stops on the road to success within the company. In fact in many enterprises the head of the union subsequently became president or director of the company. It was not uncommon to find an enterprise whose president and vice-president had been successive union presidents. Japanese managers came to regard the union leadership in very much the same light as teachers in British schools see prefects as those pupils who are full of promise for the future. This meant there was a complete calming down of the radical labour movement which for a time had resulted in a rush of strikes throughout the country; in extreme cases enterprise unions ended up by cooperating with management in much the same way as had the Patriotic Industrial Associations existing within each company during the war. The labour movement which was encouraged by the occupation authorities as part of the democratisation policy was eventually paralysed by the halt called by the same occupation forces.

Another plank of the democratisation policy of the occupation forces had been the purge of top executives of leading enterprises. This was done on the grounds that they had all to a greater or lesser extent cooperated in pursuit of the war. The vacancies created by this purge had to be filled up by younger people. These young men had plenty of military experience but could show virtually no achievements as far as company management was concerned. Japan had been at war for a period of some fifteen years from 1931. Therefore even among those who were aged forty when the war ended a large number had spent a decade as soldiers at the front, and had no more than eight years experience of working in a company. Moreover the companies in which they had been employed had been operating under war conditions, so they had no experience of company employment at a time when the economy was operating freely. Young men of this kind were hastily promoted to directorships to substitute for those purged; they were quite naturally referred to as 'third-rate directors'.

Managers of this kind conducted their labour management in much the same way as they had commanded their troops. Similarly the workers as well had long experience of the army. After the conclusion of the war all the practices and systems of the era of militarism were regarded as evil, but both management and workers had spent so long in the army that they had formed a liking for the seniority and lifetime employment systems and they all harboured no doubts as to the merits of this sort of system. Not only did these practices continue to prevail after the war, but, on the contrary, they became more and more widespread. The young directors urged their workers to 'unite together in order to cope with the grave situation' and made factory '1' compete with factory '2' for higher productivity just as battalion '1' had tried to outshine battalion '2' during the war. Unlimited dedication to the enterprise was regarded as the highest virtue.

Large enterprises formerly connected to a *zaibatsu* were especially affected by these changes. Directives issued by the army of occupation prohibited the *zaibatsu* families from involvement in management activities, and as a result of the new property tax they also lost a large proportion of their assets. At the same time those who had acted as their loyal 'foremen' before and during the war, i.e. the top managers of *zaibatsu* enterprises, were also purged. Thus, in these enterprises management and ownership were separated in one stroke. The new young manager felt a far greater affinity towards the workers than towards the owner of the enterprise. This kind of non-capitalist, young, employed manager was far keener to improve the enterprises' national or international position than to serve its owners by striving for the greatest possible profit. The attitude of such managers was comparable to that of true scholars who believe that the achievement of academic results is more important than the accumulation of wealth. Since management believed that the support of the workers was essential for this purpose they did not demand huge salaries for themselves and were keen to provide ample welfare facilities for the workers. Prior to the war, members of *zaibatsu* families and their managers had been severely criticised by both left and right wing for arbitrarily pursuing their own self-interest; there had been frequent calls for the nationalisation of these enterprises. However one could probably say that postwar the enterprises which had formerly been affiliated to *zaibatsu* had almost no problem in dealing with this sort of criticism.

There are, of course, in Japan also other large enterprises which have never been part of a *zaibatsu*. Many of these are managed by presidents and directors who had formerly been ordinary company employees, in much the same way as the *zaibatsu*-affiliated enterprises mentioned above. There also exist other large enterprises which are managed personally either by the founder of that enterprise, or by members of his family. Such firms include Matsushita Electric, Sony, Toyota, Honda, Cannon and Suntory. The success of these managers is due in large measure to their own personal charisma, but they are well aware that without the support of both white-collar and blue-collar employees they too would forfeit their charisma and that they cannot hope to take on outstanding personnel if they treat their employees indifferently. Generally speaking, managers of this kind are rather more adventurous and full of resolution than the managers mentioned above who had formerly been company employees, but this also has a bad side in that the institution of company precepts and company mottos serves to impose the manager's own personal philosophy on every single company employee. Regardless of whether they were formerly part of a *zaibatsu* or not enterprises in Japan are now to a greater or lesser degree communities where both management and employees are bound together by a common fate and common interests; in extreme cases they are communities which share a communal philosophy and the founder of the firm is frequently revered like the founder of a religious sect.

Managers of enterprises in the postwar period required their employees to unite in demonstrating to the utmost their loyalty towards the firm. Managers were not satisfied with new entrants to the firm who had received only a school education. The primary aim of education should of course be the bringing out of the latent abilities of each individual, but there is also the kind of education which tries to fit each individual into just one mould. In most Western European countries the education given at schools is probably such as will develop individuality, but within an army the education is such as will promote uniformity. When human beings have been standardised commanding officers are easily able to estimate the total capability of those under their command. In effect the standardisation of people is a necessary prerequisite for operations involving large forces. In prewar Japan even at school the education given was that which moulded people to a uniform pattern. Even after the war, although lip service was paid to the concepts of development of individualism and liberalism, education for the purposes of uniformity was still persistently carried on. Despite this managers considered that receipt of a school education alone was insufficient to make an employee show solidarity in his work at the enterprise. New employees on their entry into the company immediately received training within the firm where there was a thorough programme of moral training and they were inculcated into the ways of the company. Thus new entrants into top-ranking enterprises had, within a very short time, been polished into first-class company 'soldiers' who would be at the manager's beck and call.

In this way large enterprises required allegiance of their employees, and medium/small enterprises were unable to demand of their employees anything over and above their normal work. As a result the dualistic structure of the prewar labour market – consisting of the first labour market, that of the large enterprises, which I earlier called the 'market for loyalty' and the second market, used by the small and medium enterprises and referred to as the 'market for mercenaries' – was preserved intact postwar. Consequently when the Korean War boom began in 1950 it was not long before great disparities in wages between large and medium/small enterprises commensurate with those which had existed prewar became firmly implanted.

Table 6A shows differences in wages according to scale of enterprise, covering all employees, both male and female, in the

Table 6A. *Differences in wages by scale of enterprise (%)*

Year	Scale of enterprise (measured by number of employees in the plant)			
	5–29	30–99	100–499	500–
1951	38	56	75	100
1953	41	54	71	100
1955	41	53	69	100
1958	44	55	70	100
1960	46	59	71	100
1963	58	69	79	100
1965	63	71	81	100
1968	63	69	80	100
1970	62	70	81	100
1973	61	71	82	100
1975	60	69	83	100
1978	61	68	83	100

Source:
1951–55: Ministry of International Trade and Industry, *Kōgyō Tōkei Hyō* (Tables of industrial statistics).
1958–78: Ministry of Labour, *Maigetsu Kinrō Tōkei Chōsa* (Monthly survey of employment statistics).

period after 1951. It shows that in the 1950s very considerable wage disparities existed between large and small enterprises, that from 1960 the disparity decreased rapidly, but that this trend halted around 1970 and during the 1970s the difference with regard to smaller enterprises again increased just a little. However, one must not be overhasty in drawing a direct comparison between this table and Table 4 which shows the difference existing in the years 1909 and 1914. As has already been explained, the large enterprise sector of Japanese manufacturing industry became more and more the province of men in the 1930s. Before then the proportion of female workers in large enterprises was high, while from the 1950s there was a high proportion of male employees. The wages of female employees were extremely low compared with those of the men both before and after the war, so the average wage in large enterprises before 1930 was low, whereas after the war it was high. As a result the figures in Table 4 indicating the difference in 1909 and 1914 underestimate the true state of affairs, while the postwar figures in Table 6A overestimate it.

Table 6B shows the disparities in wages with male and female workers separated. As expected it confirms both the overestimation

Table 6B. *Wage differentials according to scale of enterprise and according to sex (%)*

Year		Scale of enterprise (measured by number of employees)			
		5–29	30–99	100–499	500–
1909	Men	85	92	97	100
	Women	77	89	93	100
1914	Men	78	84	89	100
	Women	74	85	89	100
1960	Men	54	71	83	100
	Women	62	77	86	100
1968	Men	69	76	86	100
	Women	69	73	85	100
1973	Men	70	81	90	100
	Women	63	72	83	100
1977	Men	70	77	90	100
	Women	63	69	83	100

Source:
1909–14: *Kōjō Tōkei Hyō* (Statistical tables of factories).
1960–77: *Maigetsu Kinrō Tōkei Chōsa* (Monthly survey of employment statistics).

and the underestimation, but even in 1960, when the actual disparity was lessening, the disparity in wages was clearly greater, for men and for women, than it had been in 1909 and 1914; it is therefore difficult to conceal the fact that there was in the 1950s a very great disparity in wages, even though there are no statistical data available which give wage disparities according to scale of enterprise for men and women respectively during the years of the 1950s. Moreover, even when the difference was at its smallest (1973 for men, 1968 for women) it was still greater than that existing in 1914, let alone 1909.

Despite this there are economists who on the basis of this state of affairs conclude that during the 1970s the Japanese economy has overcome its problem of dualistic structure. I, on the contrary, believe that regardless of the facts set out above differences in wages according to the scale of the enterprise are still very much in existence. It is true that if we consider wages in the narrow sense of the sum of regular wages including overtime pay plus bonus then we must acknowledge the figures given in Table 6B, but in the postwar period, especially since 1960 when the large enterprises had completed their recovery, large enterprises have begun to provide ample fringe benefits for all their employees. It goes without saying that accommodation for workers has been provided, but there are also ample facilities in terms of clinics (some enterprise groups even have their own large hospitals), convalescent homes, and recreation centres in mountain or sea areas. In addition there is an organised system of paid holidays as well as levels of company pension and retirement pay which bear no comparison to those provided by small or medium-sized enterprises. Such items as the monthly salary received by an employee or the bonus he receives at the end of the year are no more than just one part of the total payments he receives if one takes these fringe benefits into account. Under the lifetime employment system a lot of consideration is given to company pensions and retirement payments, and those who have retired from the company are permitted to use the company's medical facilities and holiday homes by virtue of their previous employment.[3] Medium and small

---

[3] In addition, in the case of white-collar workers there is a high probability that if they have been employed in a large enterprise when they reach the retirement age they can get a post as director in a smaller enterprise within the same group. But when the normal employee of a medium/small enterprise reaches retirement he has only a small chance of obtaining this sort of opening.

enterprises are left with no surplus with which they can build welfare facilities; even if the wages appear to be high it is at best no more than a superficial adjustment.[4]

III

Even today in Japan the well-being of a person's whole life is virtually decided by whether or not he is able to obtain employment within a large enterprise. It is true that as a result of Japan's becoming affluent the employees of medium and small enterprises can no longer really be said to lead lives which are wretched by any international comparison, but domestically they suffer a severe disparity in standard of living when compared with the employees of large enterprises. In a Western type capitalist economy the most difficult problem is that of class, and in Confucian–capitalist Japan the problem of dual structure, a sort of segmentation of labour market, is no more than the class problem in another guise.

As might be expected competition to gain employment in large enterprises is fierce. The examinations for entrance into a large enterprise are open to an individual only once in his life, immediately after his graduation from school or college. Since an individual has little chance of gaining entrance to a company if the school or college from which he has graduated is not a good one there is fierce competition to get into the good universities, hence fierce competition to get into good high schools, and so on right down the education ladder. In extreme cases the competition is so relentless that it extends to getting a child into a good kindergarten and in order to get them into a good kindergarten some children even receive instruction at home. Since in a Confucian society people are ranked in the hierarchy according to the education they have, or have not, received, the large enterprises wish to recruit graduates from what one might term the more prestigious institutions, as this is clearly the most appropriate way to preserve the standing of the enterprise.

[4] It has been pointed out by P. J. D. Wiles that where unions are organised on an enterprise basis, rather than according to industry, regardless of the nature of the economic system (e.g. in both Yugoslavia and Japan) there are enormous differences in wages among enterprises. See Wiles, *The Free Enterprise Economy and the Socialist Economy* (in Japanese) (Japan Economic Research Centre Bulletin No. 310, 1978).

Since before the war Japan has been one of the countries best equipped with educational facilities and an educational system in the world. However, before the war education was geared not to the individual but largely to the purposes of the state. The first clause of the Imperial Universities Ordinance clearly states 'The aim of the imperial universities shall be to teach the arts and sciences in accordance with the priorities of the State, and to make a study of their principles', and not just the imperial universities, but other educational institutions as well, had to produce people whose talents would be of use to the nation. Since the state was frequently engaged in war, to be of use to the state was nothing but being able to contribute to the waging of war, and, especially after 1930, when Japan moved towards a quasi-wartime set up, the universities had to commit themselves to wholehearted support of the army. The arts, philosophy and basic natural science were played down while great importance was attached to engineering and such economics as would be useful for company employees. After the war the education system was remodelled along American lines and the main objective of education became to develop the potential within any individual; but this was never really more than superficial, and postwar educational institutions, especially the universities, have become completely subject to the needs of big business. Universities do no more than 'give instruction in learning in accordance with the priorities of business enterprises'; most students study only in order to gain employment in one of the top large enterprises. Consequently the situation is like it was prewar: those faculties with the largest number of students are those of engineering, economics and business administration.

Such a characteristic of Japanese higher education is apparent when contrasted with higher education in the U.K. which is of notoriously little use to industry. In the U.K. (excluding Scotland and Northern Ireland) there were in 1974 170,000 undergraduates of whom 15%, some 24,000, were specialising in engineering. In contrast there were in Japan in the same year 1,590,000 undergraduate students at national, public or private universities, of whom 21%, some 330,000, belonged to faculties of engineering.[5] As Ronald P. Dore has said elsewhere, in Japan there are a large

---

[5] In the case of postgraduate students in Britain 13% of the total of 61,000 (c. 8000) are studying engineering, whereas for Japan the figure is 33% of the total of 46,000 students (i.e. c.15,000).

number of universities 'which would admit an intelligent chimpanzee provided his guardian made a large enough contribution to the
university building fund',[6] so to compare Japanese universities *in
toto* with British universities is hardly fair. However, universities
such as these do not, as a rule, possess engineering departments
since they need so much money, so those Japanese students who
specialise in engineering tend to be concentrated in the relatively
good universities.[7] Since 1955, Japan has managed to improve her
productivity by importing and improving on foreign techniques,
but such technical improvements have only been possible because
Japan had continuously been producing large numbers of en-
gineers since the years of the war. A large number of these
improvements were quite epoch-making. From the 1960s Japanese
goods made tremendous inroads into international markets and
this was the result of this kind of technological progress.

A good many examples can be cited which fall into this category.
Japan's domination of the world shipbuilding market was due to
Japan's success in making fantastic improvements in welding
techniques. Until this success it was possible to build tankers of at
the most about 50,000 tons, but with the new techniques it became
possible to produce completely welded vessels of over 500,000 tons
weight. Moreover at the same time they also succeeded in making
improvements in engines which enabled all these mammoth
tankers to travel at high speeds. In another sphere one is justified in
saying that the 'Bullet Train' which ran on the new Tōkaidō trunk
line (Shinkansen) opened in 1964 was a technological advance such
as had not occurred in the railway world since George Stephenson;
the Japanese National Railways had decided to built this 'Shinkansen' in 1958, only 13 years after the Japanese people had vowed
that they would revive their country from the situation of total ruin
which prevailed. When a group-oriented society such as Japan has
a total command of modern technology it can easily release a
menacing productive energy, at times so great that it can be
suicidal.

However, research into natural science, which is the basis of

---

[6] Ronald P. Dore, *The Diploma Disease: Education, Qualification and Development* (George Allen
& Unwin, London 1976), p. 48.

[7] In Japan, Kyoto University and Osaka University are among the most prominent of the
leading universities. In both universities students in engineering departments account for
over 40% of all undergraduates.

ategories of professional, and large enterprise administrative, hite- and blue-collar workers as the upper classes, and the other ve categories of medium/small enterprise administration, blue- nd white-collar workers, agriculture and self-employed as the wer strata, then the figures in the top right- and bottom left-hand ctors indicate movement between these two groups. That is to y the higher the figures in the top right-hand corner the higher e rate of movement from the lower strata to the upper strata, hile if the figures in the bottom left-hand corner are high it is ovement in the other direction which is common. In Table 7, th the exception of the 9% of workers originally employed in the ue-collar jobs in medium or small enterprises now working at ue-collar jobs in large enterprises, all the other figures in the top ht-hand section are so small as to be able to be disregarded. In ntrast to this generally low mobility from strata in the lower half the upper strata (except for one small group of blue-collar rkers), mobility from the upper strata into the lower – especially o the self-employed category – is quite common. That is to say gaining of employment within the upper categories at the time graduation is a necessary condition for, but not a guarantee of, aining permanently within the upper strata. While Table 7 ostantiates my concept of dualistic structure it also shows how oortant a person's academic career is.

Next let us investigate my second conjecture, whether or not ergenerational mobility of employment in Japan is very high. In ole 8 occupations are classified into the eight categories of fessional, administration, office work, marketing, skilled, i-skilled and unskilled labour, and agriculture. Each column ws the occupation in which the father was mainly active in his ime, and each row the occupation of the son. The figures in column show the proportional distribution among each upation of all those sons whose fathers share the same occupa- . Figures below 4.5% are indicated by the symbol *. The first categories are non-physical work, and the other four categories be brought together under the heading of manual work. rgenerational mobility of occupation between the manual and -manual group is shown by the figures in this table to be far ter than the intragenerational mobility between the upper and r strata of society which we have considered. Furthermore, the nal Tominaga table shows that mobility from the manual

engineering, has been neglected in Japan. In 1974 the total number of undergraduates in science faculties was no more than 3% of all undergraduates, and even for such good universities as Kyoto and Osaka the percentage was only 10%. Compared with the United Kingdom, where 24% of all students are in science departments the Japanese figures are certainly rather poor. This kind of overemphasis on engineering and neglect of natural science which exists within scientific education in Japan dates back to the Meiji period and can be regarded as a natural consequence of the policies of 'Japanese spirit and Western techniques'. From the Meiji period Japan has paid close atten- tion to importing Western techniques with the greatest speed, to improving them and making them suitable for industrial produc- tion in order to achieve military and economic strength. The Japanese have shown little desire to involve themselves in such fundamental questions as what the academic foundation for this technology actually is. Is it not the case that, consciously or unconsciously, the Japanese spirit has rejected the science which is such a major element in what one might call the Western spirit? Japanese universities do not face up to fundamental questions but have continued to serve the needs of the state, the military or else big business. Japan can continue to purchase foreign technology in as far as she has the money to do so. Consequently, as long as Japan has the engineering knowledge sufficient to improve these acquired techniques and to incorpor- ate them into the industrial process Japanese industry will never be technologically behind other countries more than a very little. At the time of the conclusion of the war it was frequently said: 'Japan is badly off for experimental facilities and there is no prospect of an expansion in applied physics in the future, so Japanese physicists have no alternative but to engage in theoreti- cal research'; however the history of the 35 years since the war has shown quite the reverse to be true.

Japanese universities were built up with the purpose of sending their graduates into the business world and the government. Japanese children have been forced to study from morning until night with the sole aim of getting into a good university. High school students in particular, who are studying for university entrance examinations, attend special private schools (*juku*) for examination preparation after their regular school hours are over.

When they return from these *juku* a university student is waiting to give them tuition at home and they have to study for several hours more. Leaving aside those universities into which 'even a chimpanzee' can get, the normal university entrance examinations are conducted strictly and, indeed, impartially. The Japanese believe that the fairest method of rating success in these examinations is the mechanical one of adding up the total marks from all the papers a candidate has taken; therefore, in as far as possible examination questions take a form which renders mechanical marking easy. Almost all parents are very keen for their children to go to university. Such an enthusiasm for education is by no means surprising in a Confucian society where a person's worth is estimated not on the basis of whether or not he possesses money, but on the basis of whether or nor he has been educated. Naturally one would expect *inter*generational mobility of occupation, between parents and children, to be high in Japan. On the other hand, once an individual has taken up employment in a medium-sized or small enterprise he has the greatest difficulty in transferring to the large enterprise sector; one might, therefore, predict that *intra*generational mobility of occupation will be extremely low. One would expect, in effect, the level of intergenerational mobility and that of intragenerational mobility to be in complete contrast to each other; moreover that this very low level of intragenerational mobility might contribute to the high level of intergenerational mobility.

The correctness of this sort of conjecture can be tested by reference to surveys on social stratification and social mobility. In Japan the third national survey into social stratification and mobility was conducted in 1975, and it produced the picture of intragenerational mobility of occupation we see in Table 7. In this table occupation is categorised into nine sections (professional; large enterprise administration, white-collar, and blue-collar; medium/small enterprise administration, white-collar, and blue-collar; agriculture; and self-employed), and the figures in each column show the current proportional distribution among the nine occupations of all those people who initially gained employment within a specific category, say, blue-collar employment with a large enterprise. In order to clarify the pattern of distribution small figures of less than 4.5% have been replaced by the symbol *. Such figures can be disregarded and treated as if they were zero. If we now call the four

Table 7. *Intragenerational mobility of occupation in 1975 (%)*[a]

Present employment	Initial employment								
	Professional	Large enterprise			Medium/small enterprise			Agriculture	Self-employed
		administration	white collar	blue collar	administration	white collar	blue collar		
Professional	75	*	*	*	*	*	*	*	*
Large enterprise — administration	*	100	9	*	*	*	*	*	*
Large enterprise — white collar	*	*	54	7	*	*	*	*	*
Large enterprise — blue collar	*	*	*	37	*	*	9	*	*
Medium/small — administration	*	*	*	*	75	9	*	*	*
Medium/small — white collar	*	8	8	10	*	40	8	*	5

Table 8. *Intergenerational mobility of occupation 1975 (%)*[a]

	Father's occupation							
Occupation of son	Professional	Administration	Office work	Marketing	Skilled	Semi-skilled	Un-skilled	Agri-culture
Professional	37	9	10	6	6	8	*	*
Administration	15	28	14	11	8	11	6	6
Office work	24	26	27	21	14	15	10	11
Marketing	7	11	17	30	10	11	9	9
Skilled	5	10	14	16	39	25	32	17
Semi-skilled	7	10	10	11	14	23	26	18
Unskilled	*	*	*	*	6	*	11	5
Agriculture	*	*	*	*	*	6	*	30

[a] * indicates a figure of less than 4.5%. The total number of the sample was 2338. Prepared from K. Tominaga, *op. cit.*, Table 2.9c.

group of occupations into the non-manual is greater than movement the other way round, i.e. from the non-manual into the manual, thus indicating that there exists within the Japanese economy a trend towards more non-manual work.

Thus Table 8 would seem to support my hypothesis. It must be noted, however, that if we compare these figures with a table of intergenerational class mobility in Britain drawn up in 1972 it cannot be said that mobility in Japan is any greater.[8] In fact we observe that, whereas the movement from the manual sector into the non-manual is very much the same in both Japan and Britain, the reverse movement (i.e. non-manual to manual) is considerably greater in Britain than in Japan.[9] The British themselves have an image of Britain as a country with a very low level of intergenerational class mobility, and the Japanese people's image of Japan is of a country with a very high rate of mobility. This kind of self-image is not founded on objective international comparison but in-

---

[8] Recent intergenerational class mobility in Britain is set out in the following table. Class I embraces the upper levels of professional and administrative work, class II consists of the remainder of professional and administrative employment, class III includes office and sales work, class IV self-employed (small proprietors and self-employed artisans) and farmers, class V lower grade technicians and supervisors of manual workers, class VI skilled workers, class VII semi- and non-skilled workers and agricultural labourers. For a detailed definition see J. H. Goldthorpe, *Social Mobility and Class Structure in Modern Britain* (Clarendon Press, Oxford, 1980), pp. 39–42.

Intergenerational class mobility in Britain 1972 (%)

		Father's class						
		I	II	III	IV	V	VI	VII
Class of son	I	45	29	18	12	14	8	7
	II	19	23	16	11	14	9	8
	III	12	12	13	8	10	8	8
	IV	8	7	8	24	8	7	7
	V	5	10	13	9	16	12	13
	VI	5	11	16	14	21	30	24
	VII	7	9	17	21	17	26	35

Source:
Table 4.2 in Goldthorpe, *op. cit.*, p. 105. The total sample was 9434. Leaving aside rounding errors the total of the figures in each column equals 100%.

[9] Studies of intergenerational social mobility in Japan show that 31% of manual workers move into the non-manual sector, and 28% of non-manual workers into the manual. In contrast the British figures are 33% and 36% respectively. See Tominaga (ed.), *op.cit.*, p. 53 and Goldthorpe, *op.cit.*, p. 105.

fluenced by aspirations, conceit, and many other factors. In particular, in the case of Japan, the level of mobility between the lower and upper strata of society within one generation is extremely low (once a person is firmly fixed in the lower strata it is almost impossible for him to escape from these strata during the course of his life), and this fact is deeply imprinted on the minds of the Japanese, who therefore feel that their intergenerational mobility must be very high, where it is, in fact, rather low.

In any case it is surprising to see that, despite the fact that the children of nearly all social classes are caught up in the ruthless competition of the university entrance exams, intergenerational class mobility in Japan is roughly comparable to, or even less than, that in Britain. Probably this may be because those children who are from non-manual occupation households are sent to the private *'juku'* and receive home tutoring from an early age, and as a result they have a greater skill in answering examination questions than do the children of farmers and manual workers. In addition it is probably true to say that since the entrance examination questions and their marking are mechanical, success or failure in the entrance examination is highly dependent on whether or not one had acquired this skill. The social background of students at Tokyo University, said to gather the brightest students in the whole of Japan, has recently become increasingly higher in the social scale, and Tokyo University is often criticised on the grounds that it is in the process of becoming a university for the sons of the bourgeoisie rather than one for the most outstanding students. A Confucian society which decides a person's social position purely on the basis of the education he himself has received may be just as unfair as a bourgeois society where a child's social placing is decided by the wealth of his father. Moreover, since Japanese teenagers are compelled to study for 6 hours in regular school, 3–4 hours at the private crammers and another 4–5 hours in their own homes, i.e. some 13–15 hours in all per day, this degree of 'exploitation' is little different from that of child workers of Victorian Britain. Some Japanese economists say that it is as a result of having had in childhood this kind of hard work and discipline that the quality of Japanese workers is so high. But it must not be forgotten that it has also resulted in the annihilation of their own selves.

IV

The Japanese economy was in a wretched state at the end of the war. All cities of any size, with the exception of a few historical towns such as Kyoto and Nara, had been almost totally burnt down. Not only were large numbers of people without anywhere to live but Japan's productive facilities had also been completely destroyed. In addition large numbers of Japanese who had been working in the territories formerly occupied by Japan, and their families, returned home with members of the armed forces. When these people returned home living allowances and demobilisation payments were made. The purchasing power stored up during the war was now released. Predictably Japan embarked on a sharp spiral of inflation.

During the war large numbers of workers had been diverted to the machine industry and the production of munitions, and there was a shortage of labour in the production of consumer goods. During the 1930s Japan had gone to great expense and effort to change rapidly from the production of consumer goods to the production of capital goods and munitions, and she now had to carry out just the reverse transformation with extreme rapidity. However, in such an impoverished society the margin for the expansion of the industrial production of consumer goods was extremely limited. Each person obtained his vegetables directly from the farm, and fish too went straight from the boat into the individual's stomach. It was the same way with meat. Since the people of the towns devoted all their money to getting enough to eat they scarcely ever purchased a new item of clothing. Those who had been lucky enough to survive air raids took their best clothes, rescued from the flames, to farming or fishing villages to exchange them for rice or fish, so the clothing needs of the farming or fishing populations were more or less adequately supplied. It was an era when the best clothes which had been lying forgotten in the cupboard were transferred from town to country in lieu of cash. Since labour surplus to the requirements of the munitions and machine manufacturing industries could not entirely be absorbed into the production of consumer goods, one group of these people returned to the farming villages from which they had originally come. However, in Japan as a whole land was inadequate, and the farming villages' ability to accommodate this labour was no more than minimal. The streets overflowed with men unable to engage in farming. What happened was that they eked out a living either by working on the black market, or else lived off the black market by bringing goods to it.[10]

The Japanese bureaucracy, which had hitherto skilfully played the role of a second government after the self-willed Japanese military, could easily demonstrate their competence under the occupation forces as well. A strange relationship of trust and friendship sometimes develops between hostages and their captors, and in much the same way the Japanese government had before very long succeeded in establishing an amicable relationship with the occupation forces. With very positive support from G.H.Q., the Economic Stabilisation Board (subsequently referred to as E.S.B.) was established in August 1946, and in March 1947 MacArthur issued a directive calling on the Japanese government 'to adopt resolute policies, in which priority is given to the E.S.B., to find a way out of the current economic crisis'. The E.S.B. was promptly expanded to include outstanding young bureaucrats and business-men. That these men were outstanding is apparent from the fact that almost all of them subsequently made their names in the bureaucratic, political, business or academic worlds. Anyway, Japan's basic predisposition, whereby by means of this sort of 'pipeline' of the second government the first, real, government (the Allied G.H.Q. in this case) could guide the economy along the lines it thought it should follow, remained virtually intact.

MacArthur's injunction was to 'adopt resolute policies with priority given to the E.S.B.', but the Japanese government was unable to adopt resolute policies. Since the occupation forces themselves were irresolute – as we have seen they made a complete U-turn – there was little likelihood of the Japanese government, which had become its loyal 'agent', showing resolution. However, because the new course tended in a direction which was beneficial for Japan, both government and business gave a wholehearted welcome to the U-turn. Up to then Japan had had to export

[10] The occupation forces ordered the disbanding of the army and navy and the closing down of all munitions factories, but the managers and workers of these factories cleverly concealed their materials and later on used the duralumin which had originally been intended for aeroplanes for making such things as pots and kettles. In addition, instead of precision instruments they made pachinko (pinball) machines, and pachinko balls instead of bullets. Around 1950 the pachinko parlours set up in this fashion were Japan's only places of amusement.

commodities in order to be able to import foodstuffs; the situation
was such that the only thing that Japan was able to export at the
time was raw silk. Some 30–40% of the equipment used for
production in the cotton cloth industry at its prewar peak had
escaped destruction by the war, but since supplies of raw materials were insufficient even this amount of equipment could not
be operated to capacity. Export industries such as cotton goods
which are dependent on the import of raw materials might as well
not exist in a situation where imports cannot be further increased.
When the Meiji government opened Japan to the West the export
of raw silk was the starting point for industrialisation, and in the
early stages under the MacArthur regime the only means available to the Japanese government was this same one. The Japanese
people were all overwhelmed with despair which rendered them
distraught, and G.H.Q.'s U-turn was indeed a blessing for them.

When the Korean War began the 'special procurements' placed
by the American army brought to the Japanese textile industry
what was the last great boom in its history, and the iron and steel
and non-ferrous metal sectors also embarked upon a wave of
prosperity. In addition to this the cold war was worsening and
moreover Western countries apart from America were all very
occupied with their own individual recovery. In this situation it
was hardly an expedient policy for America to exact harsh reparations from Japan. If Japan were disastrously weakened by reparations America would be the only country able to confront the
communist camp, and this would further increase the burden on
the American people. In view of the prosecution of the cold war it
was necessary for America to educate the Japanese into providing
appropriate cooperation. As a result the burden of reparations
was considerably lightened. Moves such as these were criticised
by the Japanese left-wing as moves towards rearmament and
symptomatic of the revival of monopoly capitalism, but were, of
course, welcomed both by government and by business. The
E.S.B., which in this way served as Japan's window onto America
and simultaneously as America's window on Japan, was even
referred to, at its prosperous time, as 'the E.S.B. which causes
even a baby to stop crying'. This phrase was an analogy of the old
phrase 'the Imperial Army which causes even a baby to stop
crying', suggesting that the young officers of the E.S.B. were as
bumptious as the young army officers had been, so that despite

the end of the war Japan's social and economic structure had not undergone any fundamental change.

Textile products became Japan's number one export, but it became clear that economic expansion could not take place in as far as such products remained Japan's staple export. At the time there was no possibility of making advances into the Chinese market, and since the developing countries as well were in the process of becoming self-sufficient in textiles, there was a limit to how much Japan could export. With the future of light industry not very bright Japan had once again to turn to expansion of heavy industry. Precisely at this time it looked as though the 'special procurements' boom generated by the Korean war would continue into the long term; foundries were, therefore, in the process of investing in plant modernisation. The Chiba Iron Works newly built by the Kawasaki Iron Company, for example, was a huge plant of the most modern kind situated right by the sea. It was possible for Japan to use the modernised iron industry as a basis for the expansion of all sectors of the machine industry. In the face of this second postwar reorganisation of Japanese industry the Economic Stabilisation Board, which had acted as the headquarters (or rather as a deputy-headquarters subordinate to G.H.Q.) for the first reorganisation operation, was disbanded with the end of the allied occupation. It was succeeded by the Economic Planning Agency, which no longer possessed the powers to 'stop even a baby crying' as had the earlier E.S.B.

The major role in the second industrial reorganisation was carried out by the Ministry of International Trade and Industry (M.I.T.I.). The Economic Planning Agency ceased to play the main part in the open expression of government guidance to business, and willingly played a rather more hidden role in the government's industrial control as a leading administrative bureau with responsibility for drawing up the government's economic plans. In much the same way as the Meiji government had hoisted the slogan of 'a Rich Country and a Strong Army', so successive postwar cabinets clearly stated their policy aims; in 1955 the Hatoyama cabinet published a 'Five Year Plan for Economic Self-Reliance' which aimed at balancing imports and exports, and full employment, and thereafter one cabinet after another published its own particular economic plan. Among these the most famous, and, indeed, the most successful, was the Ikeda cabinet's

'National Income Doubling Plan' which aimed at doubling the national income within ten years, but others included that of the Ōhira cabinet, which publicised its 'New 7 Year Economic Plan' only to have it lapse within a year and a half.[11]

Since the government had no power to enforce these plans the actual performances of the economy were often far removed from the targets of the plans and many parts of them existed only on paper. But during the course of drawing up the plans there were frequent deliberations between the representatives of relevant government ministries, private interest groups and intellectuals, so that the 'Plans' were effective in promoting mutual understanding between different parties. In a country like Japan where the idea of harmony (*wa*) is valued, and where there is a national tendency to believe that harmony means listening to what the government says, these published 'Plans' have served as guidelines for people's activities. Thus the contribution of the Economic Planning Agency cannot really be disregarded. However, compared with the Ministry of International Trade and Industry (M.I.T.I.), which to a certain extent has had the power to coerce even in the case of a plan with no powers of enforcement, the E.P.A., though it is a reincarnation of the powerful E.S.B., has no more than a shadowy existence.

With the confirmation in the 'New Long Term Economic Plan' (1957) and the 'National Income Doubling Plan' (1960) in which the aim of government policy was the development of the heavy and chemical industries, industrial policy was carried out in the following way. M.I.T.I. first designated within the heavy and chemical industries those categories which were to be promoted. These included oil refining, petrochemicals, artificial fibres, motor cars, industrial machinery, aeroplanes, electronics and electrical appliances. These categories were then provided with absolute protection and developmental assistance. Initial measures to provide protection from competition from foreign enterprises included

---

[11] There is no question but that the economic plans of the various cabinets were of considerable quality. For example, Prime Minister Tanaka Kakuei's *Remodelling of the Japanese Archipelago* was reviewed in the *Journal of Economic Literature* published by the American Economic Association in the following words: 'Probably no other world leader could match this degree of encyclopedic knowledge of his country's problems, and almost certainly no other leader would dare to conceive and propose solutions involving such phenomenal transformations' (*J.E.L.*, June, 1974, p. 547).

However, the Tanaka cabinet itself was short-lived as a result of Tanaka's own involvement in the Lockheed bribery affair.

the limitation of imports by imposing quotas on foreign goods, directly limiting the amount of imports by such measures as the introduction of an import licensing system, and indirectly regulating imports by such means as imposing a high protective tariff on imports and introducing a preferential commodity tax for domestically produced goods.

Moreover the development of these industries was further promoted by supplying them with capital at low interest from government financial institutions such as the Japan Development Bank and the Japan Import Export Bank, granting subsidies and adopting certain favourable measures of taxation such as reduction or exemption of corporation tax with regard to income gained from exports. On top of all this M.I.T.I. and the Finance Ministry engaged in a certain amount of administrative guidance vis-à-vis enterprises. When they considered production to be too high they advised the cotton spinning, iron and steel, and chemical fertiliser manufacturing industries to curtail their operations, and when investment was regarded as being excessive they suggested to enterprises in the petrochemical, paper and pulp, and iron and steel industries that they make adjustments in plant and investment. In order to stabilise iron and steel prices M.I.T.I. also took the lead in introducing a system of open sales for iron and steel.

In normal cases this kind of administrative guidance fell within M.I.T.I.'s own administrative jurisdiction, but even in cases where this was not so, for example where it was merely the opinion of the ministry which had been passed on, the results were considerable. Since the Meiji period the business world has always been guided by the government, and has reaped the benefits by swarming around the government. It was still the case when the rule of the occupation forces took precedence over the government. The government showed extreme favouritism towards a specific group of enterprises and was quite unfeeling towards all others. Consequently, even though a government communication might be no more than a suggestion, a request or a notification and with no binding force, in as far as it came from M.I.T.I. at all any enterprise feared a cold reception should they fail to comply and therefore had no choice but to do so. In Japan to be deserted by the government is to be relegated to being a second-rate enterprise. As a result all major enterprises have not only moved their head offices to Tokyo, but also taken on as directors former high officials of

M.I.T.I. and the Finance Ministry in an attempt to preserve close contacts with the government.

Table 9 shows how far this kind of industrial policy has been successful. The figures show as percentages the ratio of the value of shipments of manufactured goods in each category to the total value of shipments of goods from the manufacturing industry in each year. We show for the sake of simplicity only the highest and lowest ratios for each category. (The lowest value is written in brackets.) For example, the ratio achieved by shipments of manufactured foodstuffs (by value) reached a peak in 1955 (18% of the total value of shipments from the manufacturing industry) and reached a low point (10.2%) in 1973.

From Table 9 it can be seen that first of all the production of consumer goods recovered, mainly in timber and wooden goods, chemicals, textiles and foodstuffs industries in that order, and that by about 1955 the shift from an industrial structure concentrating on the heavy and chemical industries which had existed during the war to one which focused on consumer goods had been more or less successfully accomplished. This was followed by recovery in the iron and steel industry, and development in the heavy industries was carried out on this basis. The 1960s showed a process of change back to manufacturing industry concentrating on heavy industry, from manufacturing industry concentrating on the production of consumer goods; the relative proportion of shipments of products of industries manufacturing consumer goods was declining, while the proportion of shipments from heavy industry was on the increase. By the 1970s this process of reconversion had been completed in certain sectors and the ratio of shipments from the machine tool (including weapons) and electrical machinery and equipment industries reached a peak in 1970. The proportion made up by metal products and oil and coal products reached their peaks in 1973 and 1975 respectively. In contrast to this the relative importance of the foodstuffs and chemical industries recorded their lowest level in 1973. However the relative contribution of machinery and equipment for transportation and that of precision machinery and equipment were still increasing in 1977, while those of textiles, and timber and wood products were still on the decrease. At all events the table demonstrates that the Japanese economy's process of reconversion to heavy industries was accomplished at much the same speed as the first such conversion which had taken place before the war.

Table 9. *Highest (lowest) ratios of value of shipments of manufactured goods within the manufacturing industries 1948–77 (%)*

	Food-stuffs	Textiles	Timber and wooden products	Chemicals	Oil and coal products	Steel	Metal products	General machinery	Electrical machinery	Transport-ation equipment	Precision machinery
1948						(7.5)					
1949			5.8	14.1							
1950		21.5								(5.2)	
1951					(0.7)		(2.7)		(3.0)		(0.7)
1952											
1953											
1954											
1955	18.0							(4.8)			
1956											
1957						11.7					
1970								9.9	10.6		
1971											
1972											
1973	(10.2)			(7.2)			5.8				
1974											
1975					5.9						
1976		(4.6)	(2.7)								
1977										12.2	1.5

Source: Kōgyō Tōkei Hyō (Tables of industrial statistics).

Some commentators have used the phrase 'Japan Inc.' to refer to the Japanese economy's being subject to this sort of strong industrial policy on the part of the government; others have regarded this kind of industrial promotion policy as a formula for cooperation between the state and the people, or else as a formula for cooperation between government, industrialists and financiers. In an economy and society of this kind those industries which are designated as strategic for the country are carefully protected and fostered, but those industries which are deemed by the government to have no prospects for development in the future receive absolutely no help from the government, receive no capital and are forced to fight for themselves. However, this kind of policy of concentrating economic growth on certain priorities – the inequitable policy whereby the government, admittedly taking into account the opinions of industrialists, financiers and other men of appropriate learning and experience, selects certain strategic industries and strengthens them through sacrificing others – has been continued postwar, and not merely those involved in those industries which are chosen for favourable treatment, but also those who are sacrificed, have had to support the measures taken by the state.

This kind of ethic which prevails among Japanese adults is in sharp contrast to the competitive ethic which prevails among their children – the judging of a child's ability by adding up all the points he has received in his examinations, and applying no other standard of judgement in deciding his success or failure in entrance examinations. At first sight the co-existence of these two ethics would appear strange; they even seem to contradict each other. However, if we bear in mind that the earnest wish of the Japanese people ever since the Meiji Revolution has been to catch up and to overtake the countries of the West, and that Japanese people since the war as well have harboured the same aspirations, it then becomes clear that these apparently asymmetrical ethics prevailing amongst parents and children in fact conform to circumstances within Japan. In order selectively to strengthen strategic industries which can compete effectively with the West, outstanding individuals must be, in as far as possible, concentrated in these industries, and in order to find out such individuals children must be forced to engage in ruthless competition with each other. Then once these talented individuals have been given their places their task is to develop and strengthen these industries, for which they receive the strongest possible backing from the government.

Moreover, the Japanese company strengthens itself by promoting the employees' feelings of loyalty towards the company and by providing them with extensive training. Therefore where company members have once banded together in this way, even if talented personnel were to be recruited from another company there would be almost no way in which they could play an active part, and the company as well would be unwilling to destroy the unity among existing company employees. It is harmony between company employees, and their dedication to the company, which are regarded as important, rather than competition between individual employees. The employees of those companies which constitute the 'national team' of Japanese industry compete with their foreign rivals as a single, united body, and competition among large enterprises to become a member of this national team and be in receipt of various favours from the government is equally fierce. The other medium-sized or small enterprises without such prospects are forced to compete for their own survival. In this sense Japanese society is a fiercely competitive society, but it does not produce competition between individuals; the individual has to work at the risk of his life on the battlefield of group competition. This was the strategy which enabled Japan by about 1975 in many respects to catch up with the countries of the West; in some respects she had managed to overtake them.

Conclusion

There are basically two kinds of religion; firstly, a religion which unites with the governing power in a state, acts as guardian of its legitimacy and whose role is to sanctify the lineage of the ruling tribe or tribes. There is secondly the kind of religion which turns its back on the ruling elements, which permeates those tribes and classes which are ruled, rather than ruling, and those who do not possess superior status, i.e. the religion which tries to bring help to people such as these. The former kind is in many cases the servant of politics; the latter, if not actually critical of the existing system, is at least apolitical. Provided that a religion whose objective is to help the ruled is rational it will be strongly critical of the existing regime, and such religions will deny the deities espoused by the ruling groups. At the same time they will also try to bring together all the non-ruling groups and form either some new, opposing political grouping, or some new spiritual movement. This kind of political or religious cohesion is securely founded on rational principles which transcend any idea of tribe – general, universal principles to which any individual must submit, whatever his tribe; the supreme duty of religions of this kind is help to the individual, not the legitimation of power. However there are also some religions which, while their objective remains the succour of the ruled, are nevertheless irrational and strongly magical and in cases such as these the subject classes are taught to turn their back on politics, to live the life of a mystical recluse, seeking only eternal youth, longevity and other items of physical well-being.

If we now categorise these three types of religion as type 1 (that which serves to justify the ruling forces), type 2 (the rational religion whose objective is to assist either the ruled or the individual) and type 3 (the mystical religion whose objective is to assist the individual), we find that Puritanism is typical of the second

194

type. In contrast Confucianism and Taoism were of the first and third types respectively. That means that in Western Europe, in England for example, there grew up a modern, civil society whose spiritual mainstay was Protestantism, whereas in China the bureaucracy advocated the legitimacy of the imperial government and the people completely turned their back on politics.

However, in Japan, which imported both Confucianism and Taoism from China, not only Confucianism but Taoism as well was modified to become a religion of first, pro-government, type. Japanese Confucianism was a far more enthusiastic upholder of the existing regime than was Chinese Confucianism; its role in the Tokugawa period was that of an ideology legitimating the Bakufu regime as one approved by the Emperor; in the Meiji period its role was the justification of the so-called 'Emperor regime' (*tennōsei*). Shintō, the Japanese version of Taoism, could no longer be called a religion of the third type but was the religion of the imperial family in their role as the ruling clan. Such a transformation must really be regarded as quite natural in view of the fact that the religion had been brought into Japan by members of the ruling tribe or ruling class. Moreover, Japan was inevitably in a position where she was perpetually aware of the overwhelming cultural or technological gap which existed between her and other foreign countries (the Chinese Empire or the countries of the West). This kind of awareness of weakness rendered Japan's ruling classes at the same time both defensive and aggressive, and all the elements which were imported into Japan from elsewhere were modified so that they could be of use in Japan's own protection and development. Even Buddhism in Japan was no exception to this pattern. As far as doctrine was concerned, Buddhism was really split between the second and third types, although it varied depending on the sect. When Buddhism had been introduced into Japan it has been used as far as possible to demonstrate the glory of the state. Since Buddhism was at the time widely disseminated throughout Eastern societies an international comparison of the cultural level of each country could be made by comparing the degree to which Buddhism flourished in each country. Behind Shōtoku Taishi's attempts to promote Buddhism there lay an attempt to reconcile by means of Buddhism the sharp conflicts which existed within the ruling class at the time, but it cannot be denied that there was also a strong desire to try and raise Japan's cultural position vis-à-vis other countries.

A different reinterpretation of the same sacred texts can lead to the development of a totally different life among the people at large, as has been made abundantly clear by Max Weber in the case of Western Europe, and the same phenomenon can be clearly perceived in the case of the East as well. In China, which possessed religions of the first and third type, the debauched lifestyle of the upper classes and the poverty and inertia of the lower classes seemed permanent fixtures (until the rise of the Chinese Communist Party). Society was being stifled, and even when a dynasty changed the change brought no transformation with it. Japan, however, which had modified those same religions possessed by China to make them ideologies strongly supportive of the existing regime, could, after the Meiji Revolution, easily and rapidly put herself in a position where she could manipulate Western technology for the development of the Japanese state.

Japan, however, possessed only this first kind of religion (an ideology providing religious justification for the position of those in power and upholding the status quo) and lacked any religion of the second type (a religion founded on the basis of individuals with the aim of helping humanity). As a result neither individualism nor internationalism developed and the people had no religion of their own, having become completely non-religious. (Shinshū, the largest sect in Japanese Buddhism, must doctrinally be included in our second category of religions, but after the defeat of the Ikko uprising by Nobunaga its adherents did not fight against those in power.) Since this areligiousness of the Japanese people led them to be materialistic, and since they were at the same time on the other hand also nationalistic, they had no hesitation in working together for the material prosperity of Japan as a nation.

Such inclinations meant that the economy in Japan could easily tend towards the right. Since each individual member of the Japanese population was deeply permeated with a nationalist awareness the force of public opinion could (quite democratically) lead to the suppression of all liberalistic economic activity, even without the appearance of a strong leader or autocrat. During the period of the quasi-war regime after 1932 the people desired the appearance of a strong rightist government. The newspapers and other information media divined this national will, played to public opinion and incited it still further, so much so that the prevailing atmosphere was one desirous of the emergence of fascism. Once the wheels of this process had started rolling there was no way of stopping them, and the economy as well was completely subjected to state control. Even when the liberal economy was, to all appearances, restored after the war it was not difficult to secure unity among public opinion.[1] As long as the intentions of those in power were communicated to the people agreement was, in most cases, easily obtained, since the people had been educated in a way which deprived them of the heart to resist. As a result, although the 'economic plans' championed by cabinets in the postwar years have had no legal force they have been acknowledged without any problem and people have cooperated in their realisation. If one terms Japan's prewar regime as a democratic fascist regime, then the postwar economy can perhaps be regarded as a kind of 'democratic "planned" economy'.[2] Whatever the case, the modern economy which prospered in Western Europe under religion of the second type (a rational religion aimed at emancipating the individual) – an economy with an industry founded on the techniques of modern science – was in Japan successfully grafted onto a religion of the first type, i.e. a religion aimed at justifying the status quo.

In Confucianism and Taoism, China possessed religions of both the first and third (mystical, individualistic) type, and was more individualistic and less nationalistic than Japan, whose ideologies were only of the first type. China can be regarded as lying midway between Japan and the West; as a result, she ended up in a position far from both the West and Japan. The situation in China was one which made extremely difficult the emergence both of modern, Western-style capitalism and of Japanese-style capitalism. China's

[1] Even after the war what might be called 'democratic witchhunts' – concentrated and exhaustive attacks on those whose views were regarded as undesirable – were conducted repeatedly. At the time not only were those who were the targets of these attacks given virtually no chance to defend themselves, but it was more or less impossible for a third person to speak for them.

[2] This kind of structure has reaped tremendous success in material terms. However, a necessary precondition for the establishment of such a regime is the absence of an ideology which will criticise and rebel against the powers that be. Individualism, liberalism and internationalism have therefore been unable to prosper under such a regime. The Japanese are strong believers in the importance of the family and of kinship; they are nationalistic and believers in the importance of race; they are warm towards their own circle, but cold towards anyone from outside. It is true that the view of how far one's own circle extends has changed over the years, but it has remained the case that there are two quite different yardsticks governing the behaviour of the Japanese, one applied to those within one's own circle, and another applied to those outside it. In this sense neither have the Japanese been logical, nor have they shown any sensibility towards the precepts of universal justice.

backward conditions lasted a long time, and she was laid waste and brought to her knees by the imperialist aggression of Japan and the nations of the West.

As one might expect, a movement did arise which hoped to save the nation. In 1900 the Boxers, a mystical religious society advocating the expulsion of foreigners, destroyed railways and telegraphs, burnt down churches and, entering Peking, attacked the settlement occupied by the legations of the major Western powers. This outbreak of violence, like the terrorist attacks carried out by the anti-foreign faction in Japan prior to the Meiji Revolution, was nothing more than a totally irrational, fanatical patriotic movement. The Chinese government assisted the Boxers, but they were eventually routed by a combined force from the Western powers and Japan.

The lesson that patriotism alone would not solve the problem was thus brought home to the Chinese. With Japan's success before their very eyes large numbers of Chinese students were sent to Japan to learn from her. However, it proved far more difficult in China, where Confucianism was less collectivist than its Japanese counterpart, than it had proved in Japan, to build on the basis of this type of ideology any structure of national unity which had the intelligentsia as its nucleus. With their orthodox ideology of insufficient use to waken the sleeping Chinese the only thing to do was to refine and strengthen the heterodoxy.

In China, Taoism had normally turned its back on politics and advocated a mystical, secluded lifestyle for its followers, but at times it had shown itself to be a revolutionary force and come into fierce confrontation with the Confucian government. Taoism was indeed a religion for the people, aiming at individual salvation, but it was unfortunately also a mystical religion quite incapable of making an analytical, rational judgement of the realities of life. Any religion capable of becoming a truly revolutionary force must not merely have as its mission the salvation of the individual, it must also be rational. Chinese revolutionaries, therefore, whether Sun Yat-sen or Mao Tse-tung, introduced liberalism, Marxism and other Western ideas, and by this means recast the indigenous spirit of resistance into a form which was both logical and tenacious.[3]

---

[3] Amongst these revolutionaries was Chiang Kai-shek, who was himself an ardent Confucian, but whose wife was Protestant. Chiang rejected a communist revolution, adhering to the idea of a bourgeois revolution.

Compared with the Meiji Revolution, which was no more than a revolution in the political structure brought about by the mental attitude of the Japanese, the Chinese Revolution was not merely a political revolution; it is noticeable that it was a revolution in attitudes so fundamental as to require brainwashing.

Such a 'spiritual' revolution was imperative in China. Viewed from a different point of view the history of the vicissitudes of the dynasties of China becomes the history of the struggle between the Confucian bureaucrats and the Taoist peasantry. Even when the dynasty changed as a result of peasant insurrection the peasantry soon came under the domination of the bureaucrats of the new dynasty and continued their subservient, spiritless existence until the next revolt broke out. Given the consistent operation of this major trend throughout China's history it was expected that following the Communist Revolution Chinese society would soon fall under the control of the bureaucracy, lose its driving force and eventually end up in a state of stagnation. Not just that, but eventually the usual peasant rebellion would also break out and the existing communist regime too would be brought to an end. Such a way of thinking suggests an understanding that a thoroughgoing criticism of Confucianism is essential in China in order to firmly implant the communist system and make it last.[4] At the same time it was essential to develop the peasants' ideology into something which was both rational and critical, and by doing so to annul the difference which had hitherto existed between the ideologies of those who had worked with their brains and those who had worked with their hands – Confucianism and Taoism. It was imperative to establish a new national ideology (for example, Maoism). Granted that the great Cultural Revolution had many excesses, if we look at things in this way it is at least not impossible to understand what it was aiming at. Bureaucratic elements and those who wielded power were thoroughly criticised, and the removal of the so-called 'three differences' (between city and village, between industry and agriculture, and between brain work and manual work) became the slogan of the revolutionaries.

The Cultural Revolution can thus really be regarded as an attack

---

[4] Mao Tse-tung himself spoke about 'succeeding with a critical eye to the historical legacy from Confucius to Sun Yat-sen', and the present Chinese Communist Party, despite its fierce criticism of Confucianism, has to a limited extent evaluated highly the reforming spirit possessed by early Confucianism.

on Confucianism (and the technocrats who supported it) by a Taoism armed and rationalised by Marxist ideology. It must be noted, however, that the path followed by the cultural revolution brought about in this way was quite the opposite of the policies adopted by the Japanese government after the Meiji Revolution. In Japan the modernisation of the country was pushed ahead so as to make ever greater the so-called 'three differences'. Modernisation did not proceed in all areas of the countries and all spheres of society in the same way and at the same pace. In each sector within the country a nucleus was created which was way out ahead and equal in every way to its counterpart in the West, and modernisation was pushed forward through enlarging these nuclear sectors. As a result Japan was rapidly able to achieve, at least in the past, the front line in terms of technological development, and utilising what she learnt in this manner also promoted modernisation in other sectors. This kind of unbalanced development, however, firmly rooted the dualistic structure in Japan and led to the emergence of a huge labour proletariat exploited by one small part of the population – capitalists and the labour aristocracy. The Chinese Communist Party, however, and especially its Maoist aspects, has to eliminate exploitation of this nature and remove the diverse 'ten thousand differences' which have existed. This means that achievement of the technological front line in all sectors will take a very long time. Especially when we consider how vast a country China is it may well be the case that this method of modernisation results in China's remaining a backward country in perpetuity. The Chinese, however, made it their absolute priority to save the manual workers and peasants of China by this means from the hardship which had been the lot of the lower strata of Japanese society, especially during the period 1915–50. One could perhaps say that whereas the Japanese had carried out a forced march towards modernisation the Chinese selected the route of the long-winded 'Long March' with peasants and workers proceeding side by side.

Whatever the case, these political and economic choices depend on the manner in which ideologies have been disposed during the course of a country's history. What is also true is that ideology itself is influenced and modified by economic developments, and even destroyed by them, and this reverse effect cannot be overlooked. What we have seen in this work, however, is not only that a given ideology frequently plays a role of crucial importance at a turning point in history, but also that it has the effect of restricting the possibilities of day-to-day economic activity to within the framework peculiar to that ideology. It is therefore true that achievements in Japan, even where material conditions have been the same, have not been limited to what has been achieved in the West. The reverse is also true. This is especially true if we limit our considerations to the short term.[5] Because of its ideology Japan's economy is very different from the free enterprise system of the West; for the same reason the Communist economy of China has a vastly different character from that of the economy of the Soviet Union. It is a mistake, therefore, merely to consider China and Japan as potential models for backward countries.

No country can progress while it disregards its own past history by which its subsequent course of development is constrained. Historical considerations are equally important for the social sciences. Any social scientific thought which has paid no attention to history, although it may be effective as a first approximation to reality, can at times even be dangerous. Economic policies which lack any historical perspective are similarly extremely hazardous. A policy which has been proved to be successful for Japan may turn out to be unworkable in Britain and vice versa, because of the differences in their ethoses, in the ways of behaviour of their peoples and in all the other cultural characteristics which they have inherited from their respective pasts.

[5] In this sense it is erroneous to assume unconditionally that one can construct an economic model in the abstract and apply the logic of the model to the realities of a country.

Index

Date Due